Islam and Morality

ALSO AVAILABLE FROM BLOOMSBURY

Comparative Studies in Asian and Latin American Philosophies, edited by Stephanie Rivera Berruz and Leah Kalmanson
Faith and Reason in Continental and Japanese Philosophy, by Takeshi Morisato
Imagination: Cross-Cultural Philosophical Analyses, edited by Hans-Georg Moeller and Andrew Whitehead
The Biographical Encyclopedia of Islamic Philosophy, edited by Oliver Leaman
The Qur'an: A Philosophical Guide, by Oliver Leaman

Islam and Morality

A Philosophical Introduction

Oliver Leaman

BLOOMSBURY ACADEMIC
LONDON · NEW YORK · OXFORD · NEW DELHI · SYDNEY

BLOOMSBURY ACADEMIC
Bloomsbury Publishing Plc
50 Bedford Square, London, WC1B 3DP, UK
1385 Broadway, New York, NY 10018, USA

BLOOMSBURY, BLOOMSBURY ACADEMIC and the Diana logo are trademarks of
Bloomsbury Publishing Plc

First published in Great Britain 2019
Reprinted 2020

Copyright © Oliver Leaman, 2019

Oliver Leaman has asserted his right under the Copyright, Designs and Patents Act, 1988, to be identified as Author of this work.

For legal purposes the Acknowledgments on p. vi constitute an extension of this copyright page.

Cover design: Emma J. Hardy

All rights reserved. No part of this publication may be reproduced or transmitted in any form or by any means, electronic or mechanical, including photocopying, recording, or any information storage or retrieval system, without prior permission in writing from the publishers.

Bloomsbury Publishing Plc does not have any control over, or responsibility for, any third-party websites referred to or in this book. All internet addresses given in this book were correct at the time of going to press. The author and publisher regret any inconvenience caused if addresses have changed or sites have ceased to exist, but can accept no responsibility for any such changes.

A catalogue record for this book is available from the British Library.

A catalog record for this book is available from the Library of Congress.

ISBN: HB: 978-1-3500-6318-1
PB: 978-1-3500-6322-8
ePDF: 978-1-3500-6321-1
eBook: 978-1-3500-6320-4

Typeset by Deanta Global Publishing Services, Chennai, India
Printed and bound in Great Britain

To find out more about our authors and books visit www.bloomsbury.com and sign up for our newsletters.

CONTENTS

Acknowledgments vi
Introduction vii
Note on transliteration xiii

1 Justice 1

2 Conflict 23

3 Sins 43

4 Health 65

5 Bodies 89

6 Nature 125

7 Choice 149

8 Sufis 161

9 Principles 185

Index 201

ACKNOWLEDGMENTS

As with all my books, I am very grateful to the people who responded to my arguments and ideas as they were developing. The most important here are my students in Kentucky, who over the years have often been a lively presence and helped me refine and expand the thesis to be found here. I must also thank audiences in a variety of academic settings—the Islamic College in London, University of Paderborn, Virginia Theological Seminary, University of Bergen, University of Edinburgh, King Abdul-Aziz Al Saud Foundation for Islamic Studies and Human Sciences—and in a variety of other places.

Although I have been critical of a central thesis about religion, that there are central principles that define it, I am grateful to those who write on the topic. As an idea this has been dealt with very clearly on the whole, and it is a popular thesis. Alas, in my view it is not true.

The translations in the book from the Qur'an are mine, but I would have found this very tough without all the other translations available in English and I must acknowledge this.

I must also thank the International Institute of Islamic Thought (IIIT) based in Virginia, United States, for having financed partially the empirical research on halal food that I refer to here.

I am grateful to an anonymous reader for comments on an earlier draft.

It would be invidious to mention particular individuals, especially as it is often a nonacademic who says something to you that has a greater impact than colleagues on the topics in question here, since morality is all about practice.

Lexington
August 2018

INTRODUCTION

I wrote this book because I often read things on Islam and morality that seem to me to be problematic. Islamic philosophy does not discuss morality in much depth; there are extensive discussions of metaphysics, ontology, philosophy of religion, and law, of course, but a rather slim analysis of ethics. To a certain extent this is because many philosophers thought that there was not much systematic to say about morality that is not already said in the Qur'an. Some thinkers also regarded moral language as operating at a lower level of demonstrative rigor than other forms of reasoning, or thought that it could be derived from general rational principles, all ideas I shall be looking at in this book.

As a result of this relative absence of discussion, a new kind of writing has become popular that could be called the *khutbaization* of ethical discourse. The *khutba* is the sermon that the imam gives in the mosque on a Friday and other important days on which Muslims gather together to pray. While giving a *khutba*, the imam includes quotations from the Qur'an and the Traditions (*ahadith*, singular *hadith*), some reflections on Islamic history, remarks on personal experience, and some reference to contemporary affairs. This can be an inspiring performance, and it is designed to assure the faithful that Islam is a remarkable religion and everything about it fits in nicely. Nothing wrong with this, but often the discussion lacks rigor and objectivity, and this sort of approach is often also there in more academic treatments. There is nothing wrong with trying to defend a religion, and often it results in excellent philosophy. When it comes to ethics though, it will be argued that there is often a lack of evidence of critical thought, and the time has come to try to put the discussion of ethics on a more sound foundation in Islam. The Qur'an already does this, but the problem is commentators who try to go further and impose a structure on the Book that really does not fit.

I have written a number of books recently that discuss many of the same issues, and I hope this does not duplicate much of that material. In this book I am largely interested in metaethics, the theory behind the formulation of ethical principles in Islam. The other books are more oriented toward trying to understand how moral rules in Islam work. In this book, I am particularly interested in trying to understand the idea that there are general moral principles in Islam and that these form the basis on which we can allow rules to change to fit in with social changes while remaining faithful to the original intentions of the law. Those who are not interested in changing anything think that the idea of general principles underlying law establishes the rationality of the system and ultimately its benign character. These principles are what the Qur'an is arguing for and they express the moral essence of Islam. This is a popular strategy and has been for a long time, but it will be argued here that it really does not do justice to the Qur'an. The remarkable thing about the idea of basic principles is that it is popular with very different kinds of Muslims—those keen to reform the religion and those who see it as important to base society on what they take to be traditional Islam. The idea resonates with both conservatives and radicals, but it will be argued here that it does not really resonate with the Qur'an.

This seems wrong, since we are familiar with ideas like the pillars of Islam and generally we think of religions as having basic principles on which they rest, similar to the way in which any rational system is deducible from its axioms. We often talk about Islamic ethics, Christian ethics, Buddhist ethics, and so on as though these terms make sense, and if they do then there must be something distinctive about what they describe. Hospitals often ask their staff from different religious groups to expound on what in their religion counts as death, for example, or appropriate treatment, and the assumption is that often the responses would be different. Sometimes no doubt this information is used to decide on the treatment of patients, although just because a patient follows a particular religion does not necessarily mean that they will go along with any specific view on end of life or treatment issues at all. When we come to look at the issue of food it will be argued that many Muslims have only a vague idea, or a wrong idea, of what they are supposed to be eating and drinking. There are often few recognizable principles at work here, although that might just be to say that many people in a religion just do not understand what they are supposed to do. That does not show there are no principles, just that many people do not know what they are. But it does show that they think they can be members of a group without signing up to what are taken to be the principles. Perhaps they are wrong, yet we should be cautious before we dismiss their claims to be in the group. After all, people can speak poor English and still count as English-speakers. Many people are very interested in sport without being able to participate in it in any direct way. The idea that we have to accept principles before we can get properly involved in something is suspect.

At many universities there are principles that students have to sign up to, often called a pledge of excellence: "As a member of . . . , I dedicate myself to intellectual inquiry, life-long learning, and critical thinking. I pledge to demonstrate personal and academic integrity both in and outside of the classroom. I pledge to always be willing to engage my peers in earnest and respectful discussion with an open mind." This is a familiar form of words seen in American higher education institutions. The extraordinary collection of platitudes are fortunately difficult to understand, since if students really thought about it they would be reluctant to sign. Why should they promise personal integrity outside the classroom, for example, and what does it mean? Does it mean they should always tell the truth, do the right thing, not throw litter on the floor? Why should they dedicate themselves to lifelong learning, since they might after a bit decide they want to take it easy for the rest of their lives and who are we to insist they are wrong? Why are they agreeing to engage their peers in earnest and respectful discussion? This makes one wonder—Does this only apply to their peers? How should they speak to everyone else, with contempt perhaps? These earnest and respectful discussions sound rather boring; one would hope that young people would find some room for passionate and unbalanced debates in favor of ideas that later on may come to embarrass them, but at this stage are worth trying to see how far they can be taken. So this vague ragbag of principles designed to help organize those involved in a fairly narrow academic exercise is difficult to accept or even really understand.

How much more difficult is it to make specific the principles said to be behind a religion? In this book there will be a good deal of criticism of the idea of such principles, and yet it has to be accepted that it seems obvious that there are such principles. It makes life much easier for us if we think in terms of such principles, and it makes religions seem far neater. But this is the religion of the people in the streets who hold up a religious book and proclaim that Jesus died for our sins or that Muhammad revealed the word of God. For these people religion is simple, based on a few principles that can be clearly grasped. For most of us, fortunately, it is something else. Nowhere is this clearer than when morality is at issue. Morality is complex and has the unusual feature that we may think someone is wrong in their moral views and yet respect their sincerity in getting to those views. Similarly, we may agree with someone's views and yet not think highly of how they got to them—perhaps because they just accepted them as part of a package of ideas that have not really been interrogated in any way.

Another aspect of religion is the issue of how it should be interpreted. Those who think it is simple to understand what their religion requires of them, and how to understand their holy book, fail to grasp the nature of any religion. That is very much a theme of this book. Islam like other religions has a complex variety of hermeneutic methods to help us understand what it requires of us. First of all there is the Qur'an, or so everyone always says, but often the Qur'an is not really considered as important as the material interpreting Islam. There is the *sira* of the Prophet, his history and what we can learn from it, his *sunna*, how he acted according to the reports we have, and the hadith, the conversations he and his companions had on a number of issues relevant to how we should behave. Then there are different theories of how reliable these stories actually are. For the Shi'a there are also the sayings of the imams and sometimes different hadith. Then there is our understanding of Qur'anic Arabic, the language of the Qur'an that we are trying to understand, and of course this is different from modern Arabic and the Arabic of the commentators who worked some centuries after the original revelation. Then there is the issue of whether some of the verses of the Qur'an actually are designed to replace other verses, something that makes the text especially complex to grasp. Part of working this out involves the *asbab al-nuzul*, the circumstances behind a particular Qur'anic revelation, and what order of priority can be established. Then there are interpretive principles established by the different schools of law, and for the Shi'a by the imams.

In modern times there are the principles defended by popular legal thinkers who often do not align themselves officially with a particular school of law. I could go on and on with layers of interpretive complexity. There are also a huge number of theories of the grammatical and linguistic structure of the Qur'an designed to help us understand how it all fits together, since the pattern is not obvious when we read the Book for the first time. On the contrary it is often not clear what goes with what, and why one topic appears in one place and another elsewhere. This is true of small parts of the text, and of the whole Book also, and different approaches connect the parts to other parts in distinct and often very interesting ways.

What this suggests is that the rhetoric of identifying the Qur'an as the basis of Islam is often misleading. This is because what we take to be the Qur'an is often more a function of a whole range of interpretive techniques than anything else. That is the normal situation for religions; they have to support a heavy parasitical growth of commentaries and often the skirmishing that goes on is in the undergrowth rather than in the scriptures themselves. In this book I try to steer close to the Qur'an throughout and not get involved in much of this supplementary material, except to point out how far it often is from the Qur'an itself. This is a very simple interpretive principle of this book: Are the descriptions of the morality of the Qur'an in the works of commentators like what we find in the Book? It may be a rather naïve way to approach the text, but it is probably one that is followed by many believers. It will be argued that the Qur'an has a sophisticated account of moral behavior, and to bring this out one needs to do little more than read the Book. There is no argument here that the Qur'an represents the correct position, nor one that was really sent to humanity by God. This is not a book setting out to establish any religious truths. This is a book defending a particular account of how the Qur'an works to defend its view of morality, so it has very limited aims. Since many commentators on the issue have unsatisfactory opinions and arguments, it may be useful to show why they are wrong and how we should think of Islamic morality if we follow the Qur'anic paradigm.

Bibliography

Campanini, Massimo (2010), *The Qur'an: Modern Muslim Interpretations*, London: Routledge.

Campanini, Massimo (2014), *Philosophical Perspectives on Modern Qur'anic Exegesis: Key Paradigms and Concepts*, Sheffield: Equinox.

Eggen, Nora S. (2011), "Conception of trust in the Qur'an," *Journal of Qur'anic Studies* 13/2: 56–85.

Leaman, Oliver (1996), "Secular friendship and religious devotion," in *Friendship East and West—Philosophical Perspectives*, Oliver Leaman (ed.), Richmond: Curzon: 251–62.

Leaman, Oliver (2000), "Can rights coexist with religion?," in *Studies in Islamic and Middle Eastern Texts and Traditions in Memory of Norman Calder*, Gerald Hawting, Jawid Mojaddedi, and Alexander Samely (eds.), Oxford: Oxford University Press, *Journal of Semitic Studies Supplement* 12: 163–74.

Leaman, Oliver (2001), *Introduction to Classical Islamic Philosophy*, Cambridge: Cambridge University Press.

Leaman, Oliver (2003), "Appearance and reality in the Qur'an: Bilqis and Zulaykha," *Islam Araştırmaları Dergisi* 10: 23–37.

Leaman, Oliver (ed.) (2006), *The Qur'an: An Encyclopedia*, London: Routledge.

Leaman, Oliver (2008a), *Islam: The Key Concepts*, with Kecia Ali, London: Routledge.

Leaman, Oliver (2008b), "The developed Kalam tradition," in *Cambridge Companion to Islamic Theology*, T. Winter (ed.), Cambridge: Cambridge University Press: 77–90.

Leaman, Oliver (2009a), "Islamic philosophical theology," in *The Oxford Handbook of Philosophical Theology*, T. Flint and M. Rea (eds.), Oxford: Oxford University Press: 556–73.

Leaman, Oliver (2009b), *Islamic Philosophy: An Introduction*, Cambridge: Polity Press.

Leaman, Oliver (2012a), "Identifying God: How far is the God of Judaism, Christianity and Islam the same God?," in *Dios in las tres culturas*, J. Choza, J. de Garyu, and J. Padial (eds.), Sevilla: Themata: 143–54.

Leaman, Oliver (2012b), "Theism in Islam," in *The Routledge Companion to Theism*, C. Taliaferro, V. Harrison, and S. Goetz (eds.), London: Routledge: 66–76.

Leaman, Oliver (2013a), *Controversies in Contemporary Islam*, London: Routledge.

Leaman, Oliver (2013b), "The Corpus Coranicum project and the issue of novelty," *Journal of Qur'anic Studies* 15/2: 142–48.

Leaman, Oliver (ed.) (2015), *Biographical Encyclopedia of Islamic Philosophy* (2nd ed.), London: Bloomsbury.

Leaman, Oliver (2016a), *The Qur'an: A Philosophical Guide*, London: Bloomsbury.

Leaman, Oliver (2016b), "Economics and religion or economics versus religion: The concept of an Islamic economics," in *Value and Values: Economics and Justice in an Age of Global Interdependence*, Roger T. Ames and Peter D. Hershock (eds.), Honolulu, HI: University of Hawaii Press: 272–82.

Leaman, Oliver (2016c), "Islamic philosophical traditions," in *Philosophy: Sources, Perspectives, and Methodologies*, Donald M. Borchert (ed.), Farmington Hills, MI: Macmillan Reference: 245–56.

Moosa, Ebrahim, and Mian, Ali Ataf (2012), "Islam," in *Encyclopedia of Applied Ethics* (vol. 2, 2nd ed.), San Diego, CA: Academic Press: 769–76. [8pp].

Nanji, Azim (1991), "Islamic ethics," in *A Companion to Ethics*, Peter Singer (ed.), Oxford: Blackwell: 106–18. Available at http://iis.ac.uk/islamic-ethics

Nanji, Azim (1996), "The ethical tradition in Islam," in *The Muslim Almanac. A Reference Work on the History, Faith, Culture, and Peoples of Islam*, Azim Nanji (ed.), Detroit, MI: Gale Research: 205–14. Available at: http://iis.ac.uk/academic-article/ethical-tradition-islam

Nasr, Seyyed H., and Leaman, Oliver (eds.) (1996), *History of Islamic Philosophy*, London: Routledge.

Rahman, Fazlur (1980), "Man in society," ch. 3 in his *Major Themes of the Qur'an*, Fazlur Rahman Minneapolis, MN: Bibliotheca Islamica: 37–64.

NOTE ON TRANSLITERATION

The transliteration system here ignores diacritics and macrons and includes *'ayn* and *hamza*.

Dates are given in this way: CE/Hijri

1

Justice

*You are the best community ever raised up for humanity.
You enjoin what is right and forbid what is wrong,
and you believe in God. (3:110)*

This inspiring *aya* or verse from the Qur'an seems to suggest that Muslims are a wonderful group of people, since they behave well, avoid sin, and believe in God. It is not entirely clear, however, since it could be that Muslims are just better than everyone else or perhaps the claim is that if they live up to the standards of Islam they would be, but this is more of a challenge than a report on a fact. It calls on people to think about whether they really pursue justice and avoid evil and believe in God. It is of course very easy to claim such ambitions and beliefs but something quite different to actually embody them in one's conduct. What we do get in this claim though is the idea that the Islamic system as a whole is especially close to morality and also correct religious belief, and that these are all related to each other in some way. But in what way? It is worth pointing out that the Arabic term for ethics, *akhlaq*, is linked with the words *makhluq*, created, and of course to the creator, *khaliq*. To attempt at being a bit more precise on this issue is important since otherwise we are left with some vague platitudes about law and ethics bearing a relationship to each other that really does not tell us anything about either law or ethics. It will be argued here that the relationship, although it clearly exists, is far more complex than is often appreciated.

It is often said that law is very important in Islam, and no doubt it is. Here we are more interested in how law brings out moral ideas and helps us see how they operate in practice. In law there is often a question of how someone ought to behave, and this in turn refers us back to how God expects us to behave, and there is some degree of unclarity about the precise nature of our duty. The various schools of law in Islam provide a variety of views on these issues, and like all religious law they refer us back eventually to the source of the law, God. It would seem then that the situation is quite clear; we wonder how to act, we refer back to God and His teachings, and we act accordingly. It is not easy to disentangle ethics in Islam from law, or so it is often claimed. Law is certainly very significant in Islam, but then it is in other religions also, such as Judaism, and this leads to a number of problems. Traditionally philosophers have felt it was important to distinguish between certain distinct kinds of language, since often the rules that apply to each kind is itself distinct. Legal language is not ethical language, although each may refer to the other in a variety of ways. Trying to develop an idea of how law and ethics relate to each other in Islam is an important task, and it is the aim of this chapter to move us along in that direction. Commentators often make vague claims about the connection between law and ethics in Islam, and we should be suspicious of many of these. In this book a number of legal issues will be discussed, and since this is not a book on Islamic law but on ethics the obvious assumption is that they are relevant. But why are they relevant? One way of answering this question would be to look at four ways of linking law and ethics. This gets us to what are four fallacies in working out the nature of the link.

Fallacy of basing ethics on law

Religious law, we are often told, comes from God. There is certainly plenty of law in the Qur'an, and that comes from God according to Islam, so law comes from God and is the basis or perhaps part of the basis of informing us how to act. There is much more to it than that, though, since on the basis of the Qur'an and other sources such as the hadith and the teachings of the imams, depending on what sort of Muslim one is, there is a development of a variety of legal doctrines and schools. To actually work out how to act in a particular case one would normally look at the religious sources in the Qur'an and so on, plus make some acknowledgment of the legal school to which one adheres. Of course, normally this is the school of the region or the one to which your family or group belongs. At least within the Sunni tradition there is general acceptance of all the groups, and this has been extended recently even to Shi'a and Ibadi legal schools being accorded the same respect, although this is very much an official policy of governments and not necessarily often followed by most Sunnis.

A problem here is that ethics is about working out how to behave, and law gives us a variety of different kinds of advice. It is not like being given different directions about how to get from A to B. B is the same for everyone, but in the case of law we do not end up in the same place, in the sense that we are often told to do different things. For example, some schools of law regard particular behavior as acceptable, while for others it is not, and there is a whole continuum of views on many issues. Perhaps B is the same because it represents the will of God. But how can God want us to do different things? He could perhaps value the process of disagreement and debate, and not care especially how people behave, yet this seems far from what we know about how Islam describes human action and its consequences. We do just have to accept that different legal opinions can be given in a particular case, one judge goes in one direction, and others in different directions, so it is not as though one could just read ethical conclusions from legal statements. There are of course different legal schools, and even within one school lawyers differ on the correct judgment. Basing ethics on law would be basing it on a range of theoretical approaches that would tend to go in a variety of directions. How people ought to act ought to be based on something more solid than that. We tend to think there is a right and a wrong here, and we have to work hard to get the right line on the issue. From a religious point of view, ethics is closely linked with God, hence the idea of justice being something objective, yet law is obviously very different, based as it is on the changing perceptions of particular fallible lawyers.

Fallacy of basing law on ethics

A more plausible line might seem to be that law embodies ethical principles, and these are variously interpreted by the different legal thinkers. They can be identified in the Qur'an and other sources, and the point of law is to accord with them. Here we are seen as taking a variety of routes from A to B and B really is the same terminus for all the journeys. B can be seen as justice or mercy or happiness and so on. It is not difficult to argue that in religion the legal rules are aimed at such ends. Islam proves to be an exception here, however. Think of the protracted discussion between Musa and Khidr. Musa, the prophet Musa, seeks to understand what happens in terms of familiar moral categories, and he always gets it wrong. What we should do is a matter of being guided by someone with real knowledge and the ultimate source of such knowledge is of course God. He is presumably the source of both law and ethics, ultimately at least, and it is wrong to see the latter as grounding the former. Only God "has the keys of all that is hidden" (6:59) and the prophets' role is to interpret the signs of God. So, after having interpreted the dreams of Pharaoh's dignitaries, Yusuf adds: "Did I not tell you that God has made known to me things you do not know at all? . . . O my father, this is the meaning (*ta'wil*) of my previous dream; my lord made it true" (12:96-100). God is the truth and He produces the truth both in His various revelations and in the world He created. Our scope for understanding our duties based on what we know prior to or without revelation is limited indeed. Even after revelation our scope for knowing why we need to behave in the way we do is also limited. After all, tradition is no guide since the customs and practices of the past are often based on nothing more than just being old. If we do not understand our moral duties in various situations, basing law on what we do in those situations will be to base them on something very weak. We just have to accept that without divine guidance we are in very bad shape morally speaking, and even with it there is much about morality that is still obscure to us.

Some argue that we can work out our duties by using reason alone, since reason will enable us to decide how we ought to behave. This is very far from the view of the Qur'an, though, which is full of comments on the need for guidance through revelation. It might be suggested, and some philosophers made this argument, that while most people need guidance, philosophers can do it by themselves. We will consider this view in due course, but even these thinkers did not think that law could be based entirely on reason. Law clearly has a public function and needs to engage with the entire community, and although it clearly has a rational structure, it has a complexity that makes it distinct from ethics. There is much in it that has no apparent reason apart from the fact that God advocated it, and we shall see how pervasive this theme is in the Qur'an.

Fallacy of separating ethics from law

We might feel like throwing up our hands in the air and giving up on linking ethics with law, and saying they are entirely distinct. But they are not at all, the Qur'an refers time and again to the ethical import of what it urges us to do. It is not just a matter of what God wants us to do, although this is clearly how we are expected to acquire our information about our duties. Law would embody that ethics in practice in some way. Not all rules are ethical although their rationale might be. Prayer is an example that is often used. It is obvious that we should pray but the manner in which we should pray is not at all obvious. This is what is often said, but it is not entirely clear why we should be grateful for something that is not necessarily something we wanted. It may be that we would prefer never to have been born. In any case, since the creation is something we did not request why should we be grateful for it? Someone who asks for something might want to thank his or her benefactor, but someone who receives help they did not request may or not like to thank their benefactor. After all, in the case of God he creates out of pure grace—it is not a transaction of any kind and he might feel embarrassed to be thanked. It is a bit like someone going to a café and buying two coffees, one for herself and one for someone else she does not know who cannot afford a coffee but would like one. She neither expects nor wants to be thanked and similarly for many acts of virtue of a similar nature. Many people who give to charity and do not give to beggars and panhandlers do it because they do not want to receive the unctuous thanks of those they assist. They want to do good without that personal contact, and we would normally say that was a superior form of doing good. It seems strange that God should seem so intent on being thanked.

We are told that "were it not for God's grace and His mercy for you in this world and the hereafter, you would have suffered a great punishment for what you did" (24:14, see also *ayat* 10, 20 and 21 of the same sura, and 2:64, 4:83, 113). There are many references to *fadl* or grace in the Book and the central theme is that God is far kinder to everyone than they deserve, and that this happens without any expectation or even scope for a return. The Qur'an often reads superficially as a rather grim text, with its emphasis on justice and punishment in the next world, yet really in the idea of grace we do receive what it calls "good news" at 33:47 (see also 10:60). The idea is that on the whole people do not deserve to be treated well, but they are, and this has obvious implications for how we should treat each other. Justice is certainly important and should underlay the basic rules of morality, doing good and urging against evil. There is a higher morality though where we put up with people who go wrong on occasion and forgive them, or forgive them in general, as we hope God will do with us. Would this not suggest that we do not need to bother to try to act well, since God may well forgive us whatever we do? He may, of course, but He might also be critical of our having this sort of motive behind our behavior, and this could have serious consequences for us. The point is that our eventual fate looks quite arbitrary if we could be rewarded even though we do not really deserve it. Yet this might be taken to be a rather realistic angle on morality. We do not know how we are going to end up in our daily affairs, we may plan for one thing and get something else, we may deserve a particular result and someone entirely undeserving gets it, and we get nothing. It is often said that this is a problem of evil-type issue, and there is no such problem in Islam. The problem is only a problem if we think that justice should prevail in the world. When we see that it does not we could hope that it will take place in the next world, and so balance out what happens in this world, as the Mu'tazilites suggest. On the other hand, we might prefer to live in a fairly unpredictable world, one where God is always ready to forgive us even when we slip up, and we have to cope with the idea of evil people being eventually successful on occasion.

The Qur'an does seem to value some kinds of diversity, and one kind is where people do different things and have to try to work out what they ought to do and what they should avoid. Although God has given us this information at every time through his messengers and prophets, some people perhaps do not get the message or understand it or even want to obey it. We do not after all always do what is in our interests. For example, we should all be careful crossing the road, we should stop, look, listen, and think, but we do not all do this and that makes life for drivers and pedestrians more interesting. As pedestrians we do not know if drivers will always obey the law, sometimes they just do not stop when they are supposed to, and accidents may result. It is very unpleasant to be involved in such an incident, but on the positive side it does make life much more interesting. We never know when we leave the house if we are going to get to where we want to go, and of course we never know even if we stay at home whether we shall be safe. When something goes wrong we are naturally upset, yet a society in which everything ran smoothly and without anyone breaking the rules, a society of angels, would be a poor place to live. Some people would no doubt prefer it, but they would be wrong, since such a society would lack flavor and excitement, and these are aspects of what counts as a valuable life for human beings.

If prayer is required by religion, as it is by Islam, it is for some reason that has nothing to do with what God needs or wants and much more about what is helpful to us. Presumably, if God creates effortlessly, as He presumably does since He is omnipotent, it is difficult to argue we should be grateful for what he does, since it did not cost Him anything, no effort was involved at all. This view is only given support by our description as slaves or servants, since despite the suggestion of some recent apologists for colonialism, and especially Islamic systems of slavery, slaves are often not treated well. The Qur'an claims we are treated fairly, taking into account both this and the next world. Perhaps that is something we should be grateful for, since our normal experience is that often we are treated very differently. But the evidence before us is very different. We do not appear to be treated well, nice people get sick and die young, leaving their children to fend for themselves, while evil people live for a long time and seem to encounter few problems in life. It could of course be sorted out more equitably in the next world, but right now we have no evidence that it is. Religious law, the law established by God for our conduct, must be designed to help us flourish in some way, if God is benign, as we are told He is, and so it must be connected to our behavior, to ethics. But how close is the connection?

Fallacy of identifying ethics with law

Although ethics and law are clearly linked, precisely how they are linked is the matter at issue here. As so often, religion is much more subtle in its description of itself than are those who seek to explain it. Ethics is not the same as law. The reasoning processes involved in each are distinct, as the *mashha'i* or peripatetic thinkers often pointed out. Religion is an explanation that resonates with the public at large and explains how we should behave. Law is largely dialectical, it starts with principles that it itself establishes as true and works from there to their implications, the whole process is valid but its demonstrative strength is limited by the scope of the initial premises. This might seem to be wrong since surely law is so important in Islam that we cannot think of Islamic ethics without also thinking about law. One of the objections made to IVF is that the precise identity of the father of the eventual child may remain hazy, yet in Islamic law it is important to know the father of the child, since it is through the father that a child receives his legal identity. If IVF means that the paternity of a child is thrown into doubt, then it is better avoided. It could be argued that the point about paternity is that in society, especially the societies in the past in which most Muslims lived, being without a father was a source of considerable social stigma. The Prophet himself must have been aware of this from his own experience. So if one is to bring about a child without a father then already a problem is established, the child may have an unfortunate start in life and we should prevent that from happening if we can.

On the other hand, in a society where lineage is not significant this might not be a huge issue, especially when it is balanced with the prospect of having no child at all. This would not work as an argument that the legal significance of lineage was no longer important given societal changes, but it would work as an argument that it no longer had the importance it had in the past. The principle that one should not make someone suffer unnecessarily remains ethically valid universally, but the legal principle that is a means to this can vary from time to time, and probably will. The issue is which kinds of suffering are unnecessary. Some suffering is sanctioned and held to have a purpose. Perhaps not everyone is meant to have children, however much they would like to do so. On the other hand, paternity is no longer such a significant social source of identity as in the past, and it would be difficult to argue that it is always worse to be born without a clear route to a father as compared with not being born at all, even within a predominantly Muslim society. Not having children may be taken to have a point. It may be that God thinks we are not the right people to have children, or He has some other task for us with which children would interfere. It may be that eventually we will have children but through a more difficult process than is the case for most people. There is a reason for this, and it lies with God.

It is often said that Islam is too closely linked with law, a complaint that in the past was made about Judaism. Judaism was seen as far too rule-bound a religion to function well in modern society, and Jesus was taken to have criticized this aspect of the religion in his lifetime. Shylock in *The Merchant of Venice* insists on his pound of flesh since that is what the law demands, or so he thinks, and it would be wrong to go against the law. In some ways that complaint against Muslims provides detractors of Islam a way of attacking the religion that can be framed as an attack on *shari'a* rather than on Islam, as though these are distinct. In the past Jews were often criticized for their dependence on the Talmud, it would hardly have done for Christians to criticize the Bible that is obviously also their Bible. The Talmud is full of law, and lots of other things also, and was often a particular target of those critical of Judaism. There is plenty of religious law in Christianity though, as anyone who has tried to have a Catholic marriage annulled will know, and other denominations in the religion also often have quite comprehensive legislative principles to which their followers must adhere. The recent turmoils in the Anglican church, for example, often take place in attempts to change the law, and the ways of doing this are highly legalistic also. Although Jesus is often taken to be a much more spontaneous religious leader than those in the Jewish establishment against which he struggled, he did say "I have not come to abolish the law " (Mt. 5:17). More significantly, the various churches have developed into large bureaucracies and these require rules to follow as do their followers. Law is omnipresent in the Abrahamic religions and should not be identified with only one or two members of that group.

One reason why Islam looks so legalistic is the fact that when ethical issues are discussed they often end up being described legally. That makes it look as though ethics and law are the same. A point worth making is that the law provides ethics with a very useful set of examples and ideas to be used to work out what the moral situation actually is. For example, there are some harsh punishments in the Qur'an and in *shari'a* and so it looks like Islamic morality countenances severe penalties on the whole. It is worth adding that in practice there are governments and groups which call themselves Muslim and they carry out the harshest sanctions for what most people would regard as minor offenses or not offenses at all. They naturally justify what they do on religious grounds. There is also much in Islam about forgiveness and mercy, and indeed the latter is a way in which God is frequently described, and surely if He is merciful His creatures might be expected to learn from this and be the same, in so far as they can. So law and ethics cannot really be identified. Someone may require a sanction legally yet be forgiven ethically, and there is nothing problematic about such a dichotomy.

The source of ethics in Islam

There is one issue that was at the heart of early discussions of the nature of ethics in Islam, and it dealt with the foundation of ethics. One might think that there is no issue here at all since presumably God is the foundation of ethics, in the same way that he is what grounds everything like our world and our fates. But one theological group, the Mu'tazilites, were unhappy with this position. Surely some things just are right and other things wrong, and of course we do depend on God to help us work out what these are, but He does not establish their rightness or wrongness. To give an example here, God is surely better at mathematics than we are, but he does not ground mathematics. The latter is a rule governed system that operates independently of anyone and it is no insult to God to suggest that He is not its cause. We can certainly think of him as the cause of our understanding mathematics, since we are created in a way that makes that possible. We could have been created in some other way, like cats, for instance, who despite their pensive attitudes are probably not thinking about quadratic equations.

The thesis that morality is independent of God could be made stronger and it might be suggested that our access to it is also independent of God. That would mean that we could in principle work out how to behave regardless of revelation. That means that had we not come into contact with a revelation of some kind, we could still know how we should behave. This would be like the mathematics example again, of course we could only think in moral terms if we had been constructed in certain ways, but once we have been, then we can work it out for ourselves. This is important since it means that there is something about rationality that makes it independent of revelation. The debate between the Mu'tazilites and their enemies looks like a debate about rationality, they value it and their opponents do not, or value it less. We shall come to see that this is an error, however widespread it has become, and it requires examination.

Mu'tazilites and Ash'arites

The opponents of the Mu'tazilites were the Ash'arites, a group who came to dominate Islamic theology and who argued that morality is based on God. There is no morality without revelation, and earlier revelations are to be replaced by the latest and last, the Qur'an, if we are to grasp our duty. This could mean that it is not possible to be good without divine guidance in some form, or that it is easier to be good with such guidance, generally the thesis was the former. The reason for this is that action itself has no character at all from a moral point of view, it is all a matter of how it is identified by God. Charity (*zakat*) is a good thing, we are told this in the Qur'an, but had we not been told it by a reliable source in this way we would have no reason to think it is a good thing. There is nothing in it that makes it good, its label has to come from without. It is rather like another Ash'arite theory that supports occasionalism, the idea that causal powers do not reside in things, only in God. We normally link causes with effects, indeed, our lives are based on this but it is a mistake to think that the power to create something new lies in a thing, it lies solely in God who has power over all things. God helps us by creating a world that is lawlike as a reflection of his desire to create an environment in which we can flourish and feel at home. Similarly, in moral life God has established laws and rules that fit in with our propensities, with our nature, but he did not have to do this. He could have done things in any way he wanted, more inconveniently for us perhaps. He is not obliged to create in any way at all, or even to create in the first place. He has created and very kindly provides his creatures with rules of nature and morality and all these fit in with how we are. He did not have to do this, he acts purely out of grace, and so moral and scientific life has to be credited entirely to His decisions.

It is often said that God could do anything He likes with us since we are His possessions, and in the Arabic the phrase often used for a human being is *'abd* or slave. Right now I am typing on a word processor and it belongs to me, so I could do anything I like with it. I could bang away at the keys with gusto, perhaps risking damaging them. I could be typing relevant material or just nonsense. On the other hand, just because it is mine does not mean I can do anything at all with it. I am not allowed to hit people over the head with it, for instance. We might even not be impressed were I to destroy it or mistreat it, not that I do not have the right to do so but it is a waste of resources and arbitrary use of an artifact that would have value for others were I to decide not to use it any more. Of course I am not God and I did not create this computer, but I did create the money to buy it and if there are people in the world who would like it and make use of it, for me to destroy it and deny them that opportunity appears to be morally dubious. To take another case where someone has really created something, when writers die they often instruct their executors to destroy their work, work which they themselves exclusively created. Sometimes the executors ignore those instructions and as a result we have some wonderful material by Virgil, Kafka and so on. How do they justify their actions? They sometimes say that although the artist created the work, he does not have the right to destroy it just because he created it. If it has a wider significance to the world as a whole then it might be wrong to go along with the artist's wishes.

This of course is to use the idea of wrong being something independent of the wishes of the Creator, but it is worth examining the idea that just because someone makes something it is then entirely at the maker's disposal. This is not what we say about human beings and the example is often used about human beings and their ability to control what they themselves create. Even in places where slavery was legal owners could not do anything they liked to slaves. Servants also cannot be treated in any way at all, there are rules and regulations, although of course how far they are observed is a valid point. It is an important part of the Ash'arite position that our lack of power with respect to our creator means that we are entirely dependent on Him to tell us how to behave. There are two sides to this and it is important not to conflate them. One is that God determines the meaning of morality, the other is that He determines our access to that meaning. The latter is weaker than the former and seems more plausible from a Qur'anic point of view. After all, we constantly apply moral terms to God as His names, and it is difficult to argue that what we mean by saying that God possesses a virtue is that He possesses what He regards as a virtue, and by default we do too. The Qur'an seems to assume that its audience knows what morality is, what they have problems with is knowing how to apply it.

This is not a good argument, though, since the fact that it is awkward to translate ordinary moral language into language about what God wants merely reflects a difficulty about technical translation. Philosophy is full of arguments that strictly speaking we ought to reformulate ordinary language in order to bring out the logical structure of a sentence, and of course those reformulations do not tend to be very elegant. A utilitarian might unpack a moral claim in terms of its consequences for human welfare, for instance, and some epistemologists would convert ordinary language about objects into language about what can be perceived at a particular time and place.

To the objection that when we use moral language we do not necessarily mean to reflect what God wants comes the response that what we think it means is wrong, and its real meaning is for it to be in line with divine wishes. So when we read, "You who believe! Be upholders of justice, bearing witness for God alone, even against yourselves or your parents and relatives" (4:135), there is no problem in translating justice into something like "the state of affairs that God wishes to prevail." We can understand something similar from the verse "You who believe! Show integrity for the sake of God, bearing witness with justice. Do not let hatred for a people motivate you into not being just. Be just. That is close to piety (*taqwa*). Fear God. God is aware of what you do" (5:8).

The first quotation reminds people that our conceptions of justice may be at fault, as may those we acquire from others, even those close to us and in authority over us. God is the source of true information about justice and we should not be confused by either tradition or our passions, as in 5:8. This is further emphasized in "And when they do something shameful they say: 'We found our fathers doing it and God has enjoined it on us'. Say: 'God really does not command us to do what is shameful.' Are you saying about God what you do not know?" (7:28). People tend to refer to God as encouraging us to do things that are entirely the reverse of the truth. Muslims often refer to tradition as supporting what they do but we need to recall how critical the Qur'an is of tradition.

It might be argued that the earlier revelations constitute a process of moral education for humanity, and once we arrive at the final revelation those teachings have prepared the way. It is worth noticing that these *ayat* address believers, with the assumption being that they know something about divine intentions. Piety is precisely not allowing our feelings to overwhelm what we know God wants us to do. Believers could include non-Muslims, People of the Book perhaps also, since they are all in receipt of a revelation and can use it to find out how they are to behave. Muslims thinkers differ on this issue, some like al-Ghazali (d. 1111/505) argue that only people who accept the main points of the Qur'an are really believers. Jews and Christians do not give any sort of religious role to the Prophet Muhammad and so are seriously awry (Leaman 2016: 58–59). There is also the theory of *tahrif* or corruption, according to which the original scriptures have been so corrupted by their users that they are useless in telling us how to behave or what to believe. It would be difficult to argue then that Jews and Christians could be regarded as genuine believers.

The role of revelation

Could people have worked out how to behave without any sort of revelation at all? It is worth pointing out that the position that ethics is linked with knowledge of God has a variety of gradations of strength. They range from the idea that we can work out our duties by using reason alone to the principle that we have no hope of getting anything right morally if we rely on ourselves to work it out, and everything in between. For instance, it might be that we could use our independent thinking to work out the bare bones of our duty but need revelation to find out about the detail. Or the other way around. It is worth mentioning this continuum here since the bald argument about the link between ethics and the divine really tells us very little about either. We need to know precisely what the link is supposed to be and then we can assess how plausible that claim is.

The Ash'arite claim that there is a problem with making God dependent on a moral system separate from Him is a bit overdone. God is dependent on all sorts of things presumably like the rules of chess. It could be that He would prevent people from developing the idea of such a game, but once it is invented it is what it is, for God as well as for us. It could be changed of course but then perhaps it would not be chess. Morality consists of rules and they apply to all agents, including God. It is not as though He should be troubled by the rules in the sense of finding them hard to follow. Justice is justice, although our understandings of it might differ, of course. When God revealed the Qur'an to the Prophet he followed the rules of Arabic, a language that the text is proud of at least in terms of its style, and with earlier revelations he used the local language. He followed the rules of grammar, since otherwise nothing would have been comprehensible. Saying that He is restricted by being obliged to follow the rules of justice is rather beside the point. It is like saying the Qur'an is restricted by following the rules of Arabic.

If God establishes moral rules, as he does in the Qur'an, we need to ask whether we could have developed such rules by ourselves. Some obviously not: "He has only forbidden to you dead animals, blood, the flesh of swine, and that which has been dedicated to other than God. But whoever is forced, neither wishing nor going too far, there is no sin upon him. Indeed, God is forgiving and merciful" (2:173). So we have rules about not eating certain things, hardly an extensive list, and we are told at the very same time that if these forbidden foods are necessary for us, presumably if they stand in the way of our life and death, we can forego the ban on them. This is repeated (16:115 and 5:3) and we can take it that severe circumstances are meant here by looking at the end of the *aya*, "But whoever is forced by severe hunger with no inclination to sin then indeed, God is forgiving and merciful" (5:3). We could not have worked out the list of things not to eat by ourselves, apart maybe from animals sacrificed to other gods. On the other hand, this is hardly a substantial list nor does it seem that important since in the same *aya* in which it is raised circumstances appear which mitigate it. It looks like the major moral rules might be those we have acquired from our upbringing and through our use of rationality. The same qualification does not appear when murder or theft or adultery are mentioned.

An example of an important rule not accessible through reason alone is the obligation to pray and fast. Even fasting is mitigated when it is mentioned: "O you who believe, fasting is prescribed for you as it was upon those before you that you may become righteous" (2:183). In the next *aya* this is qualified and we are told that the fasting will only be for a fixed number of days and can be postponed by those who are traveling and sick. Verse 2:184 ends with the familiar phrase that this is something that is in our interests, although we may not understand why. We shall take up this passage again in the chapter on nature.

The form of prayer is also not provided in the Qur'an, this along with all the rules that emerged are more the province of the analysis of the hadith and the *shariʿa* that developed over the early centuries of Islam. It is sometimes argued that we can derive the significance of prayer from reason, although not its particular form, of course. This is because when someone does us a gratuitous favor, like creating us, we are obliged to thank them. It is sometimes said that the *fatiha*, the first *sura* in the Qur'an, represents the Book as a whole because it makes this point, referring to our need to praise God. It also refers to his showing us the straight path. Yet are we obliged to thank someone for creating us, especially if we did not ask to be created? It may be that we would have preferred not to have been created, some of us at least, and some people are definitely born with so much wrong with them that we often wonder what sort of quality of life they can be said to enjoy if any. God presumably is behind their creation in that particular way, and one wonders if they would really thank him for it. Of course, this is not the case for most people, but a large number of people have a rough time of it in this world, they may be slaves with human masters, they may be very poor or heavily persecuted by others, with lives nasty, brutish and not as short as they would like. Thanking God might appear then to be ironic were it to take place. Most people are not in that position, of course, and yet even for them it is certainly polite to thank someone for helping you, but is it a rational imperative? When gratitude is part of the mutual relations of people it serves the purpose of encouraging gratuitously beneficial behavior, but when it is directed at God one wonders what precisely it means. Of course, we may get something out of being grateful to God, the Qur'an often suggests so, and in that case it is worth doing, but that information could hardly arise without revelation.

Sin as error

There is a suggestion that people who go in the wrong moral direction make a mistake. Without revelation we are in trouble knowing how to act and are likely to go awry. This is very much a theme of the Qur'an: "Evil as an example are people who rejected our signs, and wrong themselves" (7:177). They get lost, they fall off or were never on the straight path, and they do not know how to get back to it or onto it in the first place. Are these people who deny all revelation, or some, and who seek to use reason alone, or perhaps they rely on what tradition tells them? We have seen that the latter is not supposed to be a good idea. The suggestion is that revelation is a necessary condition of moral behavior. Does this mean for everyone or for those who cannot use their intelligence to work out their duties at least in general terms by themselves? It is by no means clear although for al-Ghazali the rule applies to everyone. Morality just is not the sort of activity we can work out for ourselves however rational we are, we need to rely on what we learn from others and ultimately from God, since the world is not organized in such a way that it reveals moral truths to us. The Mu'tazilites are just wrong about this, they ignore the ways in which people may argue and disagree about morality. They do not understand that reason and morality are actually not in contact with each other most of the time since they deal with very different objects, rules of valid argument on the one hand and human action on the other. Sari Nusseibeh claims that "Mu'tazilism represents the most daring voice of rationalism in Islam" (2016: 78). This is a point which is constantly made, the Mu'tazilites are rationalists (according to Nusseibeh, more than the philosophers), their opponents are traditionalists or hostile to reason and Islamic culture suffered long-term damage from the fact that in the theological debate between the two groups the latter won and the former retreated into the Shi'i world or completely disappeared. This familiar claim needs to be questioned.

Ethics and rationality

The first thing to notice is that when al-Ghazali and others challenge the Mu'tazilite position they are being just as rational as their opponents. This seems wrong, since the Mu'tazilites give the leading role to reason, so how can anyone who challenges them be as rational? What we need to notice here is that when al-Ghazali produces an argument for his position, he bases it on an analysis of the difference between moral language and other sorts of language. He argues that it is false to see the former as capable of being generated univocally from our experience of human behavior. That is, we can interpret actions in a variety of ways if we have no criterion from elsewhere to help us discriminate between actions we should admire and those we should reject. There are a variety of different legal ways of defining actions and again for that to be possible we need a legal methodology to apply to the action, not a logical methodology. The logic of action and the logic of theoretical statements are distinct from each other, so if we are to talk about action in a way that respects their rule-governed character, we need to apply some sort of rule to them. It does not emerge from them, it needs to be imposed in some way. There is nothing unreasonable about this position, which is not to say that we should agree with it, but we should acknowledge that it is a perfectly well argued and rational argument. Al-Ghazali argues against his opponents, and his arguments are of course much better than those of the Muʿtazilites. We cannot just read off the moral qualities of actions by observing them as though the qualities were like weight or color, we have to think of morality as applying to the world in a rather different sort of way. Different people may assess the same action distinctly although they have exactly the same facts before them, something with which we are very familiar. Al-Qaradawi makes the point that God "has made permissibility and prohibition dependent upon intelligible grounds which relate to the welfare of human beings themselves. It thus became known in Islam that the prohibition of something is linked with its evil and harmfulness" (1980: 28). Even those linked with Ashʿarism seem to see the law and ethics as having a purpose which makes it rational, no one seems to think that God would command absolutely anything He wishes. He could but why would He? When we are told that God has chosen Islam for us as the best religion, one of the things that means is that it fits in with who we are, something that He knows well since He has designed us in that way. Whether we accept this argument is not at present the issue. What is the issue is whether it is an argument at all. It is, and a perfectly rational one. The argument is that the rules of religion have a basis in who we are and what we should do and avoid doing, and these are topics which can be rationally discussed and assessed.

We can see this in much of Islamic law, such as the laws of war, to be discussed in much more detail in the next chapter. Shaybani, for example, provides many restrictions on what a Muslim army is allowed to do to non-combatants, especially Muslim non-combatants. On the other hand, there are instances where they have to be harmed, since they are deliberately put there by the enemy. Besieging a city is a good example, as projectiles are hurled over the walls and the army rushes in it may easily be the case that civilians are harmed, and the enemy uses them to help preserve themselves. In such a case one other is prepared to harm them or just go away, and Shaybani is clear in the acceptability of harming them, using a variety of the law of double effect. One does not have to feel guilty about harming them or pay compensation since it is the fault of the enemy that they are harmed in the first place, they are not the target. It is easy to see the point of flexibility here, it fits in with how we act and try to reach our ends, making allowances for the particular difficulties that stand in the way of general principles.

This approach seems to fail to do justice to the idea of there being some rules that really defy explanation. What is wrong with eating pigs, for example? Plenty of people do it and seem to suffer no ill effects as a result. Here we need to defer to the idea of a lawgiver knowing more than we do and having to advise us on how to act. We do not know everything but our creator does and there are many matters where we have to defer to Him. This is not a challenge to rationality either. It is an acceptance that there are areas of life over which someone else has far better knowledge than we do. Such an attitude is not confined to religion, of course. When drawing up a legal document my lawyer carries out my instructions, I hope, but the document itself I have little grasp of, which is why I went to a lawyer in the first place. I just sign where I am told. If he made an error then I am in trouble as a result of what I signed, but it is rational for me to trust someone who I have some idea about and whose work in the past I have perhaps examined and approved. How much more trustworthy, one might say, is our creator, the person who with no self-interest brought the world into existence. It is just as rational to argue that reason has limits beyond which it should not go as it is to claim the contrary. So when we read "But it is possible that you dislike a thing which is good for you, and that you love a thing which is bad for you. But God knows, and you know not" (2:216), we can recognize the truth of the first two claims even if we reject the second statement. There are experts in many areas of life but are there moral experts? *The New York Times* column *The Ethicist* suggests there might be, but reading that column will soon disabuse one. The BBC's radio program *The Moral Maze* is similarly bereft of ideas beyond smug platitudes and self-important posturing. Morality is more than just clichés and lazy reflections of those accustomed to pontificating in public on ethical issues.

The problem of evil

It is often said that there is no problem of evil in Islam. The problem of evil is the idea that there is a problem in reconciling an omniscient and omnipotent deity who is also perfectly good with the ordinary events of the world. These often look arbitrary and cruel. If God is in control over everything, why would he allow these things to happen? The Book of Job in the Jewish Bible is a good example of how God's role is questioned thoroughly and there is a lot of skepticism of the traditional theological responses. Even God at the end of the book wants to punish those who give the traditional theological responses! Job or Ayyub in the Qur'an is very different, he suffers but just prays that his suffering will not change his relationship with God. In the Bible Job's faith never varies but he does raise some challenging and quite impolite charges about God's role in our world and how He carries it out. Job's problems arise due to the actions of Satan, of course, and in the Qur'an Satan is told: "Indeed, over my servants you have no authority. Enough for you is your Lord as the organizer of things" (17:65), and 15:42 goes a bit further and admits Satan will be effective with those who follow him. Satan will have authority over those who do not regard themselves as God's servants, presumably, they are ripe for temptation and the consequences that has for them in both this and the next life. This does not mean that bad things could not happen to anyone but that if they do they have a purpose and eventually there is reward for those who act in the right way. People are sometimes taken to be free to make their own decisions and if they go awry then they risk punishment, although God is always ready to forgive. We are assured that everything will be alright in the end, divine justice will prevail, although we may not now understand what that is, evil will not prevail.

Now, this is not a solution to the problem of evil which we might find easy to accept. For example, when it is a matter of innocent people suffering, the classic issue that arises for believers, we have to accept that it will all come right for them in the end, and of course with an afterlife there is scope for this to happen. On the other hand, as al-Ghazali says, the idea that such a consequence would make it alright is like having a king who slaps someone for no reason and then compensates him. It all seems rather futile, and unworthy of him. It is better to be compensated than otherwise, but if it was in the power of the king to avoid the injury in the first place, he should do so. This is a real problem with the Mu'tazilite position, although we are often told how rational it is. The idea that in the next world everyone who suffers unfairly in this world is recompensed, including animals, is banal. It is better than nothing, but not a lot better. A child who is born with many things wrong with her and lives a painful life for a period and then dies cannot really be compensated for that, even an infinity of pleasure and unfettered activity could not make it right. There are some pleasures that are enhanced coming as they do at the end of a period of deprivation, like when we are training for a sport and endure the hardship in order to achieve the final end of being good at the activity. Even not eating and drinking for a bit in order to enjoy the eventual feast makes sense, going out in the cold to appreciate the central heating more, and so on, these are all instances where temporary suffering results in longer term pleasure and are quite comprehensible as activities we might choose. Starving to death or being beaten with electric cable really cannot be followed by a life which would make it all better. That is not to say that people cannot endure terrible experiences and put it all right in the end, sometimes it is possible, but can we really make sense of a deity who could prevent such things happening not doing so?

The Ash'arite complaint that if morality is objective then God is forced to act in accordance with it is overdone. Whatever something is, if anyone wants to get involved with it, they will have to abide by its rules or features. If God wants to play chess he will have to regard the fate of the King as being a serious matter. He is not forced to follow any rules unless he wants to engage in an activity that has rules. Does morality have rules? We have argued so far that it does not in the sense of being a game like chess with clear and distinct rules and working principles. Different people may dispute what is right and wrong, ideas of justice vary widely and this is something that the Qur'an itself seems to hint at is a divinely organized fact: "Don't you see that God sends down rain from the sky? With it We then bring out produce of various colors. . . . They really fear God, among His servants, who have knowledge for He is powerful and often forgiving" (35:27-28). These *ayat* stress the different colors of the things that God produces in the world.

The varieties are considered natural and are called "God's signs" at 30:20-22:

> And from amongst His signs is this that He created you from dust . . . among His signs is this that He created for you mates from among yourselves that you may live peacefully with them, and He has put love and mercy between you. In fact there are signs there for those who reflect. And among His signs is the creation of the heavens and the earth and the variations in your languages and colors, in this are surely signs for those who know. And among His signs are the sleep that you take by night and by day, and your efforts out of His grace; there are certainly signs for those who listen. (30:20-23)

What is the point of this variety? We are told: "O people, We have created you from a male and a female and made you into races and tribes so that you may know each other. Surely the most honored of you in the sight of God is the one who is the most righteous of you" (49:13). There could have been uniformity in creation but

> To each among you have We prescribed a law and an open path. If God had so willed, He would have made you a single people, but to test you in what He has given you compete in virtue as in a race. The goal of you all is God; it is He that will show you the truth of the matters on which you disagree. (5:48)

Showing us the truth does not necessarily mean that we will understand it, just some idea of what we are supposed to do.

Different views on how to act

Islam does not consider all viewpoints correct or of equal value. However, there is the suggestion that very often the differences of opinions (*ikhtilaf*) are also evidence of divine mercy. If God had so willed, says the Qur'an, He could have forced people to come together on all important issues, but He did not do so. God did send His prophets and messengers, and imams, according to the Shi'a, from time to time so that the right path might be made clear through them. As regards the final judgment as to who followed the truth and who did not, that will be made known on the Day of Judgment by God Himself. In keeping with this principle, God prevented His prophets and followers from having recourse to coercion in religion: "There is no compulsion in religion" (2:256). It is not a difficult step from here to the idea that there is no compulsion in morality either, in the sense that we can allow differences of opinion to exist and be tolerated. There are limits here of course, we would be ill-advised to allow people to think it is a good idea to kill others if they were so inclined, but a wide range of other moral issues are in play for many communities and one of the major controversies will be precisely about the notion of justice. Plato discusses this in *The Republic* and comes to the conclusion that everyone has different ideas and they all need to agree that behind their differences there is just one real notion of justice, and once we grasp that the debate is at an end. But of course that one real notion became itself yet another competing notion. The suggestion of 5:48 is that God knows the answer to the problem, and if he knows the answer is he forced to act in accordance with it in his judging us?

It is difficult to think of a good argument why this should not be the case. If we know something is true then presumably we should act upon it, human or higher. We do often say that we have no choice. Presumably this is true of the deity also. It is no restriction on our freedom to act on the truth, only people who act arbitrarily would base action on anything else, and we should assume that God acts accordingly. To return to a previous couple of *ayat*:

> Don't you see that God sends down rain from the sky? With it We then bring out produce of various colors. And in the mountains are areas white and red, of various shades of color, and dark black. And so there are various colors among men and crawling creatures and cattle. Those truly fear God, among His servants, are those who have knowledge since God is powerful and merciful. (35:27-28)

The diversities of races, families and tribes also have a healthy and constructive purpose, that "you may know each other." In the words of the Qur'an: "O people, We have created you from a male and a female and made you into races and tribes so that you may know each other. Surely the most honored of you in the sight of God is the one who is the most righteous of you" (49:13). This *aya* is constantly quoted by those in favor of pluralism. Yet it does not accord with our experience, in many cases diversity leads to disruption and hostility, and religions often have a tendency to emphasize the significance of everyone being the same and doing the same sort of thing. Some religious groups are offended at the behavior of other groups, or other religions, and actually murder them when they can. Some go so far as to murder them through killing themselves. As so often, the Qur'an is arguing for a state of affairs that seems quite distant from our experience of how people behave in the world, (those who call themselves) Muslims included and there is nothing unusual about that. Religions call for humanity to behave in particular ways and often they do not.

The Ash'arite position is surely right in thinking that religion has to leave room for mystery. Islam, like so many other religions, does this often. Insisting that God adheres to just one concept of justice, the Mu'tazilite idea, is to think we can pierce that mystery and it leaves God with a rather banal notion of justice. All He does is watch what we do and eventually judges us for our actions. When the Qur'an refers to the significance of variety and diversity we might wonder how to square this with the idea of just one notion of justice. One of the interesting things about living in our sort of world is that everyone sometimes seems to have a different view on what justice is. The reference to colors is helpful here and we might wonder what the point of having different colors is. One answer is that it makes life more exciting and of course vivid. The movie *Pleasantville* brings this out nicely. In the movie the main characters are enchanted with an old black and white TV series with that name. In that fictional town this soap takes place in black and white, everything is comfortable and safe, everyone knows their role in society, there are no conflicts and divisions of any major kind. The fathers go off to work in the morning with their briefcases, the mothers stay home with the kids, the fire brigade never has to deal with fires, it just rescues cats from trees. The main characters are transported to that world and at first enjoy the experience but soon it starts to break up, color starts coming in, and it comes in through the introduction of passion. People start to have strong feelings and they interrupt the smooth flow of agreement and ritual. We start to move from a safe and regulated world to a more dangerous and unpredictable place, and the Qur'an suggests that is a good thing for us. That is how God has designed the world for us. At the same time religions have a tendency to try to regulate away those differences and insist on conformity, and Islam is no exception here.

This is not a bad analogy for ethics. We could follow a very simple set of rules, or try to, and leave it at that. Stealing is wrong and will be punished. There are certain things people are not supposed to eat and drink. Lying is a sin and should be avoided. Adultery is evil and is not to be committed. These are among the rules that Muslims are supposed to follow, and they do not only apply to Muslims but to everyone of course. Would this be how a good person would behave? Not necessarily, since there are situations where it might not be appropriate to do these things. If you are starving might you be allowed to steal? In conditions of starvation the penalties for theft were in the past suspended to recognize the difficulty of acting in such a situation of *darura* or necessity. If only the wrong food is available, it would be a mistake to die of malnutrition. And so on. We can often think of situations where we have to vary our behavior to come as close as we can to getting things right, and this often throws up what lawyers call hard cases, examples where we really cannot see what the right line of action is. Or better, where whatever we do seems either wrong or right.

It is difficult to account for this sort of (familiar) moral dilemma on either the Ash'arite or the Mu'tazilite view. Basically, on the former we are trying to think what God would call right, and that is very unhelpful. He has told us in the Qur'an what he thinks about this, and we have assistance from other sources too, the sunna, the hadith, the imams, and so on, but it is not all black and white. These general principles need to be applied and we often do not know how to apply them in particular cases. Hence the dilemma. We do have some idea of what God would say in general terms but how to use that in a difficult case is often a mystery. Similarly with the Mu'tazilites, the reference to some objective standard of justice tells us almost nothing that can be used. Of course we are trying to work out the most just solution to the problem, but what is it? Often the Qur'an wants to cash this in using utilitarian kinds of language, but we know how problematic that can be in coming to a solution. Whose happiness, whose welfare, how do we measure it, in both this and the next world, or just in this world? How far can future pleasures compensate us for present pains? These are all familiar issues and any moral theory that implies we can easily solve them is just wrong.

The trouble with Ash'arism and Mu'tazilism is that they both see the link between ethics and law in rather crude terms. The Qur'an itself seems to suggest with its emphasis on the significance of diversity and variety that we should not expect a simple link to exist here. Things change all the time, people are all different, the situations that arise in our lives are complex and often themselves different from each other. Any account of Islamic ethics that does not describe this accurately is going to be incomplete and not in line with the Qur'an. The Qur'an emphasizes the significance of balance, there are ethical principles we are supposed to follow but in certain circumstances they need to be qualified, perhaps, and other factors taken into consideration. This is a feature of ethical debate one cannot help noticing, perfectly sincere people can come to different conclusions as to how to act, and how to act in accordance with religion, and we have to respect that fact and not denounce one conclusion and accept the other as the obvious "Islamic" position. Law and morality do not have a clear relationship, although they are obviously related, and the Qur'an itself is very sophisticated on this topic. It is far less interested in specifying a definite link between law and morality than do its commentators, and this is a theme we shall follow in the rest of this book.

Bibliography

Abu-Lughod, Leila (1986), *Veiled Sentiments: Honor and Poetry in a Bedouin Society*, Berkeley: University of California Press.

Abu-Lughod, Leila (1989), "Zones of theory in the anthropology of the Arab world," *Annual Review of Anthropology* 8: 267–306.

Asad, Talal (1986), *The Idea of an Anthropology of Islam*, Washington, DC: Centre for Contemporary Arab Studies: 59–88.

Al-Attar, Mariam (2012), *Islamic Ethics: Divine Command Theory in Arabo-Islamic Culture*, London: Routledge.

Cook, Michael (2000), *Commanding Right and Forbidding Evil in Islamic Thought*, Cambridge: Cambridge University Press.

Draz, Muhammad (2009), *The Moral World of the Qur'an*, trans. Danielle Robinson and Rebecca Masterton, London: I B Tauris.

Fakhry, Majid (1994), *Ethical Theories in Islam* (2nd ed.), Leiden: Brill.
Hallaq, Wael (2001), *Authority, Continuity, and Change in Islamic Law*, Cambridge: Cambridge University Press.
Hallaq, Wael (2004), *The Origins and Evolution of Islamic Law*, Cambridge: Cambridge University Press.
Hourani, George (1985), *Reason and Tradition in Islamic Ethics*, Cambridge: Cambridge University Press.
Hovannisian, Richard (ed.) (1985), *Ethics in Islam*, Berkeley: University of California Press.
Izutsu, Toshihiko (1966), *Ethico-Religious Concepts in the Qur'an*, Montreal: McGill University Press.
Leaman, Oliver (2016), *The Qur'an: A Philosophical Guide*, London: Bloomsbury.
Nusseibeh, Sari (2016), *The Story of Reason in Islam*, Stanford, CA: Stanford University Press.
al-Qaradawi (1980), *al-Halal wa'l-haram* [The Permitted and the Forbidden] 28, Beirut: al-Maktab al-Islami al- Saduq.
Rahman, Fazlur (1983), "Some key ethical concepts of the Qur'an," *Journal of Religious Ethics* 11/2: 170–85.
Reinhart, Kevin (1983), "Islamic law as Islamic ethics," *Journal of Religious Ethics*, 11/2: 186–203.
al-Shaybani (1996), *The Islamic Law of Nations: Shaybani's Siyar*, trans. M. Khadduri, Baltimore, MD: Johns Hopkins Press.
Vasalou, Sophie (2008), *Moral Agents and their Deserts: The Character of Muʿtazilite Ethics*, Princeton, NJ: Princeton University Press.
Vasalou, Sophie (2015), *Ibn Taymiyya's Theological Ethics*, New York: Oxford University Press.

2

Conflict

Those who believe fight in the cause of God. (4:76)

One of the moral issues that arises as soon as there are people all with their own ideas and interests is how to regulate conflict. There is a complex and sophisticated legal Islamic discussion about how to conduct conflict in accordance with Islam. Most people think that peace is a desirable state of affairs, and the Qur'an supports such a position, but there are situations where conflict occurs and is even required. This could be when the community is attacked and needs to defend itself, and this is sometimes extended to cases where it thinks it is about to be attacked or might conceivably be attacked one day. It could be that violence is justified when some group of people are prevented from finding out about the divine message in the Qur'an by their leaders, or where they could find out about it but it is presented in the wrong sort of way, and those rulers and their supporters need to be fought and overcome in order that the truth be more widely broadcast. Difficult ethical issues arise here as always in political life. Often rulers have to deceive, dissimulate, make agreements they have no intention of keeping, forge alliances with disreputable groups, betray friends, and so on, and these are all in themselves immoral actions. Innocent people are often harmed, and this is also in itself immoral. We know that violence often leads to consequences for innocent people, and we need to find some justification for such behavior if we are to be able to justify our actions. In modern times the debate is even more relevant given the vastly more destructive power of weapons; however, even in the past when conflict was a matter of spears and swords innocent people clearly were affected, often enslaved and made homeless, or just through being left destitute through the deaths of their main providers.

If we approach violence as a category of justified punishment, there are two familiar theories of how we should act. One position suggests that only the guilty should be punished, and innocent people should never be punished.

The point is to target only those guilty of crimes for punishment, and in the case of war this means only those directly involved in the conflict. On the other hand, some argue that punishment should be used as a deterrent; this is a more effective strategy if the target of punishment is broadened to include more than just the guilty. After all, innocent people are inevitably harmed as a side-effect of punishment, and if people are likely to be deterred from immoral behavior by contemplating the suffering that will be caused to a large number of people, this is to the general good. In warfare, armies tend to target those who are threatening them on the battleground, but if punishing innocent civilians behind the lines—and all civilians whatever their views on the conflict count as innocent in warfare—will dissuade the enemy, then that may result in fewer deaths overall than otherwise. Armies will worry about their friends and relatives at home and may be dissuaded from aggression or even defense. We often make a big fuss about civilian suffering, but whenever a guilty person is punished, others connected to that person also inevitably suffer even if they are not directly targeted. Criminal parents are not able to insulate their children or significant others from problems. From a consequentialist point of view, collateral damage is no bad thing since it might serve as a disincentive to commit crimes. If an army can induce the enemy to destroy a civilian group of people and buildings, that is often helpful from the point of view of public relations, and may hasten the end of the conflict, as a result minimizing the eventual loss of life and damage to property. In the end then using civilians quite cynically may help bring about "better" consequences than an opposite strategy. Sometimes it is helpful to dissimulate about what was really going on. An army may deny that it targeted or even harmed civilians; most armies always deny what is obviously true even when the evidence is incontrovertible, while the other side may deny that it had forces in the area. In these examples it is the consequences that are important, and they may result in our doing something that otherwise would not be acceptable.

To take an example from recent history, in 1979 the most important mosque in the world, the *masjid al-haram* in Mecca, was captured by a violent anti-Saudi group which was led by someone claiming to be the *Mahdi*. The Mahdi is someone sent by God to start the process terminating in the end of the world. There was a discussion on whether it was legitimate to use violence to defeat and expel them. The judicial authorities first of all suggested that unarmed troops be sent in to get the building back in government hands—unarmed due to the sanctity of the site—but unsurprisingly they were all immediately killed by the insurgents. Then, quoting 2:191, the authorities permitted violence to defeat the interlopers, and this obviously caused a lot of damage to the building as well as, no doubt, killing many innocent bystanders who had been caught up in the encounter. It was the fact that there were many innocent people around in the first place that made the mosque such a tempting target for the insurgents, no doubt. They would not have deliberately set out to kill them, but it would not harm their position if some of them were to die, since it would have revealed the relative inefficiency of the Saudi authorities as protectors of the mosques, an important aspect of their political legitimacy. In any case the people who died could be rewarded in the next life if they deserved it, while the others would receive their eternal punishment. The consequences of the attack and the response to the attack are justified in terms of the consequences, as the verse from the Qur'an suggests, so does this mean that in matters of violence it is always the consequences that are the crucial factor? Again we seem to see very much of a utilitarian flavor in Islamic ethics. The point is not that the consequentialist logic justifies what happens, just that this is the approach to be applied as appropriate to the situation. What justifies behavior is going along with what God tells us to do, and the Qur'an seems to value the consequences above everything else.

The rules of war

In many ways this seems generally to be the position of radical movements seeking to challenge the status quo. The beneficial consequences of extreme measures might make those measures morally appropriate. They argue that the Qur'an itself points to the importance of frightening the enemy and the *sira* of the Prophet refers to many instances of violence that were apparently sanctioned by him and his followers, such as beheading and humiliating the enemy. The Prophet and his companions were throughout much of their lives involved in warfare and rather gruesome battles of one kind or another. Those connected to the enemy soldiers are said to have suffered greatly as well, through being killed, enslaved, and dispossessed. What is often called terrorism is action that kills innocent people, but for a purpose that is religiously valid we might wonder about using that label. So, for example, attacks on foreign tourists are designed to retaliate against those radical forces in other parts of the Middle East by hurting and killing their civilians. Such attacks in the home country may be even more effective. Of course, the people being targeted have nothing to do with the conflict, and in many cases are not even nationals of that country, but the important thing here to consider is the point of the violence. It may help motivate those countries to change their policies. Normally, it would not be thought to be right to attack innocent civilians, but if the consequences suggest it might be effective in bringing about a greater good, then some would argue it becomes a legitimate action.

The Shi'ite thinker Mutahhari (d. 1979) in his account of acceptable uses of violence argues that 2:251—"And if God had not repelled some people by others, the earth would have been corrupted"—can be taken with 22:40: "For had it not been for God's repelling some men by means of others, monasteries and churches and oratories would have been pulled down." Mainly concerned with the rules of initiating jihad, discussion of the rules of war tend to point to the major moral motives as helping the oppressed, whether or not such intervention is requested. According to Mutahhari, this was the nature of most of the early Islamic wars, and another legitimate cause is the removal of political obstacles to the propagation and spread of Islam or in other words, fighting in favor of the people that are otherwise condemned to isolation from the call of truth and against regimes that suppress freedom of speech. If people were free to hear the message of Islam, the implication is, they would obviously embrace Islam, so energetic measures need to be taken to ensure that the message is effectively broadcast, sometimes by force. Defensive wars like the defense of life, wealth, property, and land, of independence and of principles are all legitimate. However, the defense of human rights Mutahhari places above the defense of individuals. The last of Mutahhari's legitimate causes of war goes beyond any notion of defense; he supports a policy of moral expansionism. That is, when dealing with corrupt societies, whether democratic or otherwise, the Islamic state should seek to challenge the false ideas that persist there due to the ignorance of the truth and it may be necessary to invade them or at the very least confront them militarily in order to convey the proper principles as to how they are to live.

This is clearly a very broad rationale for conflict and perhaps would sanction all kinds of aggressive behavior albeit described as defensive toward others. Challenging false ideas would be a never-ending task especially as they do not only exist in the non-Islamic world. There are plenty of Muslims who have unusual ideas on important issues who may need correcting. It is a bit like getting one's retaliation in first in rugby, where a violent player on the other side is attacked before he can be aggressive. The slipperiness of religions on violence and their dependence on important individuals to interpret the religion makes it likely that in particular situations the judgment will be made to countenance it for reasons that are perhaps not that compelling when seen objectively. The religion and its followers become very dependent on the views of particular people. Justifying violence by looking at the consequences is always problematic, since the intention may be to achieve certain ends but perhaps the damage that is done to innocent people as a result may be far worse than one initially calculates and so the calculation is difficult to get right. Muhammad Sa'id Ramadan al-Buti argues that in Islam jihad is more of an offensive war, and does not take seriously the idea that it is defensive. Its main goal is the spreading of the divine message on earth. In this way he clearly advocates the offensive type of jihad. This is a view shared with Sayyid Qutb, Hasan al-Banna, and Mawdudi, all staunch representatives of Sunni Islam. It is not difficult to see how a concentration on the *maqasid al-shari'a* fits in with this approach. Once we start thinking in terms of what the rules are all about, it is quite a smooth move to basing the approach to conflict on the positive aims of broadcasting God's word generally, and that is such an important aim that perhaps anything goes in helping it along. This results in collapsing morality into any behavior in line with the general principles, and this leaves no room for saying that certain things should never be done, nor even contemplated as acceptable actions however positive the consequences might be. This really narrows the scope of morality and might be thought to reduce it to a set of formulae that prevent us from thinking seriously about the issues themselves.

There is an internal problem relating specifically to consequentialism. Once we think in terms of doing something violent in order to bring about an end we think is worthwhile, we have the problem of determining whether it will bring about that end. How likely is it to achieve its end, and if it does, was it worth the cost? Wars of liberation can be very bloody and harm many innocent people, and if the result is independence then it might look as though it was worth it. But is the happiness of those now in charge of their own affairs more weighty on the welfare scale than the losses of those who suffered due to the struggle? It may seem an easier calculation if we include religion in the mix. A war to spread Islam surely results in more people having the opportunity of learning how to live according to the divine plan, and this has consequences perhaps for the afterlife also. On the other hand, there are many *ayat* suggesting that people can expect to do well in the next life provided they are good and believe in God whether or not they are Muslims. It is not clear in any case what being a believer entails, sometimes it seems enough just to believe in one God and a few other basic religious principles, while on other accounts it is important to believe in the Prophet as the final messenger of God. On the more universal definition the effort in bringing Islam forcefully to their attention seems a bit unnecessary since they are already believers. One answer that those who harm innocents often produce is that when they die God will know if they are really innocent and reward them accordingly. It hardly matters if they are going to go to heaven anyway if they go a bit early; in fact, it is perhaps preferable to waiting a bit longer. If they are going to hell then they are not really innocent and so an earlier arrival is morally acceptable, although perhaps not something they would choose. There is a problem in that this might be taken to get in the way of the divine ability to determine when people are going to die. This is not a real problem of course, since God could be taken to know that people would die at a particular time He determines since He knows about the event that is going to kill them earlier than they expect. He is behind everything that happens, he always knew what was going to happen, the terrorist does not in any way preempt anything that God wishes to happen (see Chapter 7).

One of the familiar issues with consequentialism is that so many factors have to be considered that it is difficult to know how or when you have got the calculation right. In conflict there are the emotions of anger, revenge, the desire to win and so on, and whether or not these are helpful to welfare. On the whole they are a problem since, although on particular occasions they can help us do what we ought to do, on many occasions they are obstacles to wise judgment and calm consideration. These are important aspects of getting things right morally. Being *wasat*, being moderate is not just a matter of what we do but how we think, and the Qur'an emphasizes the importance of patience accordingly. There is the problem of deciding whose welfare is relevant, is it just one side in a conflict, our side, or both sides, and how we calculate those in any case. There is the huge problem of making a reasonable assessment of likely costs and benefits. For example, armies and air forces say they take account of collateral damage and do all they can to restrict it, but how do they know they have been successful and what counts as success? They do not generally have people on the ground in the enemy areas, and it is difficult to judge. One may not intend to harm innocents, but it can and often does happen. It may be that armed people hide behind civilians, and often they live with their families, who perform a variety of tasks for them while they are in action, they are difficult to avoid when attacking those regarded as soldiers. How significant is intention for consequentialists? It could be taken to be important since if we intend not to harm innocents, then this might be helpful for general welfare. On the other hand, if we have that intention and yet accept that despite that we often get things wrong, and innocents suffer, is this an indication of self-deception and the general irrelevance of motivation for the moral assessment of conflict? Weighing up the consequences has the virtue of making the ethical assessment objective. It is easy for someone to say he is worried about harming innocents but if his actions constantly do so what does it mean? A problem with the Qur'an is that it talks in general about things being good or bad, and legal thinkers have followed this up with concepts like *maslaha* and *darura*, welfare and necessity, and it is unclear what principles are actually being applied here. On the one hand, we know what these terms mean and think they are important morally. When we act we want to make things better and we are aware that a particular situation may require us to modify our behavior to avoid a worse outcome than would otherwise occur. Yet what that means in practice and how we get the calculation right is not formulaic. We have guidance of course, but it is difficult to know if one gets it right.

This kind of policy of assessing the moral status of the consequences contrasts with some verses, such as the verse comparing killing someone to killing everyone. This verse suggests that there are absolute principles, such as the proscribing of murder that can never be contravened, whatever the consequences. Similarly, the much quoted 49:13 is often used to suggest that God created different communities, and so it is pointless to try to make everyone believe in the same things. The Grand Mufti of Egypt, Shawki Allam, uses this passage to criticize those radical groups that kill others of a different religious background just because they have that background, quoting also 5:32: "If anyone kills a person it is as if he kills all humanity, and if anyone saves a life it is as if he saves the life of all humanity." It is also often said that there is a reference in the Qur'an to *din*, religion, and not to religions, as though the Book values all religions. It certainly says positive things about some religious groups like Jews and Christians. On the other hand, there is a suggestion that some groups are better than others, and that the original scriptures may have been corrupted by those in those religions. Shaykh Allam produced this verse about killing as an argument against ISIS and its supporters. These groups are both violent and also intolerant of difference, and there are many such groups in the world today. They have the view that those with different approaches to religion, or no religion at all, are appropriate targets for murder as a result. Yet legal thinker Shaykh Allam surely did not mean to suggest that Islam condemns all killing or even praises all saving of life, since there are many other passages which certainly seem to go in a very different direction. Even the verse comparing killing someone with killing everyone allows killing for murder and corruption on earth, *fasad*, and this famously can come to describe virtually anything. Sometimes litter is called *fasad* to emphasize its significance, and indeed when ISIS controlled parts of Syria and Iraq they would execute people for even minor infringements under this sort of label.

Of course, there is always the problem of which verses abrogate which others, but it is unlikely that Allam is arguing here that this verse abrogates all the verses about conflict in the Qur'an. Surely he also would not think it a bad thing if everyone became a Muslim, in the narrow sense of committing themselves to the specific religion and acknowledging Muhammad as the final prophet. Although the Qur'an refers to diversity as the starting position set by God, it is very unclear if it is supposed to be the final position. Certainly there is little in the Qur'an suggesting killing people just because they are not Muslims, although there are some rather hostile expressions on occasion about those regarded as having different views. On the other hand, there are many verses that make sharp distinctions between Muslims and others. One problem is that it is often not clear who the unbelievers are supposed to be, whether as some argue they include Christians and Jews or otherwise (Leaman 2016b: 62). The Qur'an says that *shirk*, idolatry, is the sin for which there is no forgiveness and *shirk* can be a broad brush. It can mean bowing down to other gods, but in a wider sense it can also mean respecting ideas and people that a particular group dislikes. Radical groups tend to find some reason for killing people and try to legitimate that reason in religious terms by finding appropriate and different authoritative sources. They may well be wrong and certainly casuistic in their approach to texts, but refuting them requires more than just referring to the way in which God created different communities in the world. Some Muslims believe that the diversity of faith should be seen as a temporary stage of humanity, until everyone comes to accept Islam. After all, Islam is seen as the primordial religion, so in effect when a non-Muslim becomes a Muslim he or she merely returns to the original and natural religion. Hence some converts do not call themselves converts but reverts—they are returning to the original monotheistic faith. The notion of *fitra*, our original disposition to be certain kinds of people, is realized best within the boundaries of Islam and some conflict is perhaps worth indulging in if it results in more people achieving such an end. Or so the reasoning would go.

Whatever the verse suggesting that killing one person is like destroying all of humanity means, it surely cannot mean that killing is completely ruled out. It would be very difficult to give the Qur'an a pacifist interpretation, although it has been given a whole range of implausible interpretations so it probably has been done. When we look at more sources of authority in Islam like the hadith and the *sira* of the Prophet, and for the Shi'a the sayings of the imams, we get yet more material advocating killing, in certain circumstances. Surely that is in principle right, there are always circumstances that look like exceptions to the rule and it then looks overly rigid to stick to the rule. There are even plenty of judicial punishments that involve killing and the blanket assertion that killing someone is wrong has to be qualified. These very general moral assertions are impressive but once they come up against reality they have to be qualified and this often involves taking account of the consequences. It might be thought that there is a problem in both valuing life and killing people, although it should be remembered that one of the crimes for which one can be killed are those which themselves take lives. Nothing can be ruled out, it depends on the consequences, and these seem to be the criteria we need to take into account to decide how to behave.

The importance of considering the consequences

The consequences of action often are the crucial factor in determining Islamic morality. Joseph Alagha shows how two very different groups of Muslims, Hezbollah in Lebanon and the Muslim Brothers in Egypt, use the principle of considering the consequences to countenance a problematic activity, dancing, if it is directed to the appropriate political ends. They recognize that while in itself dancing might be regarded as objectionable on religious grounds, specifically because of its implications for modesty, men and women mixing and touching, and so on, it can be provided with a positive role in promoting the message of resistance and encouraging solidarity among those in the movements concerned. It depends what people are getting together to go dancing *for*. If it is to have fun and meet members of the opposite sex, then there is a problem. If it is to cement political relationships and further a campaign, it is useful and even necessary. Similarly, when it comes to violence the principle of *darura* or necessity is often regarded as significant, the idea being that in particular circumstances necessity demands that things are done which normally or otherwise would not be acceptable, which again is in line with the principle that what is important morally are the consequences. The consequences then need to be cashed in terms of welfare. How this works is quite clear. In a violent confrontation one has the ultimate aim of overcoming the enemy, and, of course, the aim is to prevent the enemy from threatening Islam and Muslims, and there are things one is allowed to do to achieve this end.

The thesis is that there are acceptable principles of conflict and we need to play by the rules if the competition is to be morally sound. It may be, though, that in the particular circumstances it is necessary to put aside these principles if victory is to be attained, and in that case such a suspension of the principles is permitted. This could mean treating the civilian population in a particularly harsh way, or it could even affect how one behaves oneself. There is evidence from accounts provided by those involved in surreptitious violent missions that they are instructed to blend in by shaving off their beards, drinking alcohol, going to clubs and so on, all activities which they should avoid otherwise, but in the circumstances might find effective in realizing their goals. There is some evidence also that those who suddenly become very observant may have preceded that change with especially questionable behavior, as though they were intent on having a good time, as it might be described, before observing rules of modesty and restraint. Their example might encourage others to emulate them. Observers of their behavior before the change would assume they were "normal" and so not dangerous, and this could provide effective cover for a mission. Governments often encourage Muslim communities to police themselves and point out to the security services those who are sympathetic to extremism. Being religious suddenly looks dangerous, and those who are dangerous understand this and can take steps to downplay their religious views in public, while maintaining them in private. This is for a purpose, for a religious purpose, and drinking whisky and going to dances would all be seen as undercover activities. Often when someone is revealed to be an extremist, those close to them are surprised because their religious views did not seem to fit in with that behavior, but then, of course, perhaps they were dissimulating in order to cover their activities more effectively.

It is worth pointing out, as Alagha does, how this sort of emphasis on the consequences is supported by both Sunni and Shi'a thinkers, and that suggests that its roots in Islam are much deeper than has previously been supposed. There is, of course, the concept of *taqiya* in Shi'ism where Shi'ites are used to living as minorities in countries where open behavior would lead to persecution or discrimination. But, of course, there is nothing specifically religious or Islamic about this at all. Everyone has to dissimulate at one time or another if they are to fit into the society in which they live, and we often say or do things we do not really believe in if it is in our interests to do so. We justify this to ourselves by saying that the consequences make it necessary and so acceptable morally. These compromises are part and parcel of everyday life. We can refer here to the political flexibility of the Prophet Muhammad and also yet again to the phenomenon of abrogation. The idea that later verses can overrule and replace earlier ones is also evidence of a commitment in the religion to consider the role that changing circumstances have for what is required of Muslims. The whole process of *asbab al-nuzul*, of considering the context of revelation, is clearly important here since it helps us know which verses precede which others, and in any case once we know the situation that led to a verse we are often in a position to understand it better. The hadith also are set within a context, come to us through a chain of transmission, and their role is often to help ground a general principle in something more substantial, like an example. The whole process of using the hadith to help work out what Muslims are to do is an exercise in flexibility, since there are so many hadith and different opinions on their strengths and weaknesses as genuine reports of what was said in the past, that coming to a judgment necessarily involves a fine adjudication between a range of sources, as is the case in all major religions that are based on documents. So it looks very much as though in decisions about how to act during conflict and in times of peace, it is not sufficient to rest on certain principles that remain inviolable throughout. One has to employ a variety of material, take account of the particular circumstances of the case and be very aware of the nature of the consequences of acting in particular ways. The question then, of course, is whether the consequences take over the discussion entirely. What is the point of starting with the general principles if they are in the end to be overruled by consideration of the consequences? Do those principles have a genuine role or are they just a wish list that can readily be put aside when they prove to be inconvenient?

Different kinds of jihad

How does the emphasis on the status of the consequences work with divine as compared with secular law? The latter certainly varies from context to context, and also varies over time. But the Qur'an is taken to be the last and final message of God to His creatures, and it does not vary at all. God knew throughout the various revelations to prophets and messengers how we are supposed to act, and one wonders if these could vary over time. After all, the basic principles of morality surely stay the same throughout, while of course, there is scope for different conditions to make their application vary a bit. Our understanding of what God wants us to do could vary, but it should not, since the Qur'an is in its own view a straightforward and clear text. Saying that we do not understand it is an implicit criticism of its clarity. There is a passage which refers to the ambiguity of some verses (3:7), but it does not seem to be implied that many verses are ambiguous and there are many references to jihad where it is equated with *qital* that are very clear in how people ought to behave. The idea of absolute principles that could not be altered cannot easily coexist with the role of consequences in moral decision-making. Yet reformers often call for exceptions to be made in those absolute principles in order to modernize Islam or to better reflect the original intentions of God in His revelation and how it was interpreted by His Prophet in particular circumstances. The consequences then sneak in again. We do need to accept the great variety of hermeneutic tools that the commentator has at his or her disposal. The Qur'an is often seen as the most important, but others are highly influential and give scope to link the primary text in a variety of ways to many other things like context, grammar, the behavior of the Prophet and his companions, the views of the imams for the Shi'a, and so on. One of these supplementary points of interpretive material are the consequences. We may refer to a principle but then say in a particular case the consequences are negative and so the point of the principle would not be achieved by following it.

A good example of this is the contemporary popularity of quoting a hadith distinguishing between the greater and the lesser jihad, where the former is the spiritual struggle over the negative aspects of the self and the latter is physical struggle. This serves to emphasize the defensive nature of jihad and tries to dissociate Islam from those aspects of the account of jihad in the Qur'an that really go in a different and rather more aggressive direction. Jihad, of course, means struggle and there is no reason why it should be identified with physical struggle exclusively, but it is nonetheless true that throughout most of the history of term it was. A significant problem with representing this hadith as a crucial aspect of understanding jihad and peace is that it is often used in a very vague manner, as a corrective to the negative image of Islam as a violent religion. The hadith certainly does not do justice to the practice of Muslims at war, or even their disinclination to go to war, and this is not to criticize it, but it is to question how widely it was accepted and used as a basis to behavior. In any case, to say war is the lesser jihad does not mean it is not important nor that the rules for pursuing it are not important. It suggests that there is more to conflict than just physical struggle and that is worth emphasizing. In many Muslim communities aggressive attitudes to those seen as violating norms are encouraged and the idea that our efforts to control our feelings are harder to develop, and more valuable, would be a useful corrective to what we often see.

This is true for all communities, of course, not just Muslim ones. Many cultures are based on tribalism and shame, which, according to al-Jabri, is most Arab societies since the Ummayads. He refers to the phrase: "Those who listen to their Lord" in 42:38. He used this verse to praise a political period in early Islam of *shura* or consultation, since it goes on to mention "consult each other in their affairs." In the time of the Prophet al-Jabri says the state was based on the Islamic creed or *'aqida*. Muhammad's community in Medina was a real political community and could be seen as an "Islamic state." This was not to last long, the Ummayads distinguished in the person of their ruler the function of religious scholar (*'alim*) and leader of the state. Mu'awiya's *mulk* or kingdom was continued by his successors, replacing *'aqida* with *qabila* or tribalism, and an authoritarian government resulted, since one tribe had to dominate the rest if stability was to be preserved. The subsequent domineering regimes were based on tribalism, and its noxious heritage, in his view, continues to this day. It also encourages the growth of a form of authoritarianism in the family, a patriarchy based on the analogy with the ruler and the ruled, and levels of physical and psychological violence to maintain those levels of authority. This is part of the long tradition of looking to the past for a golden age which we should try to recapture, and yet it is a paradox that a religion which explicitly attacks tribalism, nationalism, and tradition should seem to find adherents who value precisely these aspects of what they regard as their religion. The more wrong we are about something often the more aggressive we become in defending our views, and we see how a conflation of Islam with a particular attitude to tradition is often violently imposed on others.

In 2:190 we read: "And with those who fight to kill you, fight in the way of God." Many early Sufi thinkers adopted esoteric interpretations of the Qur'anic verses treating conflict. The real challenge and test comes from within. The reasons why the Prophet stressed that the greater jihad must be against the carnal soul (*nafs*) is that physical wars against infidels are occasional but the battle against the self is frequent, indeed constant. There are ways to avoid the visible weapons of the military foe, but less chance to escape the invisible weapons of the temptations of the soul; and although we can achieve martyrdom in war with the enemy, there are no rewards if one is defeated by our inner enemy. On the contrary, that defeat is the normal condition of human beings. The idea of spiritual growth is often described in quite military language, and we are familiar with the idea of struggling against ourselves when we try to do something that goes against our inclinations. But before we come to the conclusion that physical warfare is not that important we need to consider the next verse, 2:191: "And kill them wherever you overtake them and expel them from wherever they have expelled you, and *fitna* is worse than killing. And do not fight them at al-Masjid al-Haram until they fight you there. But if they fight you, then kill them. Such is the recompense of the disbelievers." This is a robust account of how Muslims ought to act in conflict, even in Mecca itself. The reference to *fitna* or dissension suggests that such actions might be necessary against those who call themselves Muslims and are dissenting from the proper understanding of the religion. 9:14 suggests: "Fight them, God will torment them with your hands, humiliate them, empower you over them, and heal the hearts of the believers," a passage we will consider further. The Qur'an advises believers to deal harshly with the enemies of Islam. In the early conflict between the family of the Prophet and those who sought to rule the community the cutting off of heads of the enemy was a priority, we are told. The heads of the dead were on display before their relatives and survivors to emphasize the victory of one group over the other, a bloody episode which did much to cement the antagonism between Sunni and Shi'a Islam.

To understand the significance of this verse, as with the rest of the verses in the Book, it is very helpful to look at the *sira* and hadith of the Prophet. As with a variety of religions, there are plenty of bloodthirsty accounts of the past that can be used to legitimate acting in similarly direct ways in the present and future. For example, there is the death of 'Amr bin Hisham, a pagan Arab leader originally known as "Abu Hakim" (Father of Wisdom) until Muhammad renamed him "Abu Jahl" (Father of Stupidity) for his determined opposition to Islam. After 'Amr was mortally wounded by a new convert to Islam during the Battle of Badr, it is reported that 'Abdullah ibn Mas'ud, a close companion of Muhammad, saw the enemy chief on the ground and started abusing him. Among other things, 'Abdullah grabbed and pulled 'Amr's beard and stood gloating on the dying man's chest. Normally one would recoil at such a disrespectful way of treating a dead body, even one of an enemy, yet it is often not enough for people to overcome the opposition. They need to rub the noses of the other side in what has happened and humiliate them. After the defeat of the followers of 'Ali at Karbala there was a parade of heads apparently of the fallen in battle to emphasize that one side had won and the other thoroughly lost. This has led to some groups of Muslims today emulating such behavior when dealing with their enemies by cutting off their heads and humiliating their bodies, perhaps as a means to healing the hearts of the victors for earlier indignities they had suffered. They may also hold onto bodies and use them as bargaining chips, despite the rules insisting on quick burial. Although this may be distasteful to some, if this is the most efficient way of bringing about an end worth achieving, are there really any significant ethical objections to it? This is a point that is often made by those carrying out such brutal operations. At 8:16 we are told: "And whoever turns his back on them, except as a strategy . . . will certainly attract the wrath of God, his abode will be fire, And what a wretched destination that is." (It is worth noting here the idea of doing something strategically, of course, given the earlier discussion of the significance of taking account of the consequences of action.) The previous verse refers to fighting the unbelievers. There are plenty of verses which talk of the advantages of violence, but, of course, there are just as many and perhaps more that talk of the significance of peace and the importance of not prolonging conflict any longer than strictly necessary. How to balance them and find a common approach is a compelling but probably forlorn task. What is interesting is how the consequentialist strategy has influenced the language of conflict and made it much more instrumental, perhaps losing sight along the way of important principles that need to be preserved and defended despite the likely results of doing so.

Back to absolute principles

It looks as though it is very difficult to perceive the overriding absolute principles that ultimately govern action, since all sorts of otherwise objectionable actions are apparently contemplated in the right circumstances. On the other hand, we are often told that there are basic principles in religion and the *shariʿa* is said to have *maqasid*. We have to be careful in how we deal with those principles. Pious books defending Islam on this topic see no problem at all; Islam is based on peace, even the name of the religion can be taken to refer to peace, and the rules of war are fair, largely defensive and proportional. Those hostile to Islam interpret the references to peace and war to be based on rather aggressive principles, and it is not difficult to find verses that can be expanded into universal principles which accord with such a view. History has plenty of examples of the ruthlessness and brutality of people who do not seem to have reflected on how their religion might have expected them to behave. Not, of course, that there is anything specifically Islamic about this, the phrase "the rules of war" is oxymoronic, but it does serve to remind us that the rhetoric we often hear of how comparatively gentle, or vicious, the forces of Islam tend to have been in the past miss the point. Muslims in conflict are and were just like anyone else. They say they respect particular rules but in practice there is very little evidence of this. This seems to suggest that the idea that there are absolute principles to be obeyed in all circumstances is nothing more than rhetorical. This is not a point about practice but about theory as well, the principles do not seem to enter into the process of ethical decision-making. We know that the Prophet is supposed to have been very flexible in his political management of the nascent *umma* (community), but surely this pragmatism was based on principles, principles embodied in the Qur'an and derived from God. That is why one of his wives, 'A'isha, referred to his character as based on the Qur'an and his practice is taken as exemplary by Muslims even on very small matters like which shoes to put on first, and how to brush teeth. Presumably then his behavior should be taken to be something we should follow.

We need to think about the connection between principles in ethics and the ways in which we actually work out how to behave. In Islam, as in other religions and ethical systems, there are not just general principles that help one decide how to act. There are additional and diverse sources of authority, ranging in Islam from the hadith, the *sira* of the Prophet, the judgments of whatever school of law one adheres to, the sayings of the imams for the Shiʿa, the use of reason at some level, our understanding of the grammar of Qur'anic Arabic, and so on. Some of these consist of stories, stories which talk about what happened, what it meant, how people reacted and so on, and these are very helpful in teaching people how to apply theory to practice. Good teachers do not just instruct their students in the subject they are teaching but give examples, show them how to apply the theory and in this way it becomes more concrete and applicable to their everyday lives, and this is how religions also work. Such examples not only help us apply theory but also enable us to stand back from the immediacy of the situation in which we find ourselves, so pressing in the case of conflict, and calmly consider how to act. This is a point that Kant made when outlining the concepts we use both epistemologically and morally, suggesting that we need some way of actually applying them to the world we experience. He argued this involved what he calls schematism, which is a way in which the concepts are translated into a more concrete form so that they can be used to deal with the world of space and time, and human behavior. He does not actually think that we can find a clear schema of the moral law, but something rather similar to it will have to serve, and we do not have to enter into the detail of the critical philosophy here, but we should take up his main point which is that the way in which the schematism work involves the imagination, and this is how stories enter. It is the imagination that uses and manipulates the stories that are so important to us in operating in the everyday world, and the stories that feature in the hadith are precisely that, they help us work out a variety of ways of adapting the principles of religion to the practice of everyday life. It has to be said that the variety of hadith and the variety of ways of assessing their reliability makes this a very open process. That could look as though it is really being used to allow people to do whatever they want to do, finding some theological and legal support along the way, but nothing in this area seriously constrains them. This would be an error, though, imagination is not necessarily unconstrained and independent of anything else. It builds on experience and ideas we get from our lives and those we know and combines these together in ways that make sense to us as resolutions of issues we are confronting. A problem with it is that it does not seem to fit into demonstrative reasoning since such reasoning comes out with conclusions that logically follow from the premises. This is very different from what we are used to seeing in ethical decision-making, where anything often seems to go. The point here though is that it is not the case that anything goes in ethics, we do value certain principles and think it is important to try to link them with our experiences in a way that makes sense to us. This is not an arbitrary process, although different participants may come up with different conclusions, as is familiar to us in ethical discussion.

In Islamic philosophy imagination has traditionally been seen as the intermediary between heaven and earth, between the realm of the celestial and entirely abstract and the world of generation and corruption which we inhabit. As a source of knowledge it is suspect but as a way of allowing us to discover how to combine experience with general ideas it is essential. This Kantian idea has a long history in Islamic thought, and it comes very much into the ethical discussion here, since it helps us understand how it is possible for us to use moral principles in a way that makes sense both practically and yet also in a way that acknowledges the significance of those principles. Imagination is clearly involved here, the sorts of people who just follow principles without thinking about their implications or putting themselves in the shoes of the participants surely fail to act appropriately, however close their actions are to some verses in the Qur'an. They go awry since there are, of course, other verses as well, plus a wide range of interpretative material that obliges the believer to consider carefully how he should behave in a situation of conflict and not just follow a formula that represents a partial understanding of the divine will. This flexibility is a characteristic of most versions of Islam and encourages agents to take account of a wide range of consequences and think about their implications for human welfare. A legal judgment may then be produced and be regarded as definitive, at least within a particular community, but we should be careful about regarding it as absolute. The Supreme Leader of Iran, Ayatollah Khamenei, has on a number of occasions declared as not Islamic both the use and possession of nuclear weapons. Given the status of consequences in moral reasoning, though, it would not be difficult to envisage a situation where this ruling would be regarded as no longer valid. All it would need would be for the consequences of not having such weapons look worse than the consequences of having them, in which case the legal position would quite abruptly change. The Qur'an does after all say: "So get organized against them whatever force and war mounts you are able to gather so that you might deter in this way the enemies of God, who are your enemies as well, and others besides them of whom you may be unaware, but of whom God is aware" (8:60). It sounds like an excellent justification for the development and existence of a nuclear weapon, despite the obvious high civilian death toll that is likely to arise were it to be used. In any case, the idea here is to prepare against both obvious enemies and potential future enemies, a very wide brief indeed.

Principles and how to apply them

A theme of this book is that the idea of balance or *wasatiya* in religion is crucial. It is linked with the concept of justice, as in 2:143 where the followers of the Prophet are described as *wasat*. Sometimes the term is identified with being the best (68:28; 1:6-7) in the last verse contrasting sharply with the approach to religion taken by the Jews and the Christians. Indeed, Islam often sees itself as mediating between those who believe in anything at all and those who deny everything they cannot personally prove. Hence the importance of imagination, something that is very much a concept that exists in the middle. Islam is a middle point between those who see the universe as the only important place and those who regard it as an illusion. The former treat the world as too important, the latter as too unimportant. In Islamic law we find a system designed to balance crimes and penalties, and rules such as those of inheritance are designed to preserve equity. Whatever we think of the detail of such laws we may find much in them which is difficult to accept, but the principle here is entirely acceptable, that an attempt is made to be fair to all parties, to allocate people their deserts and preserve a sense of balance. The identification of virtue with moderation is not difficult to understand since the universe itself was created in a balanced and presumably good way: "And the earth We have spread out, and set on it mountains firm and immovable; and created in it all kinds of things in appropriate balance" (15:19). Not everything should be firm and immovable, some things should be fluid and mutable, and we are told that there is a balance between all these different phenomena that marks the world as a place carefully created by a benign intelligence.

In a hadith describing what will transpire at the time the world comes to an end, there will be an epic struggle between the Mahdi, supported by Jesus, and the Dajjal, a sort of antichrist. He will be popular and will be able to persuade a lot of people to support and follow him, although finally he will be defeated. He is described graphically to have all sorts of horrible aspects, but one prominent detail in many accounts is that he has only one eye. There is a discussion about the significance of this, and one possibility is that it is to emphasize the fact that there is no balance in his perspective. He only sees what is in front of him and without being able to take into consideration anything else. He cannot balance his view of the world with any other information or ideas. This is a big problem since morality involves considering a range of views and principles and making a decision about how to reconcile them all in the best sort of way. Evil people like the Dajjal are often successful, at least initially, since they are so single-minded and determined to overcome any conflicting pressures they may experience deflecting them from their main aim. Operating with only one object in sight is dangerous, the example of the Dajjal suggests, and obviates the necessity to take account of a variety of issues and indeed people.

Applying a rule always calls for discretion, and the virtue of moderation is that the rule is applied sensitively to a particular situation or within a certain context. That is where Iblis went wrong, he applied a rule, one of his rules, that fire is superior to earth, in a way that failed to take into account God's purpose in elevating humanity over jinn. We need to remember that the Qur'an is the enemy of conformity to tradition where it does not have an apparent basis in divinity. Perhaps people did talk of fire being superior to earth, it is certainly a more active type of phenomenon, but just because this was the popular view there is no reason to think it is a view worth accepting. Iblis was not prepared to consider whether there was a point to what he was told to do, he could not moderate his sense of superiority over this creature that God was elevating over others, and the result is well known (17:61-62). The angels were quite right, of course, in making critical remarks about human beings, but when God told them He knew why they should bow to him they acceded, on the principle that God knew why and they did not. This is the basis to so much of what we are told in the Qur'an and makes it difficult to those trying to apply a natural law sort of view to the text. Iblis provides us with an excellent example of the dangers of applying a rule without being prepared to consider how experience may call for it to be varied.

Musa also applied a rule to his experiences when travelling with Khidr and could not understand what was happening, rejecting the advice to just accept what he saw. He lacked patience and humility and as a result missed what was happening. On the other hand, he raises obvious questions, the sorts of questions that arise in the traditional problem of evil. How can we reconcile an omnipotent and omniscient deity with suffering to innocents? Musa is noticing an apparent problem here and is surely not at fault in pointing it out. If Iblis is correct in what he says about fire and earth, what is wrong with his insisting on it? Perhaps it is his disregard for suras such as "O you who believe! Do not make unlawful the good things which God has made lawful for you, but do no excess, for God does not love those given to excess" (5:87). This emphasis on avoiding the extremes is significant. In criticizing the status of humanity, Iblis acted excessively, rather than waiting patiently to see how this new creation would work out. Musa is in exactly the same position. This straight path is mentioned in all the daily prayers, and it is not difficult to argue that the straight path is equivalent to acquiring a moderate disposition in our behavior. The whole structure of Islam can be seen as contributing to this aim.

There is a dangerous tendency to think that a religious believer only has to rely on what he or she is told by religion to know what to do. This is true for some of the more minor rules of religion, and believers often say that the fact that they do not have to think about the little details of how they should behave means that they have more time to think about the big details of human life. It is the big details which are difficult and where often one does not know how to act. The area of conflict is a useful one to examine here. Suppose a soldier is operating in an area where an insurgency is taking place. Sometimes the enemy packs cars with explosives and directs them at barriers and troop concentrations, hoping to exact heavy casualties. It is often unclear whether a civilian car is just that or something more sinister. Morally it is unacceptable to kill innocents but in many situations it is difficult to tell who the innocents are. A soldier mans a checkpoint and is told that if any car is warned to slow down and does not, he is to shoot at it. He can follow this general rule, but is it moral to do so? He knows that sometimes civilians in a car are talking to each other, music is playing loudly and attention wanders, and it would be wrong to kill people just for being in such a car. On the other hand, they might be pretending not to understand what they are supposed to do, and once the car arrives at the barrier with the explosives, it is too late to take preventive action. It is this sort of messy situation that often characterizes our moral world and we have to try to work out how to operate within such a difficult environment.

What is the right course of action? There is no simple rule that can be followed without further thought. It is problematic to do what one is told and just fire at any vehicle that disobeys instructions since there may be a good reason for that disobedience and it should be taken into account. On the other hand, it is wrong to do nothing since there are people out there intent on doing harm unless they are stopped, and they will pretend they are non-combatants if they think this will be effective. The middle position and the just one is to form a judgment as the vehicle approaches of what the most likely explanation is, and then act on that. There are all sorts of visual aids and noises that might help one form a judgment, and past experience is, of course, very helpful here.

God knows what sorts of creatures we are, he created us. we did not come about haphazardly, and so he knows how we ought to live. We are told in the Qur'an that He provides us with this information through his messengers and prophets, through the Qur'an itself and other authoritative works, through the hadith and the sunna of the Prophet, and for some Muslims through the imams or other significant figures. A contrast was made earlier between two approaches to moderation, one based on strict adherence to the law where moderation is damaging to the point of the divine legislation, and where it is something we are advised to pursue throughout our lives with respect to our personal and communal behavior. This contrast may itself be moderated, and we might say that the strict view of the law represents one side of it, the fact that it comes from God and cannot be altered. Yet, however divine the law may be, it has to be used and interpreted in everyday life, and it is here that moderation is significant. Moderation can be linked with the idea of considering the consequences of what might happen since it involves considering a wide range of examples that might be relevant in deciding what to do in a particular case. It is opposed to the idea of just sticking to a formula and following it.

We started by contrasting two ways of decision-making in ethics, one dependent on absolute principles and one based on the consequences of action. It was argued that both are involved and that Islam suggests this by its emphasis on moderation and through the whole hermeneutic process of considering a wide range of sources of authority. Nowhere is this more important than in issues to do with conflict since here the passions of the participants are often raised to such a level that their capacity for calmly and properly assessing the situation before them is diminished. Religions are very good at helping participants think in a sophisticated manner about the issues and at coming to a conclusion based on a rounded view of both the facts and the ethical possibilities of action. To grasp this we need to understand more clearly what scope there is for moral reasoning in religion. This chapter has been an attempt at starting on this task and applying it to the debate over violence and Islam. The argument has been rather like those in Islamic philosophy advocating describing God in terms of what He is not like, as opposed to His positive attributes. It has been argued here that whatever the rules of war in Islam might be, and how violence should be used, are issues not going to be resolved by either consideration of the consequences or through relying on some general principles that can never be contradicted. It is going to be by some combination of these ethical sources of information. There is nothing novel in this suggestion. On the contrary, it represents the practice of those involved in the debate over many centuries. It is designed to serve as a corrective to those today who seek to resolve these complicated ethical issues by relying on a simple formula to work out how to behave.

Bibliography

Damad, S. Mostafa (2005), *Protection of Individuals in Times of Armed Conflict under International and Islamic Laws*, New York: Global.
Al-Dawoody, Ahmed (2011), *The Islamic Law of War: Justifications and Regulations*, New York: Macmillan.
El Fadel, K. Abou (2007), *The Great Theft: Wresting Islam from the Extremists*, New York: HarperCollins.
al-Jabiri, Muḥammad 'Abid (2001), *Naqd al-'aql al-'arabī IV: al-'aql al-akhlaqi al-'arabi* [Critique of Arab Reason IV: The Ethical Arab Mind], Beirut: Markaz Dirasat al-Waḥda al-'Arabiyya.
al-Jabiri, Muḥammad 'Abid (2002), *Takwin al-'aql al-'arabi* [Formation of Arabic Reason], Beirut: Markaz Dirasat al-Waḥda al-'Arabiyya.
Khamenei, Ali (2012), "Nuclear weapon is Haraam; Nuclear energy is a right," August 30. Available at http://english.khamenei.ir/news/2270/Nuclear-weapon-is-Haraam-Nuclear-energy-is-a-right
Leaman, Oliver (2013), *Controversies in Contemporary Islam*, London: Routledge.
Leaman, Oliver (2016a), "Religion and violence: How symbiotic a relationship?," *Religions* 9: 34–44.
Leaman, Oliver (2016b), *The Qur'an: A Philosophical Guide*, London: Bloomsbury.
Mutahhari, Murtaza (1991), *Jihad: The Holy War of Islam and Its Legitimacy in the Quran*, Silk Road.
Roy, Olivier (2017), *Jihad and Death: The Global Appeal of Islamic State*, London: Hurst.

3

Sins

O humanity! Behold, we have made you all out of a male and a female, and have made you into nations and tribes, so that you might come to know one another. In fact, the noblest of you in the sight of God is the most deeply conscious of Him. Behold, God knows and is aware of everything. (49:13)

The notion of individual rights is not easy to understand within the context of a religion that establishes rules for everyone to follow. God informs us how we are to act and whatever rights we can derive have to come from that. The Qur'an and *shari'a* seem to countenance a lot of practices which seems, on the face of it, undesirable—slavery for example, the unequal treatment of men and women, restrictions on who can marry whom, inherit property and in what proportions and so on. We are told: "And women shall have rights similar to the rights against them, according to what is equitable; but men have a degree over them" (2:228). It is sometimes said that all the Abrahamic religions had many similar rules or even worse ones, and that is certainly true, and some groups within those religions still act in accordance with them today. That is not very helpful though; it is a bit like children arguing with each other and being mean about the parents of the other child. It could be that those rules were supposed to operate in the past and were then better than the feasible alternatives but can and indeed should be avoided now. It could be that they were not even acceptable then and were largely misinterpreted since they violate other basic Islamic rules of behavior, and yet those in charge then found it convenient to apply a law that was in their interests. We see here yet another example of the *maqasid* approach, the defining of Islam in terms of a few clear general principles and everything else can be seen as fitting in or otherwise. We can totally avoid this problem, of course, if we think that what human rights are can be seen in what God says about them in the Qur'an, and He knows and we do not, so if what He prescribes seems unpalatable, we need to take our medicine and benefit as a result. This sort of complementarity fits in nicely with the *maqasid* strategy also, so, although there are occasions when women should be in authority over men, this is regarded as rare given their biological differences and social norms. So it is worth defending a general rule which sees women as to a degree less powerful than men. As with any hierarchy there are rules of deference and things may go much more smoothly if these are widely understood and accepted. It is sometimes argued that accepting such "natural" differences leads to a good deal of happiness since in a situation where everyone is secure in the knowledge of their place stability is enjoyed at the expense of equality. If welfare is the aim of religious rules, then while individuals may suffer, it could be argued that on the whole welfare is maximized where differences are regarded as inevitable and divinely sanctioned.

Apostasy

Take apostasy, for example. If someone is a Muslim and then rejects that faith, divine punishment will no doubt eventually occur: "Those who believe, then reject faith, then believe and then reject faith, go on increasing in disbelief, God will not forgive them nor guide them on the way" (4:137). On many interpretations of law and the hadith, there should be punishment in this world also, and capital punishment at that. But should not people be free to adopt religions and then change their minds? I have friends who seem to change their religions on an almost annual basis. There are countries regarded as liberal and that do restrict free speech when it is likely to lead to disruption. It is often said that free speech does not mean being able to shout "fire" in a crowded theater in order to cause panic when there is no fire. The rules in Islam on apostasy are curious since they suggest that this is the case of someone who knows that Islam is the true religion but then denies it, presumably not caring about his or her fate in the next world or what impact this might have on others. Perhaps it is like an evil mathematics teacher who instructs pupils that 2+2=5 and enjoys seeing what transpires. She might not care what this would do to her professional career or the impact it would have on her pupils. On the other hand, we do allow parents to transmit very strange beliefs to their children, and we even permit parents to change their children physically at such an early age that the notion of informed or any type of consent is vacuous. The idea that the liberal state is one where there is complete freedom to say or do whatever one wants is clearly incorrect. People whom others find very offensive may not suffer the penalties of the state but their neighbors may sanction them in some way, or they may find it difficult to earn a living or just live in a certain place.

These sorts of arguments are often produced to challenge the idea that sanctions against Muslims who seek to abandon Islam are not that difficult to accept. Perhaps that sort of decision should be seen as dangerous and disruptive behavior requiring controlling. Once religion is seen as a private matter it runs the risk of being trivialized, yet for many in Muslim communities their faith is something very public and far from trivial as a part of who they are. Islam is not alone in this of course. This is then how we get to situations where dress codes are enforced and enforceable, perhaps mosque attendance also, a particular type of male appearance (short hair, beards, etc.), an overt heterosexuality, and so on. Challenging this on the grounds that it is illiberal is met with the response of Islamophobia since after all even in liberal societies there are norms of speech and behavior that everyone is expected to observe. It looks then as though particular practices linked with Islam are being singled out for criticism, and for egregious reasons. This search for motives is usually not that helpful though. Whatever our motives might be in opposing a practice does not affect the moral acceptability of the practice or otherwise. We might oppose male circumcision at a young age when the boy has no opportunity to give informed consent to what many regard as an unnecessary procedure in just the same way that we might object to female circumcision which is actually not only unnecessary but also harmful. Our motives might be to attack those religious and cultural groups who are in favor of circumcision, but this impure motive does not mean our moral qualms are misplaced. Why chop things off people unless they need to have them chopped off for some medical reason? This seems a perfectly sensible question and it might well be said that it violates human rights to do this.

We do tend to allow parents and guardians to take decisions on behalf of children and often we allow them to do eccentric things. There are limits of course, so that if a parent consistently tries to do dangerous things with children the state may intervene or if they have very strange beliefs that we think may make life difficult for the child that sort of parenting may be challenged. On the other hand, we do allow parents with what counts as very strange views to influence their children and bring them up to fit into their own community, at the cost of their integration into society as a whole. We recognize that there are costs to this but probably acknowledge that society is better off on the whole if parents are given a degree of latitude here. After all, there is the liberal idea that different views represent competing experiments in living and unless we allow people to try things out we shall not know what might be best or at least better than other ways of doing things. The Qur'an itself refers to views like this apparently with approval; as it sometimes says, God could have made everyone part of the same community right from the start (5:48). Sometimes a strange custom does not look that strange since a lot of people practice it. Circumcision for males is one such custom, it has a long pedigree in a variety of religions and tribes and it is worth noting that, although it is said to be useful for health reasons, this is not the justification of it in Judaism and Islam. Suppose the removal was not of a piece of foreskin but the little finger on one hand? Or an earlobe, since fingers are useful things?

Rituals

All groups have rituals that introduce new people into the group, and in American universities fraternities frequently get into trouble for having too dangerous or provocative rituals, even for consenting adults. We can always question these rituals, and there has to be some sort of defense of them. This is the state of play when we come to questioning the compatibility of human rights and many interpretations of Islam. If it seems that what the religion is asking people to do to be in it is difficult to reconcile with human rights then this is a problem that needs to be resolved. If to join a club I need to strip naked and have people hit me with bats and throw water over me, we might want to question that. To say it is just the custom does not really do very much justificatory work, one of the things we notice in the Qur'an is a persistent critique of customs, those from the time of ignorance before Islam. Don't just do things because they are traditional, is the message, since if the tradition is just based on what people have always done, it has no basis. Is it what God would want us to do?

Being an apostate is not what God wants us to do, but it is something that people go for, on occasion, and this is to go against their natural instincts, according to the Qur'an. The whole universe is full of the glory of God and all we need to do is experience it, and then we are led inevitably to belief in Him. Denying God's existence is perverse, we are told, as is wearing immodest clothes, non-heterosexual relationships and much more, and yet there are societies where one is allowed to do all these things. People are said to have the right to behave in those ways, however regrettable they may seem to others, and the state needs to support such rights. One of the benefits of having competing lifestyles is that one gets to see alternatives and this could strengthen one's own faith in doing the right thing, or it could threaten that faith by suggesting tempting alternatives. The Qur'an does not tell us much about how we should react to differences except to be skeptical of the idea of forcing people to behave in particular ways. Like all religions there are serious disputes about how people are to do things like pray or appoint leaders. On my campus in the United States, there are fraternities and sororities, and they all seem very similar to me, but presumably they all have different rules and I can observe different dress codes. Obeying those rules has a point, they initiate and solidify clan membership and identity and it is something that many people actively enjoy. We are reminded here of those Qur'anic passages that refer to the easiness and naturalness of Islam, and the *maqasid* approach that sees Islam as designed to foster our welfare suggests we should be able to work out how those sorts of actions fit in with who we are and who we want to be, they represent our interests in some way. That is why the various rules linked with them have been established for us by God. But how they contribute to our interests is often mysterious, and that is the case with many activities that religions treat with disapproval, it is not at all clear what is wrong with them.

Drinking and gambling

We need to be a bit subtle about this, of course, and when we are told to do something and we cannot see much point to it perhaps it is for some connection it has not with this but with the next world. We should not expect everything to be clear to us given the differences between our and the divine point of view. Some rules seems very sensible and obvious. For example, alcohol and gambling are both criticized and banned for Muslims, and we know that much suffering results from overindulgence in these pursuits. On the other hand, once we examine this verse more closely, some interesting features emerge. Since the Qur'an merely refers to a particular kind of wine, does it have only that in mind or all wine? If all wine then can we move from here to all alcohol? If so, how about all intoxicants? Similarly with gambling, the Book refers to a particular gambling activity but presumably that is not the only thing criticized. All games of chance are to be avoided, perhaps. How about playing snakes and ladders with one's children, though, or going out in the morning without an umbrella gambling on its not raining later on? These do not seem to be especially egregious events but perhaps they come under the ban on gambling. It is true that both intoxicants and gambling are activities human beings often overindulge in, and if they avoid them completely the problem disappears. We see here a familiar feature of the *maqasid* approach, we have a generalization about what is good and otherwise for people in general and then it is turned into a legal requirement.

Suppose that an individual was capable of indulging in one of these sins without overstepping the mark. That is, he would drink in moderation and be rather good at winning when he gambled. Could he say that the law then applied to others but not to him? Surely not, when God proscribed those activities he meant for everyone and not just for those who do not know how to behave prudently. There is no problem with this, we could say as we often do that He knows and we do not, but it is a problem for the *maqasid* approach. We cannot see how the welfare issue is relevant. There are many rules like this. Islam has a strong sense of what is necessary to preserve dignity and modesty, and yet some people think that they should be allowed to wear and indeed say more or less what they want. Islamic law places stress on lineage, which is why being an orphan in the Islamic world is often rather difficult, perhaps surprising given the status of the Prophet himself. Yet many people are uninterested in lineage, and it does not affect their relationships with others to know that they are related in a particular way. There seems to be no good *maqasid* criteria as to why lineage should be important, or clothes. They are certainly familiar and no doubt based on an Arab *'urf* or custom, but it is difficult to argue that welfare is in general increased by people wearing certain clothes in itself. If God is pleased by such behavior then that is different, but the *maqasid* we are looking for is not in the thinking processes of God but in what looks to contribute to our welfare in this world. Of course it contributes to our welfare to do what God tells us to do but for this all we need is the divine word, not any details of the *maqasid*. The *maqasid* are actually confusing since they often tell us that something is in line with our welfare, and it is not. We have all the disadvantages of consequentialism and none of the advantages. We lose the notion of a nice clear criterion of what we ought to do, by considering the consequences, since the consequences could be something we have no access to in this world. The disadvantage is that we have a formula for assessing law that clearly does not work universally. It just is not the case, for example, that in this world the consequences of gambling are always deleterious. In general they are, but that is too vague as a justification for legislation, surely, especially divine legislation.

This might be regarded as too quick, since law has to deal with generalities and not with every particular possible case. It may be that there are individuals who are capable of drinking moderately and gambling sensibly, but most people cannot, so everyone is told to avoid these activities. To take another example, there is an age at which countries make legal activities like driving. Some people are perfectly safe drivers below that age and some will never be, however old they are, and the law has to aim at the mean. This is not a good analogy though since what is at issue here is the age at which something can be done, while with the law on alcohol and gambling it is supposed never to be done. Yet there are many instances where it would be fine for people to do these things since they would not go to excess. It might be said that one could never know, but of course one could. Neither having a cocktail before dinner every night nor occasionally betting on the 3.15 at Epsom lead inevitably to depravity. It does not add to the welfare of society to ban these mild activities, whatever the *maqasid* suggests. One could go further and claim that these activities can increase welfare since they are in themselves enjoyable to some people, harm no one else, and give their practitioners experience in acting moderately, something we are told is a characteristic of Islam. A gambler, for example, is aware of the fact that she must be careful not to get in too deep and then be liable to stop thinking clearly about what she is doing. She needs always to keep her eye on the odds and make rational and balanced judgments. There is for the good gambler a real appreciation of risk and where it is going, and how to stay on the right side of it. It is a bit like someone climbing a mountain, one has to be careful to do it correctly or one falls off, and the technique often involves keeping a clear head, knowing what one is capable of and what risks are unlikely to pay off, and how to take precautions so that if something does go wrong the results are not disastrous. Any activity like that is full of risk but one can manage the risk and the skillful climber is good at doing that. This is not only true of climbing, of course.

Risk

The Qur'an seems to have a horror of risk and mentions a whole range of activities to be avoided. The idea that one would risk one's welfare on the turn of a dice, or the local equivalent, horrifies the Book. On the other hand, there is plenty of risky activity in the Book, all jihad or struggle involves risk and we know from the early years of Islam how tenuous was the grip that the early Muslims had on what was happening. Often they suffered reverses, and although they prayed for the right conclusion to their actions, they were never assured it would come about. The hadith are profoundly realistic about this, indicating the importance of being practical and cautious about the ends of our actions

However, we are told at 20:115-19 that we were created in an environment of risk. Adam was created in heaven, given a wife and everything he needs but God also makes it possible for him to risk disobeying God's command. We are made weak in nature, we are after all material things, and always susceptible to risk and hence 20:115: "We had already, in the past, received the commitment of Adam but he forgot and We found on his part no resoluteness." Iblis appeared to ask Adam to accept more risks, since his role is to distract him and send him in the wrong direction. Adam had everything he needed in the Garden but once his actions made him leave, he then had to work out how to survive in a much tougher environment. God forgave him, but he was not allowed back, and so had to survive in the much riskier context of the earth. How is he to manage that risk in an acceptable way? This is a question we often have to raise, since our lives are full of risk and we need to take some decisions on how to assess it, and what level of risk is rational for us to accept.

Risk is action that is often seen as causing harm, either through wagers where the consequences entirely depend on luck that is uncontrollable by humans, or actions that involved elements of uncertainty that are damaging. We know that everything involves risk to a degree, what is at issue here is a level of risk that is excessive, perhaps without adequately assessing the situation and the levels of uncertainty that are connected to it. Risk is a venture into the hazardous. Islamic rules seek to understand the nature of risk as both a process and an outcome in order to determine an acceptable level of risk as presented in the nature of commercial affairs since to some degree it is unavoidable. Hence, excessive risk-taking without adequate assessment or calculation is condemned. In a familiar phrase we are often told it offends the *maqasid al-shari'a*, the purpose or aim of the law which is the preservation of human welfare. When a merchant buys a product to sell at a higher price he cannot know if he will succeed, but he can work out how likely it is that things will go in his direction, and on that basis he can take an acceptable risk. By contrast, someone who puts a bet on a horse is trying to make a profit without working for it, and someone is likely to be hurt in the process, so gambling and risk-taking of that sort is condemned. The hadith make clear that the Prophet saw the appropriate business situation as one where the parties can examine each other's goods and have a discussion about what they are worth, with neither side seeking to cheat the other nor hide anything from them. Nassim Nicholas Taleb has argued that acting in conditions of uncertainty and taking risks is only morally acceptable if both parties stand to lose.

Trade must be in tangible things and any dealing in financial instruments not connected closely with something solid is unacceptable. Any trade in something intangible, like money for instance, whose price is the interest rate is also unacceptable. The futures market is also in a dubious position since it exists to buy and sell products that do not at a particular time exist and may never exist.

One of the aspects of what the Prophet sees as the appropriate rules, and those we see in the Qur'an, is equity and fairness. If someone needs money, perhaps to set up an enterprise, and we choose to support them, we should not expect anything extra just for giving them the money, such as interest, although we can of course ask for a slice of the eventual profits. If they occur, they are then real, and we can calculate the risks to a degree before we decide to invest. The Prophet did not like the idea of money changing hands for something that is entirely random, as when one is offered something like a box and has no idea what, if anything, is inside it. The person who is offering the boxes knows, the others do not so there is no risk-sharing. We are following the *maqasid* approach here and asking for the general principles behind the antipathy to risk and interest, and it is not difficult to find such principles. If everyone is honest and exchanges information then our transactions are based on fairness and this helps bring about a just state of affairs. Justice involves balance and as Shuayb tells us: "Give fair measure, and cause no loss, weigh with correct scales and do not illegitimately take things away from people. Do not withhold things justly due to people, nor do evil in the land" (26:181-4).

No one would argue about the scales but what about the different levels of knowledge that parties to a transaction have? Suppose I am asked to help finance a farm growing a crop heavily dependent on the weather. I might have better knowledge than someone else about the likely climate conditions and this could mean I have an advantage over my rivals. Is this an unfair advantage? I am not misleading anyone, just not sharing what I know, and of course I could be wrong anyway. Or suppose we make a legal agreement and the contract is heavily weighted in my direction, the other party not receiving adequate or indeed any legal advice. Is that unfair? He could have got that advice but chose not to do so, perhaps, or he thought he did not need it. It may be that I was better prepared than he was, and it does not seem to be unfair for such a disparity to exist. I did not cause him to act as he did by misleading him, he just acted in a way that turned out to be inadvisable. The *maqasid* approach starts to seem unsatisfactory since it is not obvious what fairness and justice actually amount to here. In any legal dispute the financial resources of each party is relevant to how the dispute may proceed and who is able to even take legal action in the first place. In most cases if we have a dispute with the government then we are in a far worse position than they are in terms of resources, never mind the justice of my case. The money the government spends comes from a bottomless pit while my resources are limited. If the government loses a court case it shrugs its shoulders and moves onto something else, if a private individual loses then he or she may lose all their money, their house, their livelihood, and so on.

If I am better educated than someone else, is it unfair when we come to do a deal? It might, of course, be that the disparity helps the other person, he is more cautious or tougher, or more determined to succeed, which again suggests that it is not easy to see where fairness lies. We know that gambling generally benefits the bookmaker and not the punter, but not always, and the punter could gamble intelligently without affecting his income significantly while providing him with a good deal of pleasure. It depends on what you see going on in activities like gambling. If the point is to make money, then they are clearly problematic, for one side at least. If the point is to provide enjoyment for the gamblers and an income for those who set up the activities, then no one is harmed. Similarly with alcohol, if the object of the exercise is to get drunk, that is pretty harmful for everyone, but if the object is to provide incomes for those in the industry and entertainment for those indulging, then it is all fairly benign. Of course, some people go too far, but then people go too far eating food also, taking exercise, working, even praying. There is no reason to ban those activities just because some people find it difficult to establish a moderate position in such activities, and the Qur'an does not. Of course, alcohol and gambling are addictive, and perhaps we are told not to get involved with them because they are thought to be dangerous. People who are unable to control such addictions are liable to ruin their lives and relationships and suffer accordingly. Perhaps that is why the Qur'an is so critical of them.

There are at least two aspects of action and the Qur'an seems to take a rather one-dimensional view, and this is exacerbated by the *maqasid* approach. The latter depends on asking questions about what something or some rule is for. Alcohol looks like it is there to enable people to get drunk, gambling for people to risk money in order to get more, interest acts to allow people to do nothing and get richer. A lot more is involved in these activities than just this, though. Someone who lives off his money has to work out how to keep ahead of inflation, what is a reliable source of interest income, where is the best place to put his money, the taxation regime of his country, and so on. It is not as though one could just stick it in a fund and forget about it, at least not without risking large losses of one sort or another. It is just the same if he lends money to an individual to help a business be set up, where the borrower pays the lender a rate of interest. There will need to be an assessment of how reliable the borrower is, what security he can offer, what other interest rates are available at varying degrees of risk, and so the eventual calculation is a complex one. Similarly, gambling is not just about risking money, for many people it is fun, beating the odds or trying to, meeting friends, studying the previous results of a particular horse perhaps on a certain kind of course and in different types of weather, and then assessing what the odds should be. Gambling is part of a highly complex social institution, and interest is an integral part of a vast economic system. That is no reason to think they should be acceptable, of course, but it does suggest that the *maqasid* approach, asking what they are for, is hardly likely to capture their point. It is a bit like going to a football game with someone who is unenthusiastic at best about such an activity and who comments that it is just a bunch of people running after a ball. Well, it is but it is a lot more than that also. One is reminded of an aspect of Kant's definition of marriage in his *Metaphysics of Morals* as the reciprocal use that one human being makes of the sexual organs and capacities of another. There is usually a bit more than that involved. So we can agree that it is an important question to ask what the point of something is and yet we should not expect a simple formula to provide a satisfactory account. People have been trying to work out what marriage is for thousands of years. Institutions do have points but it is unlikely that they are going to be easily reduced to a simple formula.

The trouble with the *maqasid* approach is the trouble with consequentialism and ideas linked with it such as utilitarianism. They are just not complex enough to do justice to what they are purporting to qualify. This is actually not an argument against looking for the *maqasid*, it is an argument for expecting to find a nice neat formula as the answer. The virtue of consequentialism is that it does provide a tidy solution to a complicated problem. What ought we to do in a particular situation? The answer is to look at the consequences and work it out with that in mind. The trouble is that often that does not seem right, there seems to be more to the issue than are resolved by looking at the consequences. This is exactly the same for the *maqasid* strategy, it tells us where to look for an answer, but it has been argued here that we really cannot accept that answer. It is not that Islam is wrong on gambling, alcohol, and so on. We might well think that if God tells us not to do something then we are well advised not to do it. What is wrong with those activities cannot lie in their connections with human welfare since as we have seen these connections are dubious. From a religious point of view this argument comes as something of a relief, since the *maqasid* seem so banal.

According to al-Shatibi (d. 1388/790), who is often considered to be the chief proponent of the *maqasid al-shari'a* strategy, "welfare" (*istislah*) is the eventual aim of legislation, the welfare of everyone in the community. The law is made in order to benefit humans and to serve their well-being (*maslaha*) and in order to avoid harm. Al-Shatibi divides our "interests" into three categories: (1) the necessary or *daruriyyat*, that is things essential for the achievement of human beings' spiritual and material welfare in this and in the next world; (2) things that are needed or *hajiyyat*, that is things which, when fulfilled, contribute to relieve hardship and create ease; (3) the extra refinements of life or *tahsiniyyat*, which can be considered, in a sense, superfluous, but which, when fulfilled, enhance and complete the first two categories. It is often suggested that *maslaha* means something that is useful and avoiding something harmful, and this is all part of the narrative that the rules of the Qur'an are reasonable and appropriate. Some might question their specific features, and think they need to be brought up to date, but in general, there is often agreement that the religious regulations are beneficial for us as human and social creatures, and it is very much in our interests to follow them and avoid doing anything that opposes them (Ramadan 2017).

Sukuk

It has been argued here though that it is often difficult to see how the legal requirement does provide utility or avoid evil, except in the very basic sense that it is quite possible for someone to go awry if they do what the law forbids and vice versa. Someone may gamble and it may cause misery, but then for many this may not be the case. "Whatever you pay as interest so that it may increase in value does not increase in the sight of God" (30:39). Yet private property is one of the five basic *maqasid al-shari'a*, according to al-Ghazali, and for many people interest is a part of their property and a means of increasing or preserving it. As inflation gradually or swiftly diminishes the real wealth of the individual, the ability to charge interest on savings can play some role in keeping the property owner afloat. Like many religions, Islam has strictures on economic life and the Qur'an is highly critical of interest. *Riba* represents an increase in something exceeding what is just, although this has led to some exegetical issues whereby it has been argued that criticisms of *riba* are not criticisms of all interest, just excessive interest. Most financial instruments have a rate of interest connected to them, and they represent its price. A bond is a debt instrument independent of any assets, whereas *sukuk*, an Islamic bond, represents a degree of ownership in a real asset, or something linked to an asset like a service, enterprise, or project. Investors are offered something with a face value linked to an asset. They do not receive interest for buying it, but rather a share of the profits. When the bond matures the investors may not get back the face value since what underlies the product may not have been very successful, and then the bond holder is obliged to share in the loss.

Some bonds escape this restriction, the *sukuk ijara*, where the principal is guaranteed, and we shall consider them in due course. As well as interest, Islamic banking avoids *gharar* or uncertainty, which is said to be objectionable in the sense that the playing field is not even. Some participants to the transaction are in an inferior position through access to the facts, for example. Then there is *maysir* and *qamar*, activities linked to chance and gambling and so thoroughly forbidden. Speculation is a problem since to a degree it works on the principle that anything can happen. But anything cannot happen in a world controlled by God. On the other hand, there is obviously a lot of uncertainty in everyday life, and if we are to be efficient economic actors we need to acknowledge this. The idea is that a contract is unfair if one side has more information than the other side, or better information. This seems wrong since if someone has taken the trouble to work out the likely weather, for example, before investing in agriculture, as opposed to someone who has not and suffers as a result, is this not fair? For example, a farmer may need money to buy seed to plant crops, and until the harvest and the sale of the crops has no idea what the return will be. He may plant the seed but the harvest is poor, or the harvest is good but then prices drop so he gets little for his work. Someone who is considering investing in this enterprise does not receive a rate of interest but a share in the business, and that share should represent his risk to a degree, so perhaps if she invests 10 percent of the total likely value of the business, she actually gets 15 percent ownership to represent the fact that the future is uncertain. She could lose all her investment and needs some incentive to invest and not spend the money now on something else or invest it elsewhere. Presumably, the dicier the business, or the more risk averse the investor, the greater the gap that will exist between her real share of the business and her virtual share. It is not easy to distinguish this from an interest rate, especially since she may get payments before the crops are grown and sold finally. The fact that they are called a share of the eventual profits seems more a matter of words than anything substantial.

In the case of individual transactions the position is more complex. Gambling is heavily criticized in the Qur'an (2:219, 5:90-91) and the Prophet is supposed to have been critical of buying a product before you know what it is or how good it is. Why not? He thinks it is unjust even if both sides to the transaction agree. Gambling is linked in the Qur'an, and not only there, with frivolity, polytheism, and dissipation, but is there anything essentially wrong about it from a religious point of view? Religions tend to be critical of what many regard as fun, and Islam is no exception here, but we should recall the significance that moderation has in the religion. Might it not be the case that gambling all your money away is going too far, but never taking a risk is also going too far in not being prepared to try things? A middle position is what we should be aiming at. We admire people who are brave, not those who are reckless or cowardly since the latter two go too far from the mean to strike an appropriate attitude to how they should behave. We do not know what the future will bring but we can make some plans based on what we know about the past and the present, it is entirely rational to do so, and the undoubted fact that religions disapprove of gambling is a bit of a mystery. It might be the link with *maslaha* (welfare), the idea that gambling often leads to suffering and misfortune.

A linked and more serious problem is that Islam is very realistic and appreciates that uncertainty exists and so has to be accounted for in commerce. From the hadith we can tell that the Prophet disapproved of sales when there is some uncertainty about the precise nature of what is being sold. It follows that a *gharar* contract is void and cannot be enforced. The nature of the uncertainty is either that neither party knows what the situation is or that the seller has privileged information. It is quite right to call such an agreement speculative, but of course, there is a continuum of uncertainty and this has to be taken into account. At the extreme end is complete chance where one just tosses a coin, for example, to decide on a sale. There could be some uncertainty as when one goes fishing and does not know if you are going to catch anything. You might ask for money to help finance the expedition and promise to return the loan with fish, but how does one know if any fish will be caught? It could be that a small amount of money will be the cause of getting a lot of fish worth far more, or no fish at all, or something in between. Inequality between the contractees does not seem to be that relevant here since neither party knows what is likely to happen, although presumably there is or could be some reliable predictions made about the chances of being successful based on past experience. Different legal thinkers produce different definitions of *gharar* but the most reasonable suggestion is that there are two kinds of *gharar*, one which is illegal because it is based on chance in a major way, and lesser types of *gharar* which may be acceptable since they are based on uncertainty rather than complete chance. Clearly the point of the ban on *gharar*, which might be better expressed as the regulation of *gharar*, is unfairness and placing one party to the transaction in an unjustly superior position. This might then be a useful way of working out which kinds of uncertainty are acceptable and which are not. This is a strategy that is familiar to us from looking at ethics, we wonder how to vary a general rule by linking it with its overriding rationale. If the purpose of the ban is welfare in general, then we have a problem since it might be argued against the view of the Islamic authorities that in many cases there is nothing contrary to welfare about gambling.

Gambling on faith

Here we have the familiar difficulty of wondering how far if at all to reinterpret a moral rule. One of the intriguing aspects of the discussion about gambling and uncertainty is that it is linked with the issue of who is a good person. Is someone who acts well but without the right beliefs in God and the Day of Judgment a good person? The Qur'an suggests he might be provided that he has the minimal beliefs in God and the last day, although sometimes we are told he has to have the right beliefs in order to be a strong candidate for salvation. In a sense someone who acts without the right beliefs behind his action is gambling, he does not know what the connection is between his actions and goodness since he fails to understand the religious grounding of virtue, or perhaps because he is aligned with a religion that does not provide much guidance. He is gambling on what he is doing being the right thing but he might be wrong. That is one of the things that is wrong with gambling in this sort of case, it makes ethical life haphazard. Holding onto a religion like Judaism or Christianity might be like buying an old car and gambling that it does not break down. Returning to the commercial case, advocates of Islamic banking often point out that the crisis of 2008 was caused by difficulties with credit. Marginal borrowers suddenly found it difficult to pay what they had agreed and part of that sum was interest, and the financial edifice built on that came under strain and, in some instances, collapsed. Uncertainty characterized the market, borrowers did not know if they would be able to satisfy their obligations and lenders did not know the value was of what they owned since they did not own anything real, just a financial instrument. In the end though there were real things like houses and cars and it was possible often to take them in payment for debts, but the link was not direct since interest was involved and paper could be bought and sold in the market to extend the range of ownership of financial assets. Once a problem arose with repayment, a whole chain of financial assets were contaminated and the market froze. It was quite distant from the underlying assets, the physical things that started off all this creation of paper in the first place. In the end welfare suffered and perhaps that is the basis for the critique of that approach to financing, which one could easily criticize without taking any religious point of view at all. In some ways the problem may have been connected with the attempt at providing finance for those who previously had been excluded due to their ethnicity but in the end it may have been that they were indeed poor credit risks, not just taken to be poor risks because of prejudice.

Presumably what makes people poor credit risks is the high probability that they will default. So even putting the issue of interest aside, they are poor risks. From the point of view of the lender they are high risk, but, of course, some of them would no doubt manage to make their payments and keep their property and the fact that some institution was prepared to take a risk on them might be highly beneficial for them. We often value risk takers, they may save lives or do a whole range of valuable things. They may establish an important business or even industry through what they do, or they might get a home for their family in the hopes of being able to keep their job or get a better one, and they might be right. Perhaps an aspect of suspicion about risk is connected with gambling and the idea that the future is uncertain. It is uncertain for us but not for God, of course, and everything that is to happen is completely laid out before God. The idea that we can gamble or risk is based on the fact that anything can happen, and yet that fact is not true for God. For Him the future is already established and thinking that it is otherwise is to be profoundly wrong about a vital aspect of reality. On the other hand, one could be a gambler and accept that God knows what will happen but we do not, so it is appropriate for us to take a risk on what we think is going to happen. Given the general utilitarian flavor of Qur'anic ethics, the idea might be that on the whole gambling and risk-taking imply the uncertainty of the future, and this is both wrong and denies the divine role in what is going to happen. Yet, of course, there is no reason why this implication should be drawn since a religious gambler might acknowledge the dependence of the future on God and yet assert his or her right to have a guess and put some money on that guess.

Inequalities seem to be acceptable in Islam, which endorses private ownership for both men and women—"And covet not those things that God has given more of to some people than to others. Men shall have a share of that which they have earned, and women a share of that which they have earned" (4:32)—while at the same time is not happy with wealth accumulation in a few hands—"And those who hoard up gold and silver and spend it not in the way of God, warn them about a serious punishment" (9:34). So hanging onto your money is not a good thing and might be one of the problems with interest: "Whatever you pay as interest that it may increase the wealth of the people, it does not increase in the sight of God; but whatever you give in charity, this will increase their wealth a lot" (30:39). Charity increases general wealth, not interest payments to the few, and that seems obvious but might not be as obvious as it seems. Some would argue that a situation where people are free to do what they want with their money could lead to more general expansion of wealth than where they try to be charitable, but there is then less money to circulate. The good thing about interest might be that someone can get access to money, at a price, and with that money can pay the expenses and set up an enterprise, and that could all add to the general economic activity thereby helping more people to advance in wealth. If the person who gets interest just holds onto it, then that will clearly take money out of the economy, but she might, on the contrary, use it to finance her consumption and that could lead to employment and the creation of more incomes and more consumption as a whole.

Given the general utilitarian flavor of Islamic ethics, the reason for the disapproval of interest might be the idea that it is not to general advantage that it be charged and collected. Although in some cases it might work out, on the whole it does not. Perhaps the same is the case for alcohol and gambling, we can conceive of instances where they are not harmful but on the whole they are. A feature of basing an ethical system on the moderate position, as Islam sees it to be, is that differences of those at the extreme are submerged, and an attempt is made to find the middle. There is no space for individualistic differences that might make acting at the extremes more plausible on occasion. There is an entertaining passage in the movie *Battle of the Sexes* where the male protagonist is at a Gamblers Anonymous meeting and he harangues those there with the message that they are there not because they are gamblers but because they are lousy gamblers. Of course, most people are lousy gamblers, that is why on the whole bookies are wealthy and punters are not, but the occasional gambler can make money, and bookmakers can lose it. Ethics is going to concern itself with the general rule and universal laws of welfare, not with what the extraordinary individual can do, or what unlikely series of events may emerge.

One thing worth noticing about what is called Islamic ethics is that it generally has to coexist with other forms of ethics, even in societies with vast

Muslim majorities. That is, there are usually ethical alternatives and these have to be taken seriously. For example, although gambling is forbidden in Islam, there is a good deal of gambling everywhere, not to mention alcohol or interest. Even countries with Islamic banking systems often make it possible for their citizens to invest in a traditional banking institution, so the profit-sharing funds have to live side by side with the interest-bearing paper. It is hardly surprising then that the discount price of such Islamic funds is often not that dissimilar from LIBOR, the interest rate for interbank loans set in London, interest rates are in the market and anything else that can be a target for investment has to take this into account. There may be a piety premium, as it is called, which has to be paid in order to enjoy the feeling that one has put money into something acceptable to religion, where the rate of return is less than a haram form of investment, but it should not be too wide. This is different from alcohol, since there is no alternative form of drink that is like alcohol but unlike it is acceptable. In a verse already discussed, we are told that intoxicants and gambling contain "gross sins and benefits for the people, and their sinfulness is greater than their benefits" (2:219). Here is that utilitarian argument again, it is a matter of balance. We need to regulate our lives and moods without stimulants of a major kind and learn to cope. In some ways having people around us who obey different rules is useful since it gives us the opportunity to learn from them what is wrong with what they do and helps us experience the extremes of human behavior. God takes the view that gambling and alcohol are so bad that we should not indulge in them on any occasion.

Speculation

It is not difficult to be cynical about Islamic banking, since it often seems to be a mere form of words and an artificial mechanism for doing what one wants to do anyway. Yet this could be said about many religious rules. For instance, halal meat is just ordinary meat, if it comes from the right sorts of animals of course, albeit slaughtered in a particular way and with a form of words beforehand. There is no essential difference in the meat, it has just been presented in a slightly different way compared to ordinary meat. That is why in many countries today most of the meat in some categories is halal, it makes no difference to most people and renders the meat acceptable to some in the Muslim population. With banking, an attempt is made to link the transaction to something real and to avoid interest. The linking with the real involves the creation of a new financial instrument that in some way serves as an intermediary between the financial product and the non-financial world, thereby avoiding the notion that the product is purely financial. The return one gets from it is not an interest rate but a share in the profits. This will often come uncannily close to being worth the same as the interest rate prevailing at the time, and the degree of risk will sometimes vary in accordance with the level of reward expected. You might expect to receive a higher share of the profit if the place you invest in is unlikely to provide any profit at all. Would it not be unduly speculative to invest in it, then?

It is difficult to know. As experience often suggests, a lot of ideas initially appearing very improbable end up as highly successful and vice versa. Many people who look as though they are unlikely to do well end up by surprising everyone, and a lot of investment depends on hoping for the best and diversifying, spreading the risk as it were. Bookmakers and professional gamblers do this all the time, they lay off bets so that if the expectations of those who have made wagers go awry, those who have to pay out the money are covered. That is what traders and individuals do to a degree, they think the market is going in a particular direction, and obviously their funds are invested in that direction, but they insure the risk to a degree by placing some funds in the opposite direction, so that if they are wrong the losses are mitigated. This sort of insurance does not appear to be compatible with the rules against gambling and risk in Islam, and indeed there is a particular type of insurance called *takaful* which is designed to take the place of conventional insurance. This has a more cooperative structure and the money paid is left in the system to be eventually paid out for claims, rather than going to shareholders and being invested in the general financial market. Some Muslims are critical of such a device and argue that people should just trust in God and eschew insurance altogether, except presumably in countries where certain kinds of insurance are compulsory. Here again we see problems with the *maqasid al-shari'a* approach since it might be accepted both that in Islam insurance is forbidden and yet, at the same time, that it contributes to welfare, in this world at least. Life insurance means that families receive money when family members who used to provide money die, health insurance pays for health care, car insurance compensates drivers and others involved in accidents to enable them to continue their lives, and so on. But we do not know that we are going to be unhealthy or have car accidents, so insurance looks like it is gambling on things going wrong. We do know that we are going to die, but the amount of money this might produce seems to be like *riba*, an increase based on nothing except time. On the other hand, the idea of the moderate and prudent individual so popular in the Qur'an is of someone who would be interested in insurance since he or she would want to be able to continue to help others were their own circumstances to change and to maintain their family responsibilities come what may. Similarly, the cautious trader in the market would hedge his or her trades, so that if things did not turn out as they expected, their losses would be restrained. Their profits would also be limited but then like insurance this involves taking some current money off the table in order to make sure that whatever happened in the future, things could not get too dangerous for the balance sheet.

Wealth and poverty

So far we have not had much success in working out what good ethical reasons there are for the views on risk and interest that Islam so strenuously puts forward. It might help if we look in more detail at the sorts of wider economic issues and their ethical aspects according to the Qur'an. The Qur'an discusses wealth and poverty and links them with appropriate behavior. A general theme is that what happens, either for our benefit in this world or otherwise, is organized by God and should be seen as a trial (2:155, 7:130, 7:168). If we follow Him we will benefit in material terms (5:66, 7:96, 16:39, 24:55, 72:16) and we may do well even if we behave badly but it will not last long (6:6, 6:42-44, 7:96, 22:45, 22:48, 30:41, 34:15-17). What is crucial to economic success and failure is how we behave (8:53, 13:11). If most people behave badly, it will end up in misery for everyone (11:116, 16:112, 89:15-20). We require resources and God is the source (2:212, 3:27, 3:37, 13:26, 29:62, 30:37, 34:36, 34:39, 39:52, 11:6, 29:60, 42:19) and we should be grateful (14:7). Yet this appropriate attitude to divine organization does not really do much to help us work out how to behave since we can be grateful while, at the same time, behaving in a whole variety of different ways. On the other hand, perhaps the idea is that we show our gratitude by obeying the rules that God establishes. If we do not really understand the point of the rules for us then we should just reconcile ourselves to the fact that God knows and we do not.

"No one can inform you of the truth except He who knows everything" (35:14), who is "omnipotent and omniscient" (2:220, see also 2:231) and the source of guidance (2:38 and 7:52), while all we have to work with is "conjecture" which is no substitute for truth (10:36 and 3:28). Even if we are dubious about such claims, we come up against "Say 'No one in the heavens and on earth has knowledge of the unseen except God'" (27:65, see also 53:35 and 52:41). If there is another world, then we have no access to it and would have to rely on what God tells us about it. Moral demands that we do not understand could, of course, play out in the next world in ways mysterious to us in this one, and we would then be justified in doing what we are told in books like the Qur'an since we do not know and God does. God is very much in favor of spending on others (2:195, 2:219, 2:245, 17:26-27, 25:67, 47:36-37, 57:11, 57:18, 64:17, 92:18-19), while interest is without spiritual reward (2:276). Spending on others will result in a great return for both the individual and the society at large (2:261, 2:265). *Taqwa* or thinking of God is a source of benefit (92:5-10) as is repentance (11:3, 11:52, 71:10-12). While doing the right thing results in matters going well (72:16), doing the wrong thing has the reverse consequence (89:15-20).

Clearly, this is not true in every case in this world since we know of many examples of people who disobey every Islamic rule on finance and commerce and prosper enormously. It is worth pointing out again that these are not just rules for Muslims but are for everyone, so every occasion on which someone earns interest or buys insurance or market futures he or she is going against the divine will. It might be, of course, that they privately lead lives of desperate suffering, but this seems unlikely. Religions often make these sweeping claims about things ending up well for the pious and vice versa, and yet within this life the evidence is very much against it. Is this then just a mistake or is something else being said here?

It could be that the point is to offer a different way of doing things, one superior to what we have at present. If there was no gambling, no indulgence in risk, no interest, then everyone is likely to be better off on the whole than with the present state of affairs. That is possible, and God who knows everything would know that this is how we are to behave if we are to achieve maximum welfare. This brings out again the idea of the Qur'an in particular as utilitarian, as pointing to an arrangement of the economy and society that would produce the most happiness for the most people, from the divine perspective, and since God created us and knows everything, that is useful information for us to have.

It might be argued that the present sort of system is more likely to produce the most wealth than any other system, and on the principle that a rising tide lifts all boats, even the poorest are likely to be better off under capitalism, on the whole, than on any other system. This is not the place for a debate like that, although it would be worth saying that a society envisaged by the Qur'an as better than capitalism is not that distinct from it, in the sense that free trade, private property, and competition continues, albeit with some major restrictions like no interest and very limited risk-taking. Property is so significant that Fazlur Rahman calls it one of the four fundamental freedoms in Islam, along with life, religion, and honor (1980: 31). Any attack on it he calls *fasad* or corruption on earth. It is conceivable that such a system would be viable and might not produce the wealth of the present system, yet might produce happier people, more of whom acknowledge the role that God plays in their lives. That does not seem a ridiculous idea, and from a religious perspective the present economic system has at its heart the idea that people spend a great deal of time concentrating on becoming wealthier, and this is unfortunate given the lack of significance that worldly things has for us when compared with the eternity we shall be spending in the next life. We might be getting close here to understanding what the real problem is with interest, gambling, and risk. These are all processes through which we monetize time. With interest, for example, someone who pays me interest pays it for each day or month or year, and so I think of the time as a period in which I receive an income. When I gamble I put my money on a horse, say, and then wait for it to win or lose, and the intervening time is a period in which gain is possible, and captures my attention in a very direct sort of way. Insurance monetizes risk, it makes it possible for us to benefit when things go wrong, or at least get back to where we were before things went wrong. If I insure my house and contemplate in six months' time the possibility that it will catch fire and burn to the ground, I can rest assured that I am covered and so inconvenient though no doubt it would be, it would not be a total disaster. Time appears then to come under our control and the vagaries of the world are no longer going to control us, both profoundly anti-religious attitudes. The Qur'an constantly emphasizes our dependence on God and the very word Islam embodies this by using the idea of submission. We submit to our creator out of gratitude to what He has done for us, and we will benefit by doing this not because He will reward us (although He may) but because this is to take an accurate view of how things are, and we are much better off basing our lives on something that is true rather than something that is not.

It is important to distinguish between the view that God is in charge and fatalism, a point to be made in more detail in the chapter on choice. Islam expects us to do things for ourselves, in the economy as elsewhere, but we are supposed to act always with the knowledge of our basic relationship with God. Monetizing time gives us the impression that we control it and can describe it in monetary terms, whereas in reality what happens is not our decision in the end and we require a way of looking at the world that brings this important feature to our attention. It is interesting that alcohol is lumped in together with gambling, there is a condemnation of both, and the reference to alcohol is linked with being confused when it comes to pray. We could generalize here and suggest that the trouble with the sort of intoxication that alcohol results in is having an erroneous view of things. The Qur'an emphasizes the significance of having the right attitude to the world and our role in it and of performing activities that help develop our thinking accordingly. Alcohol leads to mistakes, here and elsewhere, and prevents us from understanding how things are, and so prevents us from understanding our relationship with God. Being drunk often gives us the impression that we are in control whereas the reality is very different, and so it is quite reasonably linked with gambling. It might seem strange to accuse gambling of encouraging the view that we are in control since a common experience for most gamblers is that we are not, as most gamblers lose most of the time. The desire to gamble though is an attempt at controlling our future, the prospect of a win (and particularly a big win) indicating our ability to foresee what will happen and benefit from it.

When it comes to considering the issue of balance, is a complete ban on gambling likely to be the moderate position, or is the problem with gambling not gambling as such, but going too far? Similarly with wine and interest. A glass of wine now and then might seem fine, as with a modest rate of interest not obviously being very exploitative. If we are to treat the language of the Qur'an with respect it is difficult to take these positions since the Book is quite clear on the lack of acceptability of these practices, not just some varieties of them. We have to return to the idea of the Qur'an as a basically consequentialist moral text, and we might not understand why the consequences are always dangerous, but the Book assumes its author knows even if we do not. After all, to understand the real nature of the consequences may require more than a human grasp of the future and this fits in nicely also with the language of the Qur'an. It is an interesting issue how far we should expect to understand all the aspects of our moral behavior, and there are situations surely where the rational position is to admit that we do not know why something is regarded as a sin, but we follow someone else who says it is, and we trust that person.

This might seem to be the very worst kind of paternalism or *taqlid*, imitation, but we often do this in ordinary life. We trust someone and do what they suggest even if we do not understand why. This is what we do all the time when we take professional advice. The peripatetic philosophers in the Islamic world regard this as the basis of much religion, where people are unable to follow rationally why they should act as religion tells them, but because they trust what they are taught, they do it anyway, and no less rationally. We cannot after all understand everything we are to do in life, and there are many situations where it is best to take advice, and who is better as a purveyor of advice than God? This is the Qur'anic position and it seems to be entirely consistent and rational. Many apologists for Islam insist on trying to justify aspects of moral advice that really cannot survive rational inspection if we are supposed to see why we should follow them, as though they are aspects of something like natural law. This is often a heroic strategy but usually fails to convince since there is really no evidence that some of what Islam disapproves of has anything much wrong with it. The justification for following the law lies elsewhere.

Islamic philosophy and theology has a strong line on the inadvisability of seeking reasons where it is inappropriate to do so. Philosophers argue that the search can result in rejecting religion because the reasons one finds do not seem to link up properly with the evidence, and so the religion is unsatisfactory. It could result in hostility to intellectuals by those who maintain their religious views since the intellectuals are seen as having heretical views on the faith. Al-Ghazali has similar views on the problem of a popular theology, once it fails to grip people they may turn against the religion it is set on explaining. Skilled thinkers know how to resolve all these problems, it was argued, essentially by those who saw themselves as skilled thinkers. We may again suspect this approach as paternalist or self-deceived, but the principle behind it is quite reasonable. We cannot know everything about everything, and there are many things we just would not understand, even if they were explained to us, a familiar experience to many of us when at the shop when the mechanics of our car are discussed, or at the dentist when a particular procedure is discussed. Some people do try to find out about things like that and often go awry, talking apparently knowledgeably about what they really know nothing about. As a result they may confuse others, and sow doubt widely about whether anyone really understands what is happening. A balanced view lies in accepting that there are disparities in the knowledge that different people have about things and doing our best to trust some sources of what we hope is information and be dubious about others.

Bibliography

Beck, Thorsten, and Brown, Martin (2011), "Which households use banks? Evidence from the transition economies," European Central Bank Working Paper Series No. 1295/February 2011. Available at: https://www.ecb.europa.eu/pub/pdf/scpwps/

Dar, Harvey (2004), "Demand for Islamic financial services in the UK: Chasing a mirage?," *Loughborough University Institutional Repository*. Available at: https://dspace. lboro.ac.uk/dspace-jspui/bitstream/2134/335/3/TSIJ.pdf

Demirguc-Kunt, Asli, Klapper, Leora, and Randall, Douglas (2013), "Islamic finance and financial inclusion. Measuring use of and demand for formal financial services among Muslim adults," Policy Research Working Paper 6642, The World Bank. Available at: http://documents.worldbank.org/ curated/en /611351468337493348/pdf/WPS6642.pdf

Jeldtoft, Nadia (2011), "Lived Islam: Religious identity with 'non-organized' Muslims minorities," *Ethnic and Racial Studies* 34/7: 1134–51.

Kühle, Lene (2011), "Excuse me, which radical organization are you a member of? Reflections in methods to study highly religious but non-organized Muslims," *Ethnic and Racial Studies* 34/4: 1186–1200.

Leaman, Oliver (2013), *Controversies in Contemporary Islam*, London: Routledge.

Maududi, Abu'l A'la (1969), *Economic System of Islam: Part 2. Lahore*. Available at: https://archive.org/details/MaulanaMaududiEconomicSystemOfIslam

Maurer, Bill (2005), *Mutual Life, Limited: Islamic Banking, Alternative Currencies, Lateral Reason*, Princeton, NJ: Princeton University Press.

Pal, Izzud-Din (1999), *Pakistan, Islam and Economics: Failure of Modernity*, Karachi: Oxford University Press.

Rahman, Fazlur (1980), *Major Themes of the Qur'an*, Chicago, IL: University of Chicago Press.

Ramadan, Tariq (2017), *Islam: The Essentials*, London: Penguin.

Taleb, Nassim (2018), *Skin in the Game: Hidden Asymmetries in Daily Life*, New York: Random House.

Thomas, Abdulkader (ed.) (2006), *Interest in Islamic Economics: Understanding Riba*, New York and London: Routledge.

Visser, Hans (2013), *Islamic Finance: Principles and Practice*, London: Edward Elgar Publishers.

Voas, David, and Fleischmann, Fenella (2012), "Islam moves west: Religious change in the first and second generations," *Annual Review of Sociology* 38: 525–45.

Zuhayly, Wahbah (1997), *al-Fiqh al-islami 'adilatuh* [Islamic Jurisprudence and Its Proofs], Damascus: Dar al-Fitra.

4

Health

"We have created the human being in the best form" (95:4).

Islam sees itself as on the whole a practical religion, with a commitment to preserving life and maintaining the quality of life. So there is no problem with seeking medical help when it is needed. On the other hand, there is an *aya* warning us against altering what God has done, attributing such behavior to the devil (4:119). There is also a great deal of emphasis in the Qur'an on the importance of patience, and that might be seen as extending to putting up with physical problems of one sort or another. This might seem to suggest that if we are sick then it is just something we should put up with, and there is another *aya* (2:286) referring to God not giving anyone a burden greater than can be borne. There is not always much evidence of this, sadly some people have things wrong with them which are unendurable, and there is no reason why one should not seek medical assistance for when things go wrong with the body. The divine ordering of the world is taken to be generally benevolent and appropriate for us, yet this does not mean we do not have to do anything to enjoy its bounty. We are expected to work and apply ourselves to get the most out of the world, and the same comment could be made about our bodies as we may make about Islam being the best religion. These are indications of a project rather than something finished. We have been created on the whole in a helpful way but that does not mean we can do anything we like with our bodies and they will continue to flourish, nor that everyone's body is in good working order. In general, we are told we have been well made but we know there are sometimes problems with what we have been given. Surely a perfect deity could have, perhaps should have, created us as more perfect beings, it might be said. It is however difficult to see how anything material could be perfect, since it is essential to the material that it decays and changes, so while we could expect the material part of us to be well designed and fit for purpose in general, in particular cases we should expect problems. When they arise we are entitled to seek to alleviate them through medical assistance on the principle that the world of the Qur'an is not a finished world in which there is nothing left to do, but a dynamic environment where human effort is necessary if progress is to be possible.

The quality of life

It is far from obvious how to use the principle expressed in 95:4 that we are made in the best way when dealing with a familiar issue, whether to prolong treatment for someone who has little quality of life and who is not going to recover. Does treatment include food and drink? We are told that life is very important and anyone who saves a life is as though he saved the world (5:32), but this is not very helpful in this sort of case. Here we have a person who we think has no viable future, and the same of course goes for certain kinds of fetus with problems, and we wonder whether we ought to treat them to continue their lives or bring them to birth. Euthanasia is ruled out, although it is not clear why, given the significant relevant passages in the Qur'an, since just because something is important does not mean that it is the guiding principle in all circumstances. The basic idea is that God sets the *ajal*, the time of death, and it is not for us to intervene in the divine decision. On the other hand, we can decide not to prolong the life of the patient by not resuscitating him or her, when doing so seems pointless. Feeding the patient and giving water, as well as pain relief should be continued while life continues. Doing anything more to hasten death is to intervene on the divine prerogative.

Some sorts of medical research seems precisely to be interested in altering what God has done in a much clearer way than when one is unwell and seeks to become better. It would not be appropriate in such a case of illness to defer or avoid medical treatment on the grounds that the illness is something that God has brought about. Muslims are not expected to allow themselves to become more and more ill through failing to seek treatment; this violates the many commandments to value and preserve life. Patience and resignation are certainly virtues, but that does not imply passivity in the face of the challenges with which we are faced. Prayer is important yet not the only or even the first thing to be done; there is a famous hadith in which the Prophet advises someone to pray after tying up his camel. The questioner wondered whether God could be relied on to look after the camel while its owner was praying. The Prophet was dubious, apparently, and quite rightly so. Yet some science seems to take another step in the direction of altering the fate that we have been accorded, or which we would have been accorded had it not been used. For example, one might wish a child to be taller or blonder or more intelligent, or nicer, and gene therapy might be able to bring this about, or at least make it more likely to occur. This seems to be different from cases where it might be able to produce a healthier child, perhaps a child unlikely to acquire some unpleasant genetic malformation. Yet it is difficult to say what the precise difference here is. Of course, we could try to do some of these things ourselves by doing things to the child, or working with him or her, or bringing them up in a certain way. Parents often want their children to be certain sorts of people and take steps to encourage them accordingly, but as we well know from everyday experience such attempts often go awry. If there were a way of manipulating genes that could produce precisely the sort of child we want, it would save a lot of effort by the parents and be likely to be far more reliable as a way of getting to the desired end.

It might be thought that the issue is over the quality of life as against life itself. Manipulating genes in order to help a fetus live seems acceptable, as does ensuring that such a life is worth living. There are levels of life so unpleasant that there seems little point in preserving it. On the other hand, there are a range of issues that arise in bodies that are somewhat less serious. They might mean that someone is less able to do various things than other people, yet this would not necessarily mean they have no quality of life worth enjoying. One might want to use genes to change very serious cases to something more plausible as a valuable life. On the other hand, this seems to be a slippery slope since obviously it would be easier to have a child without any imperfections, and yet many imperfections do not mean that a child would not enjoy some quality of life. Using genes to prevent such children being born means denying a particular fetus the ability to grow up in a specific way, to replace it with another fetus with far more convenient characteristics. To a certain extent we could always do this, we could do things to fetuses and their mothers to improve their chances of developing healthily, but it was in the past not that effective and often the link between the health of the eventual baby and the earlier treatment of the mother was obscure. In some cultures children who are born with a range of problems are not allowed to survive. If we could affect the fetus earlier than birth and convert a deficient fetus to a better one, or dispose of the problematic fetus and start again trying to get a better one, is this problematic? The disposing of the problematic fetus is questionable, since if this means that we only are going to allow children to be born who have everything right with them, this is not to replace one child with another child, although that is how it might seem to the parent. We are preventing one child from being born in the first place and replacing it with another child. There are two lives here at issue, one is not allowed to proceed to birth and that looks very much like altering what God has done. On the other hand, the damaged fetus is also like everything else something that God has brought about, so we might wonder if the contrast here really makes much sense.

Ethics and the *kalam*

The Ash'arites argue that science works only because it copies what God does, and were God to do something else, it would not anymore be effective in explaining nature. Nothing obliges Him to act in any way, so we are misled if we think there is a pattern here that has anything to do with nature. Everything comes from God. This may seem to be critical of science, and it does certainly deny the necessity of science, but it has the advantage of linking how the world works with divine decisions. It might be argued then that if we can manipulate nature through genomics, or appear to be do so, more strictly speaking, since genomics is like everything else subject to the divine will, then there should be nothing inappropriate in using it to help us organize the material world.

The Muʿtazilites see the organization of the natural world as also dependent on God, but divine law follows the natural order, so it cannot take any form at all. God establishes morality on the basis of what we are like and what the world is like, so looking at the natural world is helpful in working out our duties. This is a point that many philosophers also adopted. Ibn Tufayl in his philosophical novel *Hayy ibn Yaqzan* gives the example of a child brought up on an island by himself and with no human company, although there are animals around, including a deer who looks after him. He develops perfectly accurate ideas of how to behave by thinking rationally about the topic. When in the end he meets someone, a Muslim, and leaves the island to join a larger community elsewhere he is so horrified by the hypocrisy of the community that he returns to the island. When he meets the Muslim, Absal, Hayy discovers that his ideas are in line with those that Absal has been brought up with, and the suggestion is that one can work out independently how to behave. This is an argument that many of the *mashsha'i* thinkers produced. Most people need to be told how to behave by a religion, but there are some people who are intelligent enough to work it out entirely by themselves operating from rational principles. The role of religion is to tell the community as a whole how it should act but for philosophers this is not necessary since they can work it out themselves. The idea is not that philosophers are better people than everyone else since they understand how morality works—they are just as capable of lying and stealing and so on as the rest of the world. Rather, the idea is that philosophers can get to the principles of morality by thinking about what system of behavior accords with rational life. That does not mean they actually follow those principles, of course.

The role of nature

One of the interesting ideas that arises here is the principle that nature is a source of moral information. This is not an unfamiliar idea from a religious context since believers tend to think that if the world is arranged in a particular way, this may be connected to how God wants it to be. A recent Pew survey in the United States suggests that gene editing is less popular among religious believers than among others and that is presumably connected to two aspects of the process, altering the natural state of affairs and the use of fetal tissue in the process, both of which are seen perhaps as interfering inappropriately in the natural order. Yet there is no general problem with medical treatment and one wonders why one form of treatment is found problematic while others are not. There is a famous hadith to the effect that God does not send a disease for which he also does not send a cure. This is problematic in the sense that there are diseases even today for which there is no treatment, but, on the other hand, perhaps the implication is that we should find a cure for all diseases and God has made it in principle possible to do so. Although "humanity has been created weak" (4:28), we can seek to understand the world and manipulate it to our own advantage. This is very much an argument that Said Nursi in his commentaries on the Qur'an emphasizes, seeing the Qur'an as replete with useful motivation for us to develop our scientific knowledge (Turner 2013). After all, it is not difficult to see an analogy between the *ayat* or verses of the Qur'an and the *ayat* (signs) of the natural world, and the fact that we can understand the world has a lot to do with our being guided both in a religious sense and also scientifically. It is all part of the worldview where natural law leads to religious law, where religious law leads to useful hints about the natural world and so shapes our concept of a natural world and its science, and where we feel at home. The world has been made for us, we are supposed to be in charge of it, and provided we carry out our responsibilities all will be well. Bad things happen but they have a rationale. We can expect to understand the world that God has created since He would hardly put us in it if the opposite were the case. If we use our intelligence we can work out eventually how the world operates, and more immediately, what our duties are.

According to Aristotle, leading a good life is greatly assisted by being fortunate in one's circumstances. This is obvious given the word he uses for the good, *eudaemonia (sa'ada)*, meaning being fortunate and happy, and the sharp division between our material circumstances and our moral status which has become so commonplace in later ethical thought is absent in Aristotle. His point appears to be banal. If we are healthy and wealthy and have lots of friends we are in a good situation and often that arises through chance. Many good things we acquire purely as a result of being born in a particular place or having the parents we do. We can be rich and miserable, of course, but our misery will not be a result of poverty, a source of misery for a huge proportion of humanity. Greek philosophy is often ambivalent on the link between the body and the soul. The Islamic philosophers in the peripatetic tradition could argue that Islam and its law preserves and enhances our material lives, and so represents at least part of what is good about those lives. Religion also of course develops us spiritually, but for the philosophers this was something that could be done through the use of reason alone, by the small number of people who were capable of undertaking it. Most people need religion to operate ethically since otherwise they would have little idea how to behave or even what sort of lifestyle is in their interests.

There is nothing here to offend either the Mu'tazilites or the Ash'arites. After all, the material world is something created by God so it can be used as a source of moral information. On the other hand, sometimes we see our duty as lying in opposition to what we would like to do naturally. Some religious duties, for example, are not always easy to perform, like going on hajj or being charitable. We may struggle to do them. The Ash'arites argue that whatever nature suggests, our religious duty may be anything at all, provided it comes to us from God. The Mu'tazilites see difficult rules as having a purpose; they work with our nature in order to change that nature. 'Abd al-Jabbar uses the notion of *lutf*, cunning, to express how legislation uses our nature to change our nature, so that we might be threatened with physical pain in order to help us behave morally. The fact that things sometimes go wrong is regarded as representing a warning from God, and so has a useful function, and in the case of undeserved suffering the victim will have to be compensated, according to Mu'tazilite eschatology (nicely explained in Heemskerk 2000). To some extent that reduces the scope for genomics, since there is not much point in improving things, it might be thought, if they will eventually right themselves anyway because of the compensation. Someone may regret having an accident but if compensation results then they are left in the same condition as they were in before the accident, formally at least.

Does compensation really make us whole again? It may but it may not. A familiar argument insurers have with some drivers is that the latter after a collision want their car returned to them in the state it was in before the accident, but this may now be no longer possible. It is often far more feasible to scrap the car and replace it with something else. Obviously a market has to operate in such a system of cost and benefit, and we can easily understand how a monetary value has to be placed on a loss. Yet morally should we use this sort of language? Can anyone replace a dead person for whom compensation is paid at some stage? If I am an innocent person and I suffer during this life, can we really make sense of that suffering being made good by some good things happening to me either in this or in some other life? Suppose due to slander I lose my job and my links with my family are put at risk, and for several years I am miserable and so is everyone around me. I am innocent, and eventually everything is put right again, I am reinstated and paid what I am owed and so on. That is how it should be, but does it really undo the previous period of unhappiness and dislocation? It has to be said also that when one person suffers, many others do too, and they are just as innocent of the original cause of the suffering. Are they all going to be compensated? How about the bus driver who I snarl at in the morning because I am in a bad mood? Or the baby who I shout at while changing her diaper? Pains and pleasures are not easily transferable outside of the language of insurance and law. It is difficult then to see how they can be interchangeable morally.

Islam as based on moderation

Islam instructs its followers to be an *ummatun wasatan*, and moderation is a very important concept throughout the Qur'an. The religion sees itself as coming in between the excessive asceticism of Christianity and the materialism of Judaism. The virtue of *wasatiya* might be called a second-order virtue since it is something that governs many of the other virtues in religion. The idea of balance in religion is always going to be crucial, and it is linked with the concept of justice, as in 2:143 where the followers of the Prophet are described as *wasat*. Sometimes the term is identified with being the best (68:28; 1:6-7), contrasting sharply with the approach to religion taken by Judaism and Christianity. The Qur'an often criticizes those who believe in anything at all and those who deny everything they cannot personally see, trying to establish a middle point between these extremes. It is a middle point between those who see this world as the only important place and those who regard it as illusory and unimportant. In Islamic law, we find a system seeking to balance crimes and penalties, and rules that are designed to promote equity. The principle here is entirely acceptable, that an attempt is made to be fair to all parties, to allocate people their deserts and preserve a sense of balance, that is, achieve a level of moral equilibrium. For example, *zakat* or charity is a vital aspect of religion, but how do we know how much money to give away to charity, and how much to keep for oneself? Verse 17:29 advocates taking a middle path, giving something away but not everything, which would result in personal poverty and the inability to continue to be charitable. There are hadith where the Prophet advocates his companions to not give all their money away to charity but keep some at least for their family. The identification of virtue with moderation is not difficult to understand since the universe itself was created in a balanced and presumably good way. "And the earth We have spread out, and set on it mountains firm and immovable, and created in it all kinds of things in appropriate balance" (15:19). Like most religions, Islam is realistic, acknowledging that we need to earn a living and that our desire to help others has to be reconciled with the ability to create funds and carry out our responsibilities to those who are dependent on us for their welfare.

On the other hand, is moderation always such a desirable property? Islam challenges the idea that the religion is a radical departure from what took place in earlier times since Islam is an attempt at returning to an original and purer state of monotheism. That implies that it needs to reverse centuries, indeed millennia, of *kufr* and *bid'a*, unbelief and innovation. This requires a total transformation of the situation, and the detail of Islamic law and practice, including of course the sunna of the Prophet, along with the teachings of the imams for the Shi'a, are significant steps on the way to achieving this. These rules may well go against the natural and social inclinations of people and the ways they have been brought up and there will be an attempt, perhaps, to use the concept of moderation to alter or adapt the rules to local conditions, *'urf*, a suggestion that would not go down well among those who see the religious rules as God's direct plan for how human beings ought to live. On the other hand, there is a good deal of evidence from Islamic law that local conditions were brought into the law on many occasions and continue to do so. Yet we are told in 2:208 to enter Islam wholeheartedly. Here the implication is that anything less than this is to backslide. Being moderate in the application of Islam might seem to go along with the devil. On the other hand, to endorse something enthusiastically does not mean stopping to think about how to live within that framework. We should be very cautious about using the general principles that we find in Islam as ending moral discussion and implying that we no longer need to think how to act. To give a very secular example, however keen one is on a particular sports team we know that it is just one team among many others. It may well lose, and in fact may often lose but this does not diminish our wholehearted support for it. We may support it uncritically through thick and thin, but that does not mean our support is uncritical. Often on Friday the crowds leaving mosques are talking animatedly about the *khutba* and laughing and joking about the weird things the imam said. That does not mean they are not good and faithful Muslims; just that like all adherents of religion they are capable of applying a range of ideas to their religion and its performance that allows them to stand back from it to a degree.

There are people who see religion as something to be followed without any balancing assessment; they follow what they take the letter of the law to be. There are rules and they follow the rules, and if they do not understand the rules or why there are rules, no problem, since a higher source of authority does. The latter is after all where the rules come from. We all follow rules we do not understand, anyone who has tried to solve a computer problem is familiar with this phenomenon. These are rules coming from human beings, and from sources that appear to be human. How much easier is it then to understand following rules we do not understand from God? To accept something completely does not mean accepting it unthinkingly. People sometimes follow what they take the teachings of their religion to be and then they pause and wonder if the religion can really be expecting them to do something they find strange. That pause is important, it may only be a pause and then the believer continues to act in accordance with what he or she takes the rules to be. The pause shows that they raise the question of whether their religion could really expect them to do something, given that there seem to be good reasons perhaps not to do it. The pause represents the influence of balance, and for some people eventually there are so many pauses that they change their practice of the religion. It may be that religions insist on so many minor rules that in themselves do not seem very important in order to train their followers to be followers in general. The military often require their personnel to drill not because wars are won by smart clothes and sharp parades but because the unquestioning obedience to small details involved in such practices may help people obey instructions about much more significant topics. Successful military operatives are not those who obey unquestioningly all the time, but rather those who use their initiative and opinions to work out how to behave in many situations. They have to balance their training with their own ideas and try to achieve a successful synthesis, and this does not make them less enthusiastic members of their group.

Back to the Qur'an

Many of the characters in the Qur'an are extreme, either in a positive or negative way, and it might be said that Iblis is punished because he is totally convinced of the superiority of creatures made of fire, as opposed to those of earth (like us) which makes it difficult for him to acknowledge the wisdom of the divine plan. Even though God says he knows why he is acting in the way he does, Iblis ignores this and suffers as a result. Even Musa in the experiences he has with Khidr falls foul due to a lack of moderation since he is told not to question what he sees happen, but he constantly does when he thinks it is unjust, and in the end learns from the experience. Instead of considering the reasons for what is happening and restraining his sense that it is unjust, Musa is indignant and demands precisely what Khidr tells him not to do, an explanation for what is happening (18:60-82). It might be said that moderation, like patience, is something one has to learn, the end or even part of a project that we set ourselves in life, and religions are often very helpful here in helping train us in the right direction. But moderating the word of God is to distort it and to end up creating your own way of doing things and possibly deviating a good deal from where divine guidance wants to take us. It is worth pointing out also that there are some dichotomies in religion that can be dealt with in terms of some principle of moderation, but others cannot. For example, there has often been a conflict between those who advocate *tasawwuf* as a way of being a Muslim, and others who stress *kalam* or a particular understanding of Islamic law. Mysticism seems to be specialized and based on personal training and advancement while regarding Islam as equivalent to a series of doctrines, an *'aqida*, is the reverse. Yet these could be seen as different emphases in Islam, one on *tashbih* (immanence) or the proximity of God and the other on the *tanzih* (transcendence) of God, His distance from us, like the contrast between the *batin* (hidden) and the *zahir* (open), or *'aql* (reason) and *naql* (tradition). These are all familiar religious dichotomies and it might be suggested that the balanced line is to try to reconcile them in some way, so that our notion of the divinity is of someone both affecting the world and yet far above it, someone we can to a degree grasp what is going on, yet to an overwhelming extent is completely distant from us, and so on.

As we are often told, the Qur'an addresses different people in different ways, and it appeals both emotionally and intellectually to a wide variety of constituencies (Leaman 2009). Some of these people are interested in acquiring a more personal access to the religion and they are prepared to undergo the sort of training that mystics engage in, while most people just expect to find in their religion some fairly simple rules of behavior and ritual which they can follow in order to do what God expects of them. The fact that both approaches can be found in the same religion suggests that there is flexibility to allow for different degrees of access to the truth, as one would expect given the variety of humanity that exists in the world. At 5:48 we are told that God could have created one nation in the world, but wanted people to learn from each other and selected variety instead. That does not perhaps just refer to Muslims and non-Muslims but also to different kinds of Muslims, and people in general. It is because of the variety of lifestyles that we find in the world that we can work out with some plausibility what counts for us as the right way of living, and the most moderate. It might be said that within Islamic law the fact that members of one school are supposed to respect the judgments of other schools, although they disagree with them, is evidence of this principle. The capacity to accept a legal ruling which one finds dubious according to one's own principles is not something that just arises out of nowhere. It is not something we can just discover or be taught, it is a part of a process of self-discovery and reflection on experience. The Qur'an, like many other religious texts, is well adapted to helping us work out how we ought to live in a way that fits in both with us and with our creator. It is worth remarking on the fact that we are neither *jinn* nor animals nor angels but are somewhere in the middle. Our creator is obviously aware of this and designs His laws and advice appropriately.

Genes and morality

If we take the injunction to be moderate seriously we should analyze moral issues in medicine by looking for the middle position. Gene editing opens up the possibility of creating perfect human beings. Is it then obvious that this is something that should be done? People with disabilities sometimes say that they would not be the people they are without those disabilities, they form part of their lives and personality, and they would not necessarily choose not to have them. Life would be easier without the disability (and let us continue to use that expression instead of differently abled), but it would not be the life of the person who has lived with it, developed alongside it and has a character constructed by it and perhaps despite it. The disability may have made him the person he is, as we say in a familiar expression. From the point of view of a parent considering what to do with a fetus, having a healthy baby without any problems is very tempting. If gene therapy could help bring this about, it might seem the obvious choice. On the other hand, a child and adult who grew up with disabilities might wonder where he or she would be had the parent made that decision and had the ability to carry it out. Whoever emerged into life would not be that person but someone entirely different, albeit still the children of the parent. We could interfere with nature to produce a certain sort of person, but that person would not then be the person who naturally developed. It is not that someone changes from being less to being more perfect. It is that there are two different people, and the opportunity to become one such person is taken away. It is worth reflecting on many of the hadith referring to the angel bringing a soul to the fetus since they do not just talk about the addition of the soul but also the determining of the future of the child. It is not just the addition of a soul that makes us who we are but also what we end up doing, who we become in the world and an aspect of this is what we can do, given our physical nature. One of the things that the Qur'an criticizes throughout is killing children because one cannot provide for them (6:51, 6:137, 6:151, 17:31-3, 60:12), and this must have included both male and female children at the time, although the latter are especially mentioned at 16:58-9.

This discussion of the status of the fetus brings us into the familiar and controversial territory of birth control and abortion. Every time someone uses birth control a possible person is denied the right to come into existence, but we could go further back and suggest that is also true every time someone does not become friendly with a potential partner with childbearing possibilities, or even the absence of a smile at a strategic moment. Or to take another example, it is well known that having literate carers and books in the house helps children develop into people who are more comfortable and confident when dealing with language. Children brought up by people who read and discuss things with each other do better, on the whole, in the educational system than others, and it is easy to see why. Does that mean that such carers deny the opportunity of the child to grow up ignorant and with limited vocabulary? Here we need to invoke Aristotle again and ask whether there are certain physical and mental characteristics that, on the whole, it is helpful for us to possess. It is not that it is impossible to live a good life without such characteristics, but it is harder and perhaps more limited in scope, and if possible should be avoided. There is a test which is now available that makes it easier and safer to test for Down's Syndrome, and some countries have suggested that it would then be possible to see the end of this "problem." Potential parents who detect the condition would be expected to terminate the pregnancy. Yet some people with Down's live fulfilling lives, albeit with a lot more support than most other people without the syndrome. Like all forms of disability it has degrees and some are relatively benign. On the other hand, some are not and make life very difficult for both those who are carers and those who require care. It is true that society ought to cope with people who are different in ways that they cannot control. It does not follow that we should seek to increase the number of such people if we can use science to control their numbers. There are limits to resources and there are arguments that if we can reduce the number of people with disabilities then we should. That does not mean we do not value those with disabilities. They should be valued just as people who are sick should be valued, and that does not mean we should not try to cure them. But we are not talking here about curing people with the syndrome, we are talking about doing away with them *in utero* and hoping to have a different sort of fetus with a different likely outcome in the future.

Choosing children

Is disability like a form of illness? Some people cannot do things that others can, but there is nothing wrong with them apart from that. They are not ill. This is a point worth making about pregnant women who are often treated as though they require special consideration due to their pregnancy, but pregnancy is not a disease from which they will recover at the birth. It is something that happens to us naturally, like old age, and we should not necessarily see it as a problem we need to transcend. From an Islamic point of view, life in itself is very significant, and we are told in the Qur'an that unjustified killing is equivalent to destroying the world (5:32). This refers to all life, not just those who are healthy and strong, and it is not clear how that relates to choosing between different lives, a healthy life and something contrasting with that. The role of the natural is significant here. If a healthy life needs to be constructed by using medical technology, but something different can arise just by leaving things alone, the latter appears to be more natural. To take an example from sport, it is alright to eat healthy food and exercise in order to become a better performer, but it is illegal to take drugs, or certain drugs, to improve performance. Some athletes get permission to take the drugs if they have a medical condition warranting it, and one wonders at the possibilities of pushing the boundaries of acceptability here. One way of preparing is supposed to be natural and the other artificial and so illegal. There are reasons to be skeptical of this dichotomy but where does it figure in Islamic ethics? Here the distinction between the natural and the artificial is itself artificial, since both the natural and how we alter it are based on divine decision, either directly (for the Ash'arites) or indirectly (for the Mu'tazilites). There is then little point in preferring the natural over the artificial, and the distinction is itself more artificial than natural. Children are produced through a natural process, but according to Islamic law they have the right to be born through a valid union (marriage) and to know their parentage fully. Artificial insemination and in vitro fertilization (IVF) are therefore acceptable only if sperm from the woman's spouse is used.

Adoption is generally frowned on in Muslim culture since the process involves the transfer of parental rights to the adoptive parents, while Islamic law tends to insist on paternity being a matter of the biological relationship with the actual father. As Zaynab El Bernoussi demonstrates, this has caused some legal difficulties where children are illegitimate (2018). Fostering is however positively encouraged since no similar transfer of parental rights occurs. In either case, the surname of the real father should be retained. One of the important aims of the law, according to al-Ghazali, is the preservation of lineage, and this is indeed treated as vitally important in much of Islamic law, and clearly this is linked with the significance in local *'urf* of issues like kinship and religion. If we do not know who the father of the child is then we do not know the religion of the child, although since religion can change in life, this is hardly final information. In many cases it is important in telling us who can marry whom, what obligations people have for behavior in an Islamic state and so on. On the other hand, is clarification of such issues really an aim of the law, of equal importance to the preservation of life and welfare, for example? For some people the precise parentage of a child is of no significance to the present guardians or legal parents of the child. It may have no psychological importance for the child either, although clearly there are biological issues which are relevant. It may be that a child would need to know who the parents were for particular kinds of therapy to be chosen. Apart from this, though, lineage is far more questionable as something we need to know about than many may think. For al-Ghazali it is one of the *maqasid al-shari'a*, one of the basic goods that religion seeks to defend and foster. It is an essential aspect of human welfare. This is very overdone, he is right in thinking that at certain times lineage is taken to be vital but at other times it is not, and no huge implications hang on it. It is important in the Qur'an to distinguish between claims that have to do with nothing more than tradition and those that have a source in something we can link with God. A problem with the popular search for the basic moral principles of Islam is confusing what we tend to value and what we should value. The Qur'an tends to make a sharp distinction between these two categories and we too should do the same if we are to value it as a guide to how we ought to behave.

The value of life

Is all life valuable? Are there levels of existence with such poor quality that they are worse than not living at all (see Leaman 2016: 158–60 with respect to Qur'an 17:33)? Kaya (2012) argues that euthanasia cannot be part of Islam, and bases this on an analysis of hadith and passages from the Qur'an. This does not help us though in working out the moral status of the fetus. At what stage is a fetus a person, or has enough of the characteristics of a person to be valued as such? The Qur'an, and common sense, discuss this in terms of the stage the fetus reaches. The Qur'an refers to the development of the fetus from dust, to a *nutfa* (a mixture of male and female material), to a clot, then some flesh and finally, if God wills it, to an infant (23:12-14). There are hadith suggesting that the soul is at some stage placed in the fetus by an angel. The stages of fetal growth are described as forty days in the initial phase, another forty as a clot and then forty as a piece of flesh.

At this more advanced stage the angel comes and predetermines the fate of the fetus when installing the soul. At some stage, although there is a lot of debate about precisely what stage, the angel comes to the child and then he or she becomes a person. Before this stage the fetus is almost a person, and earlier on we get further and further away from personhood. That makes it look like one can use such early fetal material medically, in the sense not necessarily that it is legally commanded but perhaps that it is acceptable since it is not actually linked directly with anything we can call a person yet. At this early stage the material is alive but more similar perhaps to a plant than to a person since it is as yet without a soul, still waiting for the angel to arrive. Having a soul is sometimes regarded as occurring at 120 days from the beginning of conception while some hadith opt for forty days from the beginning of conception, or forty-two. Although the account varies, it is clear that the fetus increases in status as it ages, and legally the compensation for harming a fetus varies accordingly. Al-Ghazali does not approve of abortion but acknowledges that the crime is greater as the fetus advances toward birth, and the penalty should vary accordingly (al-Ghazali 1993). The fetus does not lose its rights to inheritance just because it is unborn when the father dies nor does its family connections lapse when it is *in utero*. The fetus is often treated not quite as a person but as almost a person and after it receives its soul as very much a person in waiting. This cautious approach reflects the significance of moderation in Islamic ethics. To a certain extent there is the familiar idea we have of a fetus being more like a person the further along it is, since it gradually starts to look more and more like a person, and there is some logic in this, in that the older the fetus, the more it functions like a child and the more likely it is to be born, in the sense that it has passed various earlier stages when it could have been naturally aborted and this did not happen. Yet just because it looks more like a person does not make it more like a person, perhaps we should think of a fetus as having all the components to make it a person at a much earlier stage, when it is very small indeed and looks nothing like a human being. At a very early stage it has all the components to make it what it will turn out to be, so perhaps we should think of the angel coming much earlier than is traditionally believed. There is nothing in the Qur'an to make us believe that this has to happen at any particular time.

The role of genes

Human stem cells can be derived from a variety of sources and perhaps this is relevant to their moral status. There is tissue from aborted fetuses, from IVF, from adult stem cells derived from parts of the body, and from cloned human embryos. The major source is embryonic material and so the moral status of the embryo and such material is at issue here. The material can be regarded as just stuff, and we should use it if it can be medically useful for others. On the other hand, the embryo often seems to have the status of a person from some stage at conception or beyond and so is more than just stuff. The idea seems to be that after the *nutfa* (zygote) has been established in the womb the fetus is ready to receive a soul. It is often accepted that while it is not a good thing to dispose of an embryo before it receives its soul, it is not regarded as forbidden, while after the soul comes it is, on the whole, forbidden. This does not mean that genomics is ruled out completely since there is always scope to use material from adults and with their consent, but often embryonic material from other sources is used. There is no problem with using adult stem cells so long as this does not harm the donor, and it is done where the parties involved are married. Fetal stem cells are different, though. If the fetus is the product of a spontaneous abortion or miscarriage there is no problem using it if it is dead, although presumably the permission of the parents, if we should call them that, is an issue, but it will usually be disposed of in any case. Abortion is forbidden after a certain period, but suppose it takes place and as a result there is then available fetal material. Since there are authoritative Islamic judgments that one should not to be medically treated with forbidden substances, it can be argued that it is not permissible to use fetal stem cells. On the other hand, so long as the abortion is not carried out for the purpose of obtaining fetal stem cells and the fetuses will be disposed of anyway, we might be able to justify such a use since it is going to help people and there is no alternative, so this is a matter of *darura* or necessity. This would fit in with the general utilitarian flavor of the Qur'an.

How the embryos are produced is a relevant factor here. The embryos used in embryonic stem cell research are often the spare embryos from IVF treatments. This is permitted if is performed between a living husband and wife with their agreement. There are often held to be ethical problems in the production of spare embryos stored in a freezer for future use. It might be that there are excess embryos and these can be left without medical intervention to end their life naturally, in the sense that they will just stop living. We see the importance of our ideas of what is natural here. Is allowing the embryo to die different from killing a potential human being? Some argue that the use of embryonic stem cells constitutes killing the unused embryo by means of taking the cells and using them as part of some other process. However, allowing the embryo to die looks like not taking any steps to save a potential human being, and so perhaps not respecting life.

It may seem that if the creation of spare embryos is necessary for the success of IVF treatment then this should be done, albeit perhaps with the minimum number of required embryos. What we are dealing with here are potentially human living creatures. In addition, the couple should also be informed that, if everything goes well, they should consent to all the embryos being implanted. If, despite all these precautions, there are spare embryos which will be destroyed, these embryos can be used in stem cell research since they have not yet received a soul, and are therefore not real human beings. On the other hand, we are told, "They ask you about the soul. Say, 'The soul is from the command of my lord, and you are given only a little knowledge'" (17:85), which as so often suggests the situation is one we do not really understand. It might be argued that transplanting cells is preferable to destroying them or allowing them to die, the material is used and benefits people as a result. On the other hand, given this Qur'anic *aya*, are the embryos just stuff to be dealt with like any other form of matter since we do not know when the soul should be taken to have been implanted?

Another way of obtaining stem cells is by the so-called therapeutic cloning. Therapeutic cloning (or biomedical cloning) is a procedure whose initial stages are identical to adult DNA cloning. The stem cells are removed from the embryo in order to produce tissue or a whole organ to transplant back into the person who supplied the DNA. The pre-embryo dies in the process, and this represents a potential problem. The goal of therapeutic cloning is to produce a healthy copy of a sick person's tissue or organ for transplant. This technique could be better than relying on organ transplants from other people, and in some countries like Egypt there has long been acceptance of organ transplantation (Hamdy 2012), although in recent years (2018) this has become controversial again where it involves the use of organs from the dead. With cloning the supply would be unlimited, so there would be no waiting lists. The tissue or organ would have the sick person's original DNA and so the patient would not have to take immunosuppressant drugs for the rest of their life after transplants to prevent organ rejection. On the principle of *la darar wa la dirar fi'l-islam* (there will be no mutual harm in Islam) if this process is available then it should be used. Many Muslim legal thinkers argue that in the Islamic tradition therapeutic uses of cloning and research for that purpose is acceptable, provided the material comes from those in a relationship of marriage. This might seem to be more of a legal than a moral issue, of course, as is lineage in Islamic law. Marriage is more than just a legal link in Islam though, hence the severe penalties for adultery. It seems questionable to insist on the material coming from a spouse since in conditions of necessity one can surely take material from wherever it can be obtained. For example, in conditions of starvation it is generally accepted that food can be acquired from anywhere, regardless of who actually owns the field in which it is grown. Necessity (*darura*) may oblige us to set aside issues of who owns what and just take what we need to survive. The implications for having children follow quite easily, perhaps in order to become pregnant a woman will need material to be used that does not come from her husband, and she will not become pregnant with it. Is she not then in the position of the starving villager who is obliged to take food she cannot pay for from the fields of someone else?

For many Muslim thinkers it is a matter of assessing what the appropriate balance is between potential dangers and benefits. In the case of cloning specifically for the purposes of relieving human disease there is usually taken to be no ethical impediment to stop any such research if on the scale of probable benefit it outweighs possible harm. Some may question how, if Islam is critical of the project of deliberately creating an embryo by IVF to be used and eventually destroyed for stem cells, it can then be acceptable to create an embryo by cloning and then destroy it for stem cells. After all, that sort of activity tends to treat the embryo and what comes from it as just stuff and ignores its status as potentially a person. Most legal judgments suggest that cloning does not bring into question any Islamic belief in any way since cloning is a process which can only work through divine agreement. Just as the person sowing the seed is not the creator of the resulting plant, so the cloning technician is not the creator of the resulting person. God will decide what will happen. This is a questionable assertion, though. It might in just the same way be said that if I put my hands around the throat of someone and squeeze it is not me who kills the person, but God since it is God who eventually decides what will take place. Not that such an assertion is false, but it would hardly work as part of a defense in murder trial. Just because God is the ultimate agent and arbiter we are not excused from acting at the same time. Islam is not a religion that advocates passivity. There is a hadith in which someone asks the Prophet if someone should trust in God and leave his camel untied, and the response is that he should tie up his camel first and then pray. This is useful advice; just because God is the ultimate cause of everything that happens does not mean that we have no responsibility for anything that happens.

The significance of the new technology

The important issue here is whether the use of this new technology leads to new ethical problems. In the case of abortion, provided it is done at an early stage, the issue is often represented as a choice between the welfare or health of the mother and the existence of the baby were the fetus to continue to term. In the case of working with additional stem cells the issue is to choose between the possible lives of several things that might continue to become human beings, although no one wants them to, and the many people who might be helped by using that fetal material. The use of principles to promote welfare such as *maslaha* and *istihsan* might make it seem more acceptable to use embryonic material. On the other hand, in the *aya* on killing a human creature being like destroying the world (5:32) there is little to help us work out what to do where it is not clear that something that is killed or allowed to die is fully human. Of course, there is a difference between human beings and embryos, and yet they are both living things. The *aya* is quite bold in its claim and does not hedge it with considerations of *maslaha*, although, of course, there may be other *ayat* that do so. Islam has no problems with killing things to eat them, provided they are legal sources of food, so it is not a general ban on killing things but on killing people, and fetal material is only potentially people, of course. There is no problem with killing other people, either, provided they do something that makes them liable to be killed. Potential people do have a status in Islam, as the famous story of the three children by al-Jubba'i shows (clearly outlined in Ormsby 1984). God knows what is going to happen to potential people and it might be regarded as wrong for us to interfere with his decisions by terminating their existence. Presumably He knows that this is something we shall do and yet given our scope to be responsible for our deeds one wonders whether what we do always accords with how He wants things to be.

Defending life and the use of principles

We should try to avoid a general cynicism about the importance of human life, a principle whereby life is nominally honored but largely ignored. There are situations calling for difficult decisions. "God desires ease for you, and does not want to make things difficult for you" (2:185) and similar passages have been used to suggest we need to use general principles here to bring out beneficial consequences however unpleasant the route may be. Yet, the use of overriding principles like *maslaha* or welfare are often more misleading than helpful. It may represent an excuse for doing something distasteful we want to do anyway. Not, of course, that public welfare is not significant, but it needs to work with religious concepts like *taqwa* and *sabr*, piety and patience. For believers it is for God to determine where welfare lies, and we see this emphasized in the Qur'an in the long passage describing Khidr and Musa (discussed in detail in Leaman 2013 and 2016). The use of fetal material is often regarded as a slippery slope, and the trouble with slippery slopes is that eventually someone falls down. In any case, recent developments in gene therapy mean that there is now scope to use embryonic stem cells without destroying human embryos. Up to now the discussion has often been on how long it is acceptable to keep human embryos alive. There has often been a fourteen-day rule, since it was felt that after this date aspects of individuality arise in the fetus and so the fetus was coming rather closer to being a person than just being some kind of stuff. In any case it used to be very difficult to actually keep the embryo alive outside the uterus for more than that limit, which is no longer such an issue. It looked like a "natural" limit. We have already argued that from an Islamic point of view the status of the natural is questionable since everything that happens is linked ultimately (for the Mu'tazilites) or more intimately (the Ash'arite view) with divine decision. Both schools of theology were atomists and occasionalists, and opponents of the sort of philosophical view stemming from Ibn Sina where natural connections are in some way necessary. So the fourteen-day rule beyond which the fetus may naturally become more of an individual has nothing very special about it. When we say it is natural this means nothing more than that this is how God arranges it for the moment, and this could easily change at any time He wishes.

It is this sort of issue that was supposed to have led al-Ash'ari (d. 936/324) to abandon what was at his time the orthodox position in Islamic theology of Mu'tazilism. Al-Jubba'i (d. c. 915/295) contrasted the fate of three brothers: a believer, an unbeliever, and one who died as a child. Al-Jubba'i suggested that the first would be rewarded with paradise, the second would be punished with hell, and the third would be neither rewarded nor punished but would end up in the *barzakh*. When al-Ash'ari objected that God might have allowed the third to live longer so that he may achieve paradise, al-Jubba'i responded that God knew that the child would have become an unbeliever had he lived longer. Al-Ash'ari then wondered why God had not then allowed the second brother to die as a child so that he may be saved from hell. What al-Ash'ari disliked about this account was not the idea that God is the ultimate cause of everything but rather the principle that He had to act in certain ways. If someone leads a good life then He has to send him to paradise, His hands are tied by the principles of justice. As al-Ash'ari suggests, this principle sounds benign but in fact leads to the sort of paradoxes we see in al-Jubba'i, and a preferable way of looking at the issue is to argue that justice is what God does. Verse 5:64 makes clear that God can do anything He likes and insisting that He has to act in accordance with some abstract principle of justice is to attempt to constrain His actions. After all, God is not bound to act in accordance with what we deserve; fortunately for us, He often acts far more positively toward us than we deserve, and we cannot hope to predict what He is going to do. In any case, do we know what justice is? The example of Musa and Khidr shows that we might not. There is a theme in the Qur'an, and in many religious texts, that we really are limited in our grasp of reality, and this is just as true of concepts like justice as with anything else.

On the other hand, we need to use abstract principles of justice to work out how to behave, and the information we receive from Islam, the Qur'an, the hadith, the *sira* of the Prophet, and so on only take us so far in resolving moral conflicts. This is especially the case when new technology and scientific discoveries seem to change the moral landscape. In the past we had to put up with many physical ailments and abnormalities, some of which would result in an early death or restricted life. Now it is possible that some at least of these can be resolved by gene therapy, including even the having of children when in the past this was not possible. We are told that "He leaves barren whom He will" (42:50). Clearly God determines our future but we do not know what that determination will be and so we might decide to try to cure an inability to have children. Whatever the outcome no doubt God will decide, and it is for Him to say whether the treatment will work or whether barrenness will be overcome in some other way. To say that we can do anything at all to try to have children because after all it is all a matter of divine decision is surely just wrong. To use embryonic material that involves destroying life in order eventually to create life is more than doing something distasteful, it is to strike at the heart of the sanctity of life itself. Such material is more than just stuff, although it is certainly less than a person. It may help someone else to use it but that does not change its status. It remains one of those difficult moral issues that cannot be easily resolved by the application of religious law and theological inquiry. General principles such as *maslaha* and *darura* are obviously relevant but they should not be used like weapons of mass destruction to sweep away everything before them.

The conclusion is surely the case that genomics does not raise any new ethical issues for Islam. It returns us to the familiar controversies over the status of the fetus, with the difference that the debate is not over the fetus versus the interests of the mother, but the fetus with respect to other people. The ability to choose the sort of child one has, potentially, is not appropriately described in this way. It is a choice between two different people, one who would otherwise be born, and the replacement of someone else who is more desirable to the parents. Some children are obviously more convenient or easier to raise, or fit into the family better, but that means that other children miss their chance to exist. Parents who lose a child often have another, or try to, and they say that the new child is not a replacement for the old child and could not be. This brings out the effects of choosing one sort of child over another, it is not like choosing one chocolate in the box over another, since the less desirable chocolate is already there and will be eaten eventually. It is more like making one sort of chocolate, changing one's mind later on and altering the recipe to come up with something different. But here we are just talking about stuff, the potential existence of the less liked chocolate has no moral significance. This is not the case at all for the potential child, who but for the actions of the parents would come into existence and now will not.

Understanding this debate surely depends on what our notion of personal identity is. It may be that in the future we can choose to have a more rather than a less obedient child, yet it would be difficult to argue that the child is an entirely different person from the less obedient person he or she would have been otherwise. That aspect of personality is not a huge aspect of someone's personality. But suppose the issue is whether a child is schizophrenic (more accurately perhaps, is more rather than less liable to suffer from this condition), or whether it is largely healthy or unhealthy. We do regard people as remaining themselves even if they undergo huge personality changes, or if they change radically physically, so we should contemplate the possibility that the choice is sometimes not between two different children but between the same child with different traits. Sometimes people regard even a minor trait defining, and a major one irrelevant. So, for example, someone who became very disabled might well say they were the same person, albeit no longer with the same physical properties, while if something very small changed, like the sort of food someone could eat, they might think of themselves as now an entirely different person. In the *ahadith* describing the soul coming to the child in utero we are also told that God determines the future of the individual, and these personal characteristics would obviously be part of that fate. Genomics seems to replace God here, but from an Islamic point of view it is merely a process that operates in accordance with divine wishes, with the difference, of course, that whereas God knows how things ought to be, we just know how they should be if they are in what we take to be our interests.

Often people claim that gene editing and similar actions are equivalent to playing at being God. It seems to be even more so now when it is possible to create embryonic material from material that is not originally fetal at all. After all, we use these processes to design human beings, really the exclusive task of the deity. Are we seeking to take over God's powers by using genes to create certain kinds of people? There is no reason to think we are. Ultimately, it is for God to decide what will happen, and it is for us to do our best with the resources we have at hand to make our lives and the lives of those for whom we are responsible better. There are problems from an Islamic point of view with producing and killing embryos in order to use their stem cells. If we can find material that is acceptable for use and which harms no one, perhaps we should use it. God will determine in the end how useful it is and this is a point just as clear today as during the time of the Muʻtazilites and Ashʻarites, so really nothing significant has changed due to the arrival of modern technology.

The death of death

Suppose it were the case that death came to an end? At the moment life expectancy is gradually increasing in many countries, although in others it is decreasing, and given medical advances it might be possible one day to prevent people from dying for a lot longer, and perhaps forever. There will always be accidents of course, however healthy we are—being knocked off a bicycle by a truck rarely has a good outcome for the cyclist but the world of the Qur'an in which we at some stage, known to God, die could become much more distant or even disappear. There is a movement called transhumanism which suggests that in principle most if not all bodily parts could be replaced by machinery and so kept going so long as the engineering worked. Presumably this means that death could be staved off for a long time, perhaps for always. The Qur'an seems to assume that death is a constant for us, as is judgment and the possibility of an afterlife in a variety of places. Yet, suppose there was no more death, or it was very much restricted to certain groups, as it probably would be compared to now. How would that change things ethically? Would heaven stop accepting new guests and hell fewer new entries? It might be less interesting in heaven if no one else arrives, or there are only a few new people. Hell would probably not change much, although the end of widespread reward and punishment would certainly change the flavor of religious life.

The likelihood is that the eschatological language would then be taken in a metaphorical sense, and the afterlife not regarded so much as a specific place but rather as a way of experiencing this life. This would not be such a major change since for many this is how they see it anyway—the idea of God torturing people perpetually or plying them with wine and women is not the noblest conception of what our moral life should amount to. The idea of constant improvement through science is very much a motif of the Enlightenment and suspected by many religious thinkers and also, of course, by those who are skeptical of the Enlightenment. Muslims, in particular, talk about the importance of balance; we have spoken of that a good deal in this book and of valuing how God has made us. Pharaoh was someone who sought to equal the power of God in his arrogance, and it often looks as though many scientists set themselves up in the same way to seek to utterly transform human nature into something different and better, without appreciating the divine origins of what already exists. Gene technology is a good example of this, with many religious thinkers wondering if it is really likely to be as helpful as its supporters say, or whether we are going too far, playing God in fact. We are seeking to alter the basic constituents of human life, it has been said, and this is to throw doubt on how they were put together and why. When we are called upon to be God's *khalifa* and represent Him, this suggests that we do what keeps things ticking along and not radically change them. Hence, we should seek to preserve the environment, husband natural resources, and operate within the boundaries set at a transcendental level.

There is one aspect of this worth noting and that is how cautious such an approach is. Beware of radical change, it suggests, since that might be problematic. In the words of the English poem, stay ahold of nurse for fear of finding something worse. It is worth pointing out though that there is nothing inherently conservative about religion. Religions often call on us to change hugely our behavior, attitudes, and emotions. They tell us what God wants us to do and encourage us to have confidence in putting up with change and opposition. They urge us to trust in God and not in tradition, where tradition is what people have done in the past without it having any real basis in knowledge of anything. The idea that we should just jump on the scientific bandwagon and let it lead us wherever it wants is going much too far, but we might want to question the stereotype of the religious believer as someone frightened of the future, hesitant about committing to change, and ignorant of technical advances. There are believers who turn themselves against the world and reject modern developments, but surely this represents a small minority of the religious community. If God has created the world at least in part for us, then presumably science is there for us too, and there is no reason why we should tremble at the prospect of using it. On the other hand, the pursuit of science should not mean for believers that anything goes.

Bibliography

El Bernoussi, Zaynab (2018), "DNA tests in Morocco: Marking a historic turn in Islamic law." Available at: https://beta.shariasource.com/documents/3369

Brockopp, Jonathan, and Eich, Thomas (eds.) (2008), *Muslim Medical Ethics*, Columbia: University of South Carolina Press.

Al-Ghazali (1993), *Ihya' 'ulum al-din*, II, Beirut: Dar al-Ma'arifa: 65.

Hamdy, Sherine (2012), "The organ transplant debate in Egypt: A social anthropological analysis," *Droits et Cultures* 59: 357–65.

Heemskerk, Margarete (2000), *Suffering in the Mu'tazilite Theology: 'Abd al-Gabbar's Teaching on Pain and Divine Justice*, Leiden: Brill.

Ibn Bajja (1978), *Hayy ibn Yaqzan* [Living Son of Awake], ed. F. Sa'd, Beirut: Dar al-afaq al-jadida.

Ibn Tufayl (1972), *Hayy ibn Yaqzan: A Philosophical Tale*, trans. Lenn Goodman, New York: Twayne.

Inhorn, Marcia, and Tremayne, Soraya (2012), *Islam and Assisted Reproductive Technologies: Sunni and Shia Perspectives*, New York: Berghahn.

Kaya, Ali (2012), "Euthanasia in Islamic law with respect to the theory of protecting integrity of body and soul," *International Journal of Humanities and Social Science* 2/21: 292–97.

Leaman, Oliver (2009), *Islamic Philosophy: An Introduction*, Oxford: Polity.

Leaman, Oliver (2013), *Controversies in Contemporary Islam*, New York: Routledge.

Leaman, Oliver (2016), *The Qur'an: A Philosophical Guide*, London: Bloomsbury.

Ormsby, Eric (1984), *Theodicy in Islamic thought: The Dispute over al-Ghazali's "Best of All Possible Worlds,"* Princeton, NJ: Princeton University Press: 23.

Pew Research Center. Available at: http://www.pewinternet.org/2016/07/26/u-s-public-opinion-on-the-future-use-of-gene-editing/

Sachedina, Abdulaziz (1998), "Human clones: An Islamic view," in *The Human Cloning Debate*, G. McGhee (ed.), Berkeley, CA: Berkeley Hills Books: 231–44.

Sachedina, Abdulaziz (2009), *Islamic Biomedical Ethics*, Oxford: Oxford University Press.

Sachedina, Abdulaziz (2014), "Human suffering through illness in the context of Islamic bioethics," in *Suffering and Bioethics*, Ronald Green and Nathan Palpant (eds.), Oxford: Oxford University Press: 296–308.

Turner, Colin (2013), *The Qur'an Revealed: A Critical Analysis of Said Nursi's Epistles of Light*, Berlin: Gerlach.

5

Bodies

And women shall have rights similar to the rights against them, according to what is equitable; but men have a degree over them. (2:228)

Islamic law is like religious law in other religions and very interested in what we do with our bodies. The role of even the dead body in Islam has become controversial. Is it acceptable to pray at graves, since the person who used to be associated with that body is no longer in any relevant sense there? On the other hand, there are reliable accounts that the Prophet did so, and this is sometimes taken to be acceptable provided that one does not pray to the inhabitant of the grave. The Wahhabis do not accept even putting up a gravestone, but the other theological schools think it is desirable (Delong-Bas 2004). Bodies are supposed to be buried as quickly as possible, and with little ceremony. Bodies are supposed to be treated with respect and there are restrictions on what can be legitimately done to even dead bodies. Religions are very interested in bodies and generally have a lot to say on how they should be treated.

According to Islam, there is nothing wrong with sex provided it is between married adults, and the Prophet himself had a large number of wives, something for which he was heartily criticized in medieval Christianity. Catholic priests after all did not officially have any wives at all. The description of paradise in Islam is far from chaste, women are provided for those who merit salvation, although the Book is silent on what virtuous women can look forward to in that direction after death. Some of the interpretations vary and describe the women as wives, perhaps slightly less exciting, but the picture one has of the next world is a highly material one. If there are wives then, no doubt, they are expected to carry out their marital duties to their husbands. They often seem to be described as the rewards for a meritorious life, and one cannot help wondering what reward women have to look forward to. The description of women in the next world as wives raises the issue of whether they are the same wives as in this world, which might be nice for those happily married of course, and also helpful to the women themselves since on their own merits they might not have deserved to go to heaven. Or do people marry again from among the virtuous, which seems appropriate but might not again be very exciting.

The Muslim account of the next world is corporeal, and William of Auvergne (2009) criticized it accordingly. Many Muslim thinkers view the physical language as allegorical. In Spain the thirteenth-century archbishop of Toledo Roderick Jiménez de Rada (1999) asserted that Muhammad sought to attract lustful souls, and Alfonso X of Castile (1807) claimed that some become Muslims to enjoy a freer way of life (Roderick 1999; Alfonso 1807). Interestingly, Muslims made the same claim about converts from Islam to Christianity (Kassis 1990). The Christian side often made disparaging remarks on the Prophet's number of wives, accusing him of sensuality. God is sometimes described in physical terms as though he has a body. Some Muslims thought this has to be taken as literally true, some that it is allegorical and others that we have to believe it while not understanding what it means (Abrahamov 1996; Wolfson 1976). Wolfson suggests that the relative emphasis on *tanzih* (transcendence) rather than *tashbih* (immanence), on distancing the concept of God from material language in case he came to resemble his creatures too closely, is likewise a strategy to differentiate Him from any notion of competing deities. Many Sufis think in terms of many bodies linked with us, including not only the physical body but an imaginal body, intelligible body, and, finally, an entirely spiritual and sacred body. After the death of the physical body all of these are integrated in the next world into their archetypal reality. The human body is a microcosm of the whole universe, a symbol of all existence (Nasr 2007). Despite the spiritual aspects of religion, it is worth recalling that the Qur'an is often taught through the infliction of pain on the young child (Kane 2012), as though to reinforce the connection between religion and our possession of bodies.

Modesty

Religions often try to water down sexual excitement, and Islam is no exception. Within this world there are restrictions placed on what parts of the body may be displayed and what should be hidden. The central idea is that we should all be modest and not flaunt our physical attributes where this could lead to inappropriate behavior. There are parts of the body that should be covered (*'awra*) and it is forbidden to look at. Some people are allowed to look, generally relatives and spouses, but most people are not. There are even restrictions on looking at your own body. The body is a contested area in Islam and it is wrong to treat it as just something physical: it has a meaning and a role in social life that has to be protected and preserved.

The schools of law have a variety of views on the rules for covering of one's *'awra* (private parts) when in private. The Hanafis and the Hanbalis often argue that in the same way that it is not permissible for a person to expose his *'awra* to anyone who is not supposed to look at it, it is not permissible for him to expose it even when alone unless it is unavoidable, such as when bathing, etc. If someone else such as a relation is allowed to see those parts, why is not their owner surely the closest relation one can have? But the idea is obviously that these are things we should not think about too much, and our bodies are one of those things. The Malikis and Shafi'is tend to call such behavior not unlawful but reprehensible. The Shi'i consider it neither forbidden nor reprehensible when no one else is around, when in private nothing is private, apparently. The Sunni schools have different views about the parts of the body a woman must cover in the presence of her *maharim* (except the husband) and other Muslim women. The Hanafis and the Shafi'is consider it necessary for her to cover the area between the navel and the knees in their presence. The Malikis and the Hanbalis suggest she must cover the area between the navel and the knees in front of women, and in the presence of her *maharim*, her whole body except the head and the arms. Most Shi'i consider it necessary for her to cover her rear and private parts in the presence of women and her *maharim*; to cover other parts as well is a good idea though not necessary, except where there is a possibility of sin, which probably means in most cases. In front of a stranger and in particular any male apart from the *maharim* the schools tend to agree that it is necessary for her to cover her whole body except the face and hands (up to the wrists) in line with the verse 24:31. Al-Qaradawi (2004) argues that hiding the outward adornment means using something to cover the head and chest. It is generally understood that women have been commanded to cover their heads and their chests, although how far the covering is supposed to go is very far from clear. In the Qur'an believers who are men are advised to lower their gaze in the presence of women and to keep the sexually relevant parts of their bodies covered (24:30). Some follow the practice of the Prophet as he is reported to have worn long garments, and nothing ostentatious or luxurious. Hence also the fondness for beards among some groups, the Prophet is taken to have had one. The Prophet is often taken to have cursed women who plucked their eyebrows, and so that is not acceptable in many communities. On the other hand, the fact that some Muslim women can display very little of their bodies has sometimes led them to ornament those parts that are visible, and sometimes eye makeup can be elaborate. The Prophet was told to tell his wives and daughters and all believing women that they should draw their clothes close to them (33:59), which is often taken to be a reference to covering up. It is not clear if this is an instruction to everyone or just to his family. Often special conditions apply to his family, and some argue that there never was an intention for them to be emulated as they often are today. A leading motive for covering up is that in the interests of modesty physicality is restricted because of a desire to please God.

The schools differ on those parts of a man's body that others should not see and so should not be exposed. The Hanafis and the Hanbalis, on the whole, suggest it is necessary for a male to cover the area between the navel and the knees before everyone except his wife. It is permissible for others, whether men or women, *maharim* or strangers, to look at the rest of his body when there is no fear of sin. Presumably if his biceps were unnaturally attractive he should avoid displaying them. According to Shatibi (2003), the Malikis and the Shafi'is recognize two different rules for the male body. In the presence of men or those women who are his *maharim*, he only has to cover the area between the waist and the knees. In the case of women who are not his *maharim*, they should not look at any part of his body. While the Malikis exclude the face and the arms if looked at without any improper motive, the Shafi's do not even allow this. The Shi'i (Mutahhari 2010) differentiate between the parts of another person's body that can be looked at and those parts of one's own body which ought to be covered. A male is obliged to cover only his rear and private parts, though it is obligatory for women who are not his *maharim* to abstain from looking at any part of his body except his head and hands, up to the wrist. So it is permissible for a man to look at the body of other men and his female *maharim* except the rear and private parts provided no improper motive is involved. Similarly, a woman can view the body of other women and her male *maharim* except for the rear and private parts provided no sensual motive is behind the activity. At a certain age modesty no longer seems to become much of a problem. It is permissible for old women who do not expect to marry due to their old age to expose their face and a part of their hair and arms, and such other parts of their body that old women usually do not cover up. But we are told it is better if they do not, modesty has no age limits (24:60).

So there are a number of scriptural passages, and many hadith, which direct Muslims to restrict their display of their bodies in a variety of ways, both their own and those they look at, in the interests of modesty. There are sometimes said to be gruesome punishments for immodest behavior in the next world, and in some countries that see themselves as Islamic states there are punishments in this world also if people are caught and convicted. There are, of course, much more restrictive customs in some communities, where women are not allowed to appear in public at all whatever they are wearing. If they do appear they are very much shut off by their clothing. It is as though being separated is so important that they need to be removed from virtually the whole world. On the other hand, many Muslim women and men think that the rules advocating modesty does not require any particular clothing at all and do not accept any restrictions, and that modesty is all about inculcating an attitude and not making a fashion statement. It is not difficult to see that bodies are relevant issues in religion, and one context is of course represented by the rituals of prayer, which include a distinct physical element (Katz 2013). Clearly our bodies are important, physical imagery resounds throughout the Qur'an and the next life is described in very material terms. That is not to suggest that we should remain at the level of thinking about religion at this level, and some argue they are merely evocative language designed for an audience that is largely unsophisticated and sensual in its concerns. Whatever the truth of this idea may be, there is no doubt that the Qur'an is very interested in us as material beings, and that needs to be reflected in any account we give of how the Book works ethically. The concept of balance includes both the soul and the body in the familiar way of looking for a harmony to exist between them in some sense. How this can be achieved is, of course, the question.

The social body in Islam

The implications that Islamic law has for the treatment of the body has been much discussed in the literature and far beyond. It has also become a highly controversial social and political issue. France has banned covering the body in official buildings and even some kinds of covering in the street, a position supported by the *Ni putes ni soumises* (Neither whores nor doormats) movement (Amara and Zappi 2003 and website). Other countries have similar rules, and during the secular governments in Turkey preceding the repeated victories of the religious AKP in this century the restrictions on what was regarded as Islamic clothing were rigorously enforced and quite draconian. Students were prevented from entering a university if they were wearing hijabs and even sometimes from walking on the same side of the road as a government building, let alone entering it. The memories of those many decades of persecution of the religious community has played a substantial role in the success of the AKP, who remind their supporters of the egregious past and suggest that a defeat for the party would lead to a return to the bad old past. Some Muslim women experience religious clothing as something they enjoy wearing and find uplifting, while others hate wearing it and never do unless there is compulsion. The fact that such clothing is often uncomfortable and inappropriate for the climate makes no difference, of course, to fashion since we all wear stupid things on occasion if we feel we look good in them, or ought to wear them. The fact that clothing is uncomfortable actually increases its attraction for many wearers, especially if they think they are pleasing God through dressing in a particular way.

Barlas (2002) takes the progressive line that we will examine later on in this chapter and argues that the emphasis on covering is an attempt by men to control women and has nothing to do with the Qur'an, while most commentators are more accepting of traditional approaches to how the body ought to be presented in public (see many of the respondents in Lazreg 2009). Salafis advocate quite rigorous covering and the legal position here is well represented in al-Albani (2002). The complexity of the issue in a variety of environments is explored in Göle (1996). Mernissi (2001) developed a position that has become popular since it takes a sophisticated line on the topic and questions both the traditional Islamic basis of veiling and also the ways in which the body is treated generally since male control of the female body is far from limited to the Islamic world. Concentrating on this issue is often seen as an aspect of orientalism (Göle 2009) and as a way of attacking Islam and its adherents. The desire of the Western world to "rescue" women who are seen as living in oppressive situations has been roundly attacked as a covert form of intervention that brings with it much of the intellectual baggage of colonialism and imperialism. It was after all a slogan of colonial times that primitive people needed to be protected and civilized, imperialist powers often labeled their interventions as protectorates, and there was an emphasis on the grim events that sometimes took place in exotic parts of the world before the West had succeeded in its civilizing mission. On the other hand, there is no doubt that some local customs embodied in view on modesty really are oppressive however much we may resent having to admit it, and some people are oppressors, even though they come from religious groups who have been the subjects of oppression themselves. In recent times the compulsory head covering has been criticized in Iran, yet in 2018 at least it remains enforceable legally, while in the same year Saudi Arabia's Muhammad bin Salman has announced that covering is no longer to be compulsory and yet both men and women will have to dress "respectably." He did not define what that meant.

Modesty, dress, and body esteem

The teachings on the human body have led to discussion about what appropriate Islamic clothes would be. Tarlo (2010) reports on the various forms of negotiation that takes place within the boundaries of both contemporary Western fashion and what are taken to be the rules of Islam, while Özyürek (2015) describes the ways in which new converts find their clothes and body adornments criticized by other Muslims (2015). She suggests it is sartorially much easier to be a male than a female convert, and in general it must be said that the restrictions on women are far greater than on men sartorially. On the other hand, some converts in particular enjoy that fact, and take up with enthusiasm the role of pious Muslim women who need to change their outward appearance. Non-converts also sometimes experience a lot of satisfaction in doing what they think God wishes. The comparative study of body esteem suggests that covering may well increase levels of esteem (Mussap 2009; Woofenden 2012), although how far these small-scale pieces of research should be taken is a relevant point. Woodlock outlines a wide variety of views on the issue, and many informants talk about their high levels of esteem from the belief that through their covering of their bodies they are pleasing God. It adds another layer of sacrality to ordinary life as even when not praying the modest individual is acknowledging the influence of God in how she dresses. Modesty applies to men as a well, of course, but since the rules are less rigorous for them the idea that they are dressing for God is probably less prevalent. But men also can wear the appropriate facial hair and loose clothes that they identify with the Prophet, so their religious commitments may be expressed through their ordinary clothing and the modest behavior and the thinking that accompanies it.

The ethics of balance

One of the unusual aspects of moral debate in the Islamic world is that traditionally it has had far more to do with behavior than with motivation. There are many books on how people should behave, what they should say, who they can meet and spend time with. It is not surprising that Chinese Muslims should have found it so easy to combine their religion with the principles of Confucianism, which also emphasizes the role of the gentleman and explores his obligations and relationships. Aristotle was also concerned about such issues, and the Greeks were often seen in the early Islamic world as excellent indicators of how civilized people, and especially men, should behave. A type of writing often called *belles-lettres* or *adab* arose which advised men on their behavior and saw the virtues as very much part of the good life embodied in certain practices and relationships. How we should talk to people, who we should talk to, how we should deal with certain topics, these are among the subject matter of this type of writing, and one of the interesting distinctions between it and ethics in general is how it deals with issues. Ethics often discusses conflicts while the *adab* literature is all about how to avoid conflicts in the first place by arranging our affairs in such a way that we move smoothly through the world. Sometimes it rather has the flavor of books like *How to make friends and influence people*, while at other times it makes quite serious points about how people should relate to each other. There is a degree of smugness in the *adab* literature that is annoying; it gives off the atmosphere of successful and self-satisfied people who are confident that they know how to act in order that others will respect them and act toward them in similar ways. They feel they have not only a social sanction for what they do but also a religious one, and we can see this in the quotations they often produce from the Qur'an and hadith. This style of writing is often rather shallow and disingenuous since it is based on huge inequalities in society which are treated as the inevitable background against which we behave and nothing to be concerned about.

This category of literature in Islamic culture is often labelled ethics or *akhlaq* and yet does not seem to deal with ethics as we generally take it to be today. The writing seems much more like rhetoric or sophistry than philosophy, to use Platonic language, and part and parcel of *adab* is rightly translated as *belles-lettres* to bring out nicely the aesthetic aspect of how behavior is treated. It deals with how people are supposed to behave in a variety of circumstances and in different contexts and is a bit like the rules of the courtier literature. Al-Shahid al-Thani writes at length of the etiquette of the relationship between students and teachers, and goes into details of which hand a student is supposed to use to hand over a document to the teacher, how they should sit and how the student should walk in front of his teacher if the terrain is muddy, and yet at the same time be careful about not splattering mud on the person behind him. This sort of literature is all about how to be a gentleman, how to be cultivated and fit in, how to make friends and influence people, perhaps. Plato makes a sharp distinction between the soul and the body, and so issues like etiquette are not so important for him since what happens with the body is not important and manner definitely has to do with the body. It is the soul that represents everything important and defining about us. For Aristotle, by contrast, the body and soul are irretrievably linked, so our ethical development has to be described in terms that deal with how we are as both soul and body. There are two kinds of virtue, intellectual and practical. The latter is linked with emotions and feelings and is developed through habit and practice.

In some ways it is surprising that the thinkers in question came to this conclusion since they were wedded to a Neoplatonic rather than Aristotelian framework and saw the soul as entirely distinct from matter. Miskawayh (d. 1030/420) produces many arguments to establish this, along with the superiority of the soul over the body. He argues also that we are distinguished from the rest of creation by this feature. So our ultimate happiness is going to be more mental than physical, and the more our mind can control our body the better off we shall be. It is the intellect's role to distinguish between good and evil and it tries to control our emotions and appetites. As one might imagine, these different faculties are often in conflict with each other but our welfare depends on their working together, under the overall command of the intellect. This requires a balance between rationality and everything else, we have bodies and we should use them appropriately, not going to extremes in that use but acknowledging their limitations and how we should best proceed in order to attain happiness. When looking at the difficulties of combining philosophical and theological language it was suggested that often they are used together but with no obvious interaction, so they appear to be part of the same discourse but the reality is very different. Here we have a good example of how this works, since the philosophy is Neoplatonic and would tend to lead the description of how we are to behave by emphasizing the soul in contrast with the body, and yet because it is also Islamic theologically that sort of emphasis cannot really get established since so much of the religion insists on a basic balance between them.

Miskawayh spends a lot of time talking about how the most important aspects of human life can be seen as existing on a scale where it is easy to become unbalanced. For example, we might think about something so much that we become totally absorbed by it and are unable to act. On the other hand, we might forget it, which means that we have no idea what it is anymore. The mean is *zikr*, the Qur'anic notion of remembering, often used to indicate the importance of remembering God. We can become completely obsessed with the idea of God and do nothing except contemplate Him or we may totally forget about Him, the ideal is taken to be to think of Him but with enough space in our lives to do other things also. His examples are often inspired by religion so *shari'a*, for example, comes in between a complete abandonment of oneself to just satisfying one's desires, in between a total policy of denial and self-restraint and one of doing anything one fancied. Law often establishes the middle position through his account of it, and when one thinks about it this is not a bad idea. The thing about law is that it acknowledged the various poor decisions that people can make and applies sanctions to them in order to try to regulate our behavior. It appeals to our reason and also to our emotions and appetites (we do not want to suffer public opprobrium, go to prison, etc.) in order to instill in us the idea of justice. You would expect him to say that coming close to God is what we mean by happiness and the farther away we are the more unhappy we are, and this does say this, but is skeptical of the point of coming too close, the sort of relationship which Sufis called *fana'* where we are as it were dissolved in God and can do and think of nothing else. He argues for the normal religious view that happiness lies in coming close to God but also being able to carry out our social duties as members of a community. Our emotions can lead us to take an extreme position on anything, and we need religion and intellect to help control them and lead them in the right direction. One of the factors he stresses are features of religion that are practical, the law for instance, the examples of the prophets and no doubt that various stories that have developed to illustrate the difference between right and wrong. These are all ways in which we can practice using our intellect to control the other parts of our personality, using the more physical emotions to help control our intellect in the sense that we do not want to just think but also use our bodies, and a sort of harmony develops in the best sort of case, the sort of harmony that is spoken of often in the Qur'an and represents when someone is doing what he or she is supposed to be doing in tandem with thinking about God.

To take an example here, we have seen that Islam is critical of taking excessive risks. We have looked at the idea of how difficult it is to define what sort of risk is excessive and objectionable. We are not supposed to be constantly timid and fearful, though, this is to go to one extreme. We are also not going to benefit by being reckless, although sometimes we might. We need to be somewhere in the middle, brave but neither reckless or cowardly, and getting this right involves thinking about how we should behave (using our intellect) but also the instruction of religion and other ideas that helps us work out what sort of middle position we should be working to attain on this issue. Given the Neoplatonic orientation of thinkers like Miskawayh, you would expect him to be rather dubious about what we can do with the body since it is the soul which is the most important part of us. Here religion is important, of course, since religion and Islam, in particular, has a lot to say about the body and what we should do with it and also what we should not do. Islam takes on board the idea that we have a body and what happens to it is important for us spiritually, not just in material terms. This is not just a *façon de parler*, as the *falasifa* would have it, merely putting spiritual issues in material terms since for most people that is the only way to address them. They have difficulty contemplating the spiritual and so have to be spoken to in ways that resonate with their material and narrow interests. Our bodies are more important than this since we need to use them to establish some sort of middle position, and without a body it is difficult to see how this is possible. For example, when it comes to eating it is important not to eat too much, like a glutton, or eat too little, like an ascetic, but to establish a middle position. This only makes sense if we know what it means to be tempted into an extreme position, we need to know what it is like for our bodies to desire to eat and eat, and also what it feels like to restrict our consumption a good deal. We are pulled in both directions by our bodies and need to establish a middle position, and this is done by training our body to stop eating when it does not want to, and to start eating in opposition to our feelings.

Of course, from a religious point of view our bodies are not just incidental parts of us, they are there essentially and make us the sort of creature that we are. We need to take account of both the body and soul in how we plan on acting, and the Qur'an is very explicit on the need for balance here. It is not alone in this, all the Abrahamic religions, and we can go wider also, have a lot to say about both aspects of our humanity. Some Asian religions are seen as being far more oriented toward the soul and yet they also place a lot of emphasis on the body. For example, there is a significant discussion in Hinduism of karma and how people should behave, and of the importance of not harming other things in the universe, in order not to bring impurity close to us and to what will continue of us into future lives. In the end the aim is to escape the wheel of birth and rebirth, samsara, and so eventually the body, and move entirely into the realm of the real self, the soul. Yet many thinkers are critical of taking this too far and renouncing this world and our responsibilities in it for the sake of an entirely spiritual form of existence. In the *Bhagavad Gita* Arjuna is advised by Krishna to fight against his relatives and even kill them if necessary since that is his duty and since he is a fighter he should carry out this task just from the motivation of doing his duty and then he will acquire as little karma as possible. He is not told to go off and meditate in solitude on a mountain and renounce the world of matter. It is even suggested by some thinkers that people carrying out what is regarded in Hinduism as despicable trades, such as butchers, can be purer than those who do nothing but seek spiritual advancement if the former lack anger and envy in their thought processes. They do something that is regarded as unpleasant and against the principles of not harming sentient things and yet they can do it in a way that minimizes the spiritual damage that it might cause to them, and so remain relatively pure throughout. This is not the place to enter into a discussion of how religions like Hinduism deal with the balance between body and mind, but it is worth reminding ourselves that all religions reflect on this issue and perhaps do not differ a great deal on many aspects of it.

It is easy to escape from an orientation toward balance by just emphasizing one or two religious claims and then basing everything on them. This is such a common strategy, very popular theologically especially when addressing a general audience. In fact, this has been done in this book, a few passages have been selected and it has been argued that they are key to understanding the Qur'an and its ethical message. An argument has been produced, of course, to support such a claim, but then arguments always are, the statement that is privileged over others is explained and linked with other statements in the Book, and then it is provided with a wider context and looks like it is what the Book is all about, on that particular topic at least. Perhaps any *aya* could be given this sort of treatment, since even the most minor looking can be unfolded in a way that makes much rely on them, and they are all the word of God, we are told, so surely God would not say anything minor. It is for others to decide how strong such arguments are and how far they only work rhetorically. The main problem is that a case is made for the priority of an *aya* or even part of an *aya* and then a vast gamut of counterexamples occurs to the reader or listener. Perhaps they can be resolved, but once the process of dealing with the counterexamples is undertaken much of the dramatic effect of the prioritizing of one verse over another is lost. The principle of abrogation is sometimes used to facilitate this process, but then this also has to be established by argument and it is often a matter of debate what abrogates what. We have been critical in this book about the idea that anything goes, that any verse can be interpreted in any way, which does not seem to be appropriate for what is taken to be the word of God. It does not seem to be appropriate for any use of language, that use has an author, an audience, a context, a syntax and semantics, a language, and out of that combination of factors a meaning or meanings arise. It cannot just be anything we want it to be, although often it can be stretched. Yet there are always going to be more and less plausible understandings of a text and this is the bread and butter of theology, producing arguments that work with the basic material of scripture and also make some kind of sense with us and with the religion.

Motives

It will be said that Islam, like other religions, is very serious in its treatment not just of actions but of motives too. We are told that God not only knows what we do but also why we do it, what our motives are, and he is, of course, prepared in the end to reward and punish us accordingly. There is an *aya* "O you who believe! Respond to God and His messenger when he calls you to that which gives you life; and know that God intervenes between man and his heart, and that to Him you shall be gathered" (8:24) which suggests that God controls our thinking to the extent He guides us on how to feel about things. Islam stresses also the significance of humility and the *adab* gentleman is very far from the humble servant of God who feels his life is at the disposal of a greater being. In some ways the Sufi literature is a corrective to the *adab* discussions since it emphasizes our total dependence on God for everything, while the gentleman of the *adab* is in control of his life, in so far as any of us can be, and is far from humble. He is not boastful but he has a high opinion of himself where this is justified, and if it is, then he would be wrong not to have it. It would be false modesty. For many Sufis by contrast, we cannot take modesty too far since compared with God we are very inconsequential indeed. We do not even carry out our own actions, as it says in the Qur'an, when we throw something, it is not us that throws but God who throws. We are merely a side-effect, as it were, and this is a starting point on the route to spiritual growth which eventually ends up with our getting closer to God and to whom we really are.

Modesty is important because it makes it less likely that we will sin. Sexual offenses are more likely to arise if people are immodest or so it is often said. Yet there is plenty of evidence of molestation of modestly dressed women by men, even on the hajj, according to some accounts. The seclusion of women is not always that effective, El Cheikh (2010) looks at contemporary literature to suggest that harems were not always as effective at preserving female modesty as might have been thought even in early Baghdad. Yet the principle of not emphasizing the sexual nature of the human body has its advantages; it might lead people to regard each other not as potential sexual partners but as playing some other role. On the other hand, provocative clothing might encourage people to practice self-restraint and accustom them to deal with temptation. One of the features of the *adab* literature is the importance of self-restraint, and a way of encouraging it is to learn to cope with situations where we find it difficult to control ourselves. Psychologists often put us in situations we find difficult in order to help us learn to have the appropriate feelings. Gradually over time our character changes and we become more capable of behaving in the right sort of way. Modesty might be easier to acquire if we are used to seeing and wearing modest clothing, the suggestion goes. Then it would be the case that our behavior and our clothing were in line with each other. Perhaps the Qur'an, as so often, is not reporting on what we should do now so much as describing a state of affairs in the future that would come about if we managed to incorporate modesty in our character to a greater extent. Were we able to do so what people were or were not wearing would not be that significant. We would not notice, we would be concentrating on them as people with whom we are allowed to have a particular relationship. Anything else they possess is entirely incidental.

Does this though not suggest a far too serious attitude to other people? Is it wrong to see an attractive person and wonder what it would be like to make love to him or her? Obviously, it is wrong to carry out such an investigation in reality, unless of course this is a spouse, but one of the pleasures of being human is to have sexual feelings which are not necessarily confined in imagination to those with whom we are allowed to have sex. It is like imagining oneself the owner of a smart car or a big building; this does not imply an acceptance of car or home theft. Some types of Islamic law are very restrictive in what they allow people to do, trying no doubt to prevent them from falling into sin. Yet others do allow us to work with a degree of temptation and perhaps trust us most of the time to come out on the right side of it. This is a discussion held within many religions, and it comes out nicely in Islam when we contrast some of the figures mentioned in both the Qur'an and the Bible. In the former they are often represented in a much more positive light, although we should take account of the fact that these works are very different from each other in style, so this is hardly surprising. The Qur'an is much more concise for one thing and has an entirely non-historical order. Yet some of the major figures in the Bible are far from being very nice people, whereas in the Qur'an they are, they seem to be in control of their bodies and minds to a remarkable degree. Jacob in the Bible cheats his brother, runs to his mother for advice on what to do, runs away and when he eventually returns is frightened his brother will exact revenge. In the Qur'an when he hears his favorite son has disappeared and only some bloody clothing remains, he is apparently content to wait patiently for a positive outcome to the situation. In the Bible characters are very fallible, in the Qur'an they are much better. The Prophet himself is represented as having an excellent character, and we never get the sense that he is ever tired, fed up, disheartened, and so on, all human traits to which we are accustomed in even our heroes. The hadith bring out more of the personal and fallible features of the major characters surrounding the Prophet while the Qur'an tends to stay silent on this. One can imagine though that the Prophet must have felt bad at the disinclination of his tribe to receive his message from God and at having to leave his hometown and escape to Yathrib, later on called Medina. His only son dies, and his period as leader is marked by constant warfare and struggle, yet he seems to calmly deal with this without any drama or doubts.

The important thing about temptation is that it is countered by divine grace. People often ask why there is no problem of evil in Islam and fail to understand that the problem of evil is based on the idea that some people do not get what they deserve. Some innocent people suffer while evil people appear to flourish, and this does not seem fair. Yet, according to the Qur'an, if we got what we deserved, we would get a lot less than we do now. God is much more generous than we have the right to accept, and this is not just a religious claim. When we looked at the Mu'tazilite view that God has to recompense us for sufferings we do not deserve, at least in the next world if not in this, we said this was banal. On the other hand, given their emphasis on justice, it looked like a decent argument. If God is in charge of everything and has to be fair, then it looks like He has to bring about something like this. Suppose, however, we live in a far more unpredictable world, one in which we often cannot really explain what goes on. Some people meet someone they really love and spend the rest of their lives with that person, and they are both very happy. Yet other people never meet anyone like that and their lives are less pleasant. Perhaps their lives are more exciting as a result though since they meet a number of different people with whom they have enjoyable relationships and do not concentrate on their relationship with just one person. None of these very different but interesting things may have happened, we live in a world where they do and can, and we do not necessarily deserve it. Then bad things happen also and we wonder why; would it not have been better to have avoided such things? Of course it would. But would we want to live in a world where bad things could not happen at all, unless they were deserved since this would make life rather boring and without challenge? It is worth noting that this does not have to be a religious view at all, one could welcome a difficult and dangerous world without referring to God at all. What we need is the idea that wonderful things can happen, and they may surprise us, and that is the sort of environment in which we often enjoy living. Yet the world could have been a very different place; there is nothing in what we do that means we deserve to live in a particular kind of world. This is what the Qur'an might be suggesting when it emphasizes divine grace.

On the other hand, it might be thought that the problem of evil is precisely a problem because it does not resolve the question of why evil occurs. If God is in charge of everything as the Qur'an constantly insists, then the reason for what happens is to be found with the deity, although there is no reason why we should understand what it is. This would involve on our part the development of emotions such as patience, resignation, faith and, above all, submission, being a Muslim. The point about the problem of evil is often said to be the feeling that there is no reason for evil, whereas according to the Qur'an, there is a reason, and it lies with God. The problem is not that we do not know what the reason is, but that we suspect there may be no reason at all. There is no problem in not knowing the reason, since there is no necessity for everything that God does to be available to us. When the angels are told to bow down to Adam (2:34, 17:61), and they warn God that putting human beings in charge of the world is not a good idea. God says that He knows something they do not know. This does not just mean He knows more than they do, although, of course, He does, but that He knows in an entirely different way. Given the huge difference between God and His creation, it is unlikely that we would always understand why things happen as they do, and we should entertain no such ambition.

Sex and altering bodies

When talking about attitudes to sex and the body it is important to distinguish as far as possible between Islam as a formal system and local customs which incorporate aspects of Islamic language to justify what is regarded as acceptable but which may have nothing to do with the religion. Boudibha (1975) provides a brief account of the notion of sexuality in Islam, while the jurisprudent al-Shafi'i (2008) was quite ambivalent on the desirability of sex even in marriage, whereas many Sufis are either advocates of celibacy or have an enthusiastic attitude to sex as a temporal aspect of divine love. El Feki (2013) provides many accounts of women's experiences of sex in the Arab world, reflecting the fact that this is a region with a high use of internet pornography and also often repressive social customs. The desire to maintain virginity means that sexual practices short of vaginal penetration are said to be commonplace among young people, although it is difficult to know whether this is true or merely anecdotal and designed to attract the interest of a book-buying audience.

Alterations to the body made for no medical purpose are, on the whole, condemned by Islamic authorities. Male circumcision is an exception here, it is seen as an issue of cleanliness (Kamali 2002). Several Qur'anic verses indicate the perfection of creation (32:7, 82:7-8, 95:4, 23:14, 27:88, 80:17-19, 31:20, among others). On the other hand, no one uses these passages to ban cosmetics so it is not clear how far they are relevant to the topic. Of course, some changes are permanent or very difficult to reverse, yet why this should constitute a legal difference is also unclear. Some alterations to the body are acceptable, such as those involved in male circumcision since this is a practice praised by significant Muslims and taken to promote "cleanliness." It is thus recommended for converts. What makes the body unclean in religion is always significant, as Reinhart 2001 and Turner 1987 show, and there is particular controversy about female circumcision, which is popular in some parts of the Islamic world, but not only there either. Bodies are ideally washed and put in a shroud and buried within twenty-four hours. Cremation and autopsies are seen as marks of disrespect.

The equality issue

How far should religions be in favor of equality? It seems like a strange question since for a follower of a religion, it might be the religion itself that determines what attitude we ought to take to issues like equality, liberty, and so on. After all, if we believe that a religion represents the word of God, and of course His will, then it tells us everything we need to know about how far political virtues such as equality ought to be pursued, and to what extent they ought to be restrained. It is perhaps problematic if we introduce a notion like equality from another sphere of intellectual life and judge a religion by it. The religion will itself tell us what interpretation of equality is appropriate and that should be the basis of our assessment, and perhaps that is one of the factors referred to when people say that Islam is comprehensive. It includes everything that people need to know in working out how to behave, and that implies it includes everything that people need to know about equality in order to thrive. They discover that by being part of the religion and reading its texts. Anything coming from elsewhere is either innovation or heresy and ought to be avoided.

On the other hand, as is familiar to us by now, it is not always that easy to work out what views a particular religion has on a particular issue. Even when it is clear it is not always obvious how that view is qualified in certain conditions or by changing circumstances. In Islam it is often not clear what verse has been abrogated by what other verse, or what general principle may be taken to guide how we are to understand particular verses. Even religions which clearly approve of certain kinds of behavior, and condemn others, may be interpreted in such a way that this is held not to be the case, or no longer to be the case. The reason why religions have flourished and grown may be taken to be linked with their flexibility, with the fact that even in changing conditions they still seem to be relevant. That does not mean we should be expected to vary the religion to make it fit in with varying circumstances; some people enjoy the fact that religions are difficult to follow on occasion and relish that difficulty. The tougher the religion the more authentic it may seem to be, or the more interesting to try to observe down to every jot and tittle. It becomes a challenge and the harder it gets to follow, the more attractive it becomes to some people. For others the reverse is the case, and they may abandon the religion or merely observe it superficially. Others may reject it totally or see it as an obstacle toward initial acceptance. It is worth making this point since there is a tendency to accuse people of siding with religious beliefs which they find attractive or which fit in with their lifestyle. Islam does portray its beliefs and practices as moderate and in line with human nature. For some people though, they seem to be unnatural and difficult, and it is precisely that feature which they regard as attractive. Some school teachers are respected more because they are strict, while others are discounted for being too soft. On the other hand, for some pupils the reverse may be the case and they reject the harshness of one teacher while being attuned to the softness of another. We should be aware of how our emotional character makes a view of religion appropriate for us as individuals and how that may vary over time and between different people.

There is a persistent problem in Islamic ethics in reconciling *maslaha* or welfare and the *maqasid al-shari'a*, the aims of the law. To take an example, there are practices which many Muslim legal authorities do not favor, such as mixed dancing, tattoos, some kinds of pictorial art, music, and so on, but which are not clearly condemned in the main sources of law. These practices might be regarded as encouraging *shirk*, idolatry, in one form or another, or they could be associated with secularity and be regarded as the thin end of the wedge in changing what is appropriate behavior for Muslims. Modesty is a desirable aim and any activity that threatens it is questionable. What are the *maslaha* implications of modesty, however? How does it lead to welfare? We might say it helps with preserving dignity, for example, but in many circumstances this seems implausible. For example, it does not seem to be directed at welfare when people in very hot weather are obliged to cover up rigorously. On the other hand, if the aims of the law are doing what God wants, and we assume that as the Qur'an tells us, He knows and we do not, then, preserving modesty is in our interests, perhaps, but we do not understand why. It is enough that God tells us to act in a particular way. Even if the purpose is not obvious in this world, or realized in this world, it will have a result in the next world, and, in fact, the difficulties in preserving modesty in this world only adds to the merit of acting in accordance with the law in this world. For such behavior our reward is eventually available in the next world. Or so we should hope since, of course, we do not know how we will end up, the final decision is up to God. There are instances when modesty as traditionally interpreted may stand in the way of something else important, a particularly virtuous political or military end, for instance, and in such circumstances both the *maqasid* and *maslaha* seem to suggest we should suspend the rule and seek to attain the desirable end.

We need to be clearer on the role of general principles in ethics. There is certainly a problem in using the internal rules of a religious ethical system to work out how to behave if it looks like the decision is going against the general principles of the religion. It seems clear, for example, that Islam has quite specific and strict rules about sexual behavior, some is licit and some very much is not, and for the latter there are harsh punishments in many of the legal schools. Of course, this sort of law is a result of not only the Qur'an, where references to homosexuality, for instance, are slim if there at all and not always unambiguous, but also the hadith, where the feelings of the leading authorities are quite clear on the topic. Then there the rulings of the various legal schools in all the traditions, and they are all consistently, what is now often called, homophobic. They have a negative attitude to homosexual practices and thoughts, although in Islam, there is always the possibility of mercy from God for those who repent. The situation can become quite complex since we might debate the strength of particular hadith on the topic, and whether the appropriate rules were derived from them, and whether a homophobic attitude guided the direction of the legislation. These are interesting legal issues that do not go to the heart of the ethical issue here, the evident horror with which Islam seems to view particular sexual practices.

Homosexuality

Like many religious books within the Abrahamic religions, the Qur'an is generally taken to condemn homosexual acts and, in particular, sodomy (*liwat*). There are references to the people of Lot (Lut), at 7:81-82; 11:77-83; 15:61; 21:74; 22:43; 26:165; 27:55; and 29:29. The destruction of the people of Lot is linked with their sexual practices (26:165-173), although we are not told that in the Qur'an. This does leave some space for those seeking legal acceptance of homosexuality in Islam to argue that really there is no direct evidence in the Qur'an of hostility to the practice. Punishment for such practices, apart from divine wrath, is possibly referred to at 4:16, and both parties are blamed equally, something less common in much of the legal and other literature that came later. Some have argued that less severe punishments prescribed for homosexuality (anal intercourse between men) as compared with sexual infractions in male/female relationships suggest a less severe attitude toward homosexuality in Islam as compared with other religions. As with most sins, repentance and reform may lead to the avoidance of punishment (4:16), God can be relied upon always to be merciful. However, advocates of punishment for such behavior think this mild comment was later abrogated. In any case, it is not obvious that this passage refers to homosexuality at all, although it is often held to do so, given the use of the male personal pronoun. Sexual relations outside marriage are in any case condemned, so sexual relations between people who could not marry is obviously going to be sanctioned in any version of Islam, until perhaps we come to the present time when acceptance of homosexuality has become far more normal.

Within the Hanafi tradition often no physical punishment is suggested, because adultery, apostasy, and murder are not involved. For the Hanbalis, by contrast, the hail of stones that destroyed the people of Lot is an indication of the severity of the punishment that is appropriate for this behavior. The Maliki school insists on stoning, while the Shafi'i often distinguish between the active and the passive partner with regard to punishment. Strangely enough, it is the passive partner who is more criticized, although he might be seen as sometimes the innocent party. Shi'i Islam is very critical of homosexuality and punishes both partners, even where no actual penetration takes place. However, no specific punishment is recommended, and the legal opinions tend to range from beating to stoning to death. As with adultery, though, evidence is not easy to come by, and there is a debate as to whether the passive and the active partner should be punished equally. This ambiguity is reflected in the hadith of the Prophet, some of which make a distinction between the partners in a homosexual act, and many of which seem to permit homoerotic feelings, as long as those feelings are not translated into action (a position regarded sympathetically by Ramadan). This is the policy of some groups in other religions, where the religion condemns the act, but it allows the feelings that go along with it. There are also many hadith that are totally uncompromising in their opposition to *liwat*. There certainly seems to have been a strong distinction made between the role of the *ubna* or passive partner and the sodomizer, with the former being disgraced by their passivity. Stories in literature abound of men being punished by being sodomized, for example, and the serious consequences this has for them and for the status of those associated with them. This form of punishment is often used in Muslim countries to prisoners in order to humiliate them, but of course this is not limited to Muslim countries. It is strange why someone who is powerless and sodomized should be expected to feel especially guilty, yet people obviously do since otherwise the punishment would lose its point. Legally such victims are doubly disadvantaged by the fact that if the aggressor were to be prosecuted, in theory they would too, and would receive a longer or harsher sentence.

There are a variety of approaches in the academic literature to homosexuality in the Islamic world. One is to regard homosexuality as a universal practice, so there will be homosexuals in the Islamic world as elsewhere. The other is to regard homosexuality as culturally determined and so not universal but instead formed and structured in each culture. There is, of course, a serious problem in examining a practice such as homosexuality, which is a taboo in many societies, and determining how prevalent it is and was. To add to the confusion, the orientalist tradition of representing the Islamic world as decadent and "other" assumes a greater permissiveness to have existed in the past toward homosexuality in Islam than in other cultures. Visitors from the West to the mysterious Orient often found there a greater licentiousness, not perhaps because it was there but because they wanted it to be there to excuse their behavior. Sexual adventures clearly illegal at home could be indulged overseas since, to borrow an advertising slogan from Las Vegas, what happens there stays there. They do things differently there and sometimes that is helpful to those who want to do things differently also.

There should be no dispute about the existence of homoerotic literature and history in Islamic culture. Arabic and Persian poetry, history, political literature, songs, and material culture from the eighth to the fourteenth centuries CE abound in homoerotic and sexual symbols. Friendship between men and boys often plays a leading role, and the feelings between the partners are described in often frankly sexual ways. It is too easy to assume that this is evidence of widespread homosexuality in Islamic culture during this period, and this would be simplistic. It is a stylistic feature in such literature to link various forbidden motifs, homosexuality and wine is a good example, to parody the wider social and political order. Greek motifs, in particular, became widely employed in Arabic and Persian, and while in Greece they may have accurately described current practice, in Islamic literature they may have been used to allude in a negative way to the prevailing social order rather than as a description of common activities in contemporary society. Rowson (1997) suggests that in early Islam there was less fixity in gender roles than later, and there are reports of very varied forms of costume and play in court life. Also, there are in later Islam many miniatures, especially from Ottoman Turkey, that portray acts of sodomy and pederasty directly, and these may well represent activities then enjoying a certain popularity among particular social circles.

Was there homosexuality in the premodern world?

Much Islamic literature from the ninth to the nineteenth century includes phrases and themes that describe and celebrate the beauty of young boys, using an aesthetic style that emphasizes beauty rather than homoerotic content. Presumably in many cases women were less available to be viewed and so boys had to take their place, especially in institutions with lots of pubescent young men and little female availability. There are also more explicit narratives, often as part of a political satire or social critique, and young men occur very frequently as the object of adoration and as exemplars of grace and physical perfection. There is a literature warning people about gazing at boys in a wrong and sexual sort of way. Ruzibihan Baqli (d. 1209/605) discusses the topic at some length, as do many other Sufis (Murata 2017). El-Rouayheb (2005) argues that this does not imply the prevalence or acceptability of homosexuality, because that notion in its modern sense, or in the meaning it has in non-Islamic cultures, did not exist in the period he considers in depth (1500–1800 CE). It is a mistake to conclude that just because young men were the objects of love in *adab* and a wide variety of other literature, ranging from poetry to mysticism, this proves that the sexual practices associated with homosexuality were widespread. On the other hand, there is abundant literature at the time distinguishing between gazing at young boys in order to appreciate the principles of beauty and using those experiences for sexual gratification. The scope for exploitation of young boys within relatively isolated educational institutions was much discussed in Arabic literature during the premodern period, and teachers were advised to take precautions against temptation as a result of overly close relations with handsome, beardless boys. Writers within the Sufi tradition often warn others against this sort of behavior, and that could not be regarded as anti-Sufi propaganda. Sufi institutions, in particular, were criticized, generally by the enemies of Sufism, for the licentious behavior that was said to take place in the guise of religious and spiritual instruction. The lax attitude that some Sufis took toward legal rules encouraged, it was sometimes said, sexual advances toward young boys who were students or junior members of an order and, of course, in a very vulnerable position. On the whole, they were far from home, cut off from the rest of local society and at the disposal of powerful authority figures like their teachers or older school friends. The erratic behavior of those regarded as saints validated a variety of sexual attitudes and actions that would otherwise have been condemned, and the immature and relatively powerless were as ever frequently the victims of this license. It is possible that the modern notion of homosexuality is illegitimately applied to an earlier and precolonial period, and that a golden age of sexuality then prevailed until imperialist culture imposed its divisive ideas of how the genders should relate to each other. On the other hand, the references to what looks rather similar to the modern notion in the past suggests that this is probably not true. As we know, religious institutions of all kinds are perfect environments for sexual exploitation, today and in the past, and in any type of culture. Any situation in which there are powerful people in charge of the relatively powerless, where few know of what is going on and where there are no checks and balances on what happens, relies on the perfect probity of all concerned. Experience suggests things often go wrong in such an environment, however religious everyone in them seems to be.

El-Rouayheb suggests that in the Arab world of the early Ottoman Empire there was a significant difference between the portrayal in literature of young men as objects of desire and how they were actually treated as sexual partners. Such treatment would have been illegal and in any case would have brought social stigma along with it. Modernity has led to more questioning of the prevalent poetic and mystical idioms that center on the beauty of young men. Much of the literature from this period describes levels of power, because the objects of passion often come from minority groups, such as Christians or even slaves and servants. The 2007 movie *The Kite Runner*, based on a novel of the same name, is set in Afghanistan, where the Sunni Pashtuns have relatively high status. In one scene a Pashtun man rapes a Hazara (Shi'i) boy, replicating in modern times the tradition of seeing sodomy as much about differences of power and status as about sex. This point is often made about rape in general. In recent years the greater influence of Salafi views has also led to a greater disinclination to use imagery that could be taken to describe forbidden relationships, even obliquely, and is hardly friendly to those who explicitly represent homosexual acts in any sort of Islamic context. The celebration of beauty as personified in humanity and the view of its divine origins are features of Sufism and so are suspect from a religious point of view by those who adhere to what they see as a more literal version of Islam. There is a view of religion as a very serious activity and anything that looks like fun is treated with a good deal of suspicion. Traditional bawdy literature such as *The Arabian Nights* has been expurgated to remove stories with homosexual aspects, and poetry that celebrated the beauty of young men and seemed to countenance love for them by older men, however chaste this was supposed to be, is not acceptable in much of the Islamic world today given the relatively new prevailing climate of modesty. Homosexuality is often regarded by Salafis as a feature of Western decadence and something that does not and should not exist in Muslim communities, and if it does, then it is merely a reflection of the unwelcome spread of corrupt ideas from without. Often the severe penalties are designed to wipe it out before it manages to infect too many others.

It is certainly true that there are very few references to homosexuality and especially to lesbianism in religious or even literary material, although there is plenty of speculation about them in the journals and reports of early travelers to the Arab world. It is often unclear how accurate these are and how far they are just orientalist fantasies or wishful thinking. Those antagonistic to Islam have often criticized it for having a lax attitude to homosexual activities, no doubt as a way of distinguishing between "normal" behavior in their home countries and deviant sexuality. The nineteenth century saw the rapid decline of the Ottoman Empire, and one of the themes of orientalist visitors to the empire was the putative contrast between the sexually transgressive Muslims and the much stricter morality that then persisted in Europe. The situation is entirely reversed today, so in some Western countries prospective immigrants are obliged (pretend) to accept the permissibility of homosexuality before they can become citizens. In the past there was concern in the Islamic world about the literature dealing with love for young boys, and writers such as Ibn Taymiya (d. 1328/728) and his disciple Ibn Qayyim al-Jawziya (d. 1350/751) criticized *nazar*, or "gazing," the subject of much of the literature describing the way in which the poet contemplated the object of his affection. In fact, the topic of who it was permissible to gaze at became a controversial issue in Islamic theology, a permissive line being taken by 'Abd al-Ghanī al-Nabulusi (d. 1731/1143), who seemed to allow gazing at anyone, man or woman, provided one was able to distinguish between appreciating the aesthetic form of the object contemplated from its actual matter. Gazing at an actual person was likely to lead to lust and sin, he accepted, but he held that this could be separated from the act of contemplation of the form of the person alone. Here he represents the spirit of the literature dealing with young boys in premodern Islamic literature. This took itself not to be describing homosexuality and thus desires likely to lead to illegitimate actions, but instead aesthetic attitudes celebrating beauty wherever it was to be found.

In a speech at Columbia University (September 2007) the Iranian president Mahmoud Ahmadinejad told his audience that there were no homosexuals in Iran. This is a common belief in the Islamic world, although treated with incredulity in New York. There is an LGBTQ community in the Arab world but it tends to stay out of the limelight in the cause of self-preservation ("The Kingdom in the Closet"). Many religions in recent years, including Islam, have discussed opening themselves up to different forms of sexuality, and have tried to find resources within their faith to allow this to happen. As in other religions, many Muslims insist on a rigid ban on the practice, although as we have seen there is some scope within Islamic tradition to accept the feelings if not the actions associated with homosexuality. This is also the case, of course, in some Christian and Jewish groups. Advocates for homosexuals in the Islamic world argue that there is space for homosexuality within the *umma* (community), but it is unlikely that this issue will come to the forefront of discussion in Islam—as it has in Judaism and Christianity—for some time to come. On the other hand, the 2017 issues of the *Journal of the American Academy of Religion* and the *American Journal of Islamic Social Sciences* had significant discussions of the topic, so it is clearly coming far more to the surface, especially with those who see themselves as modernists in the Islamic world. Despite this, some use the references in the Qur'an to the divine nature of the diversity in the world (49:13) as the basis of an argument that diversity in sexual relationships might also be acceptable. It has to be said though that many countries that regard themselves as Islamic have strict penalties for homosexual behavior, including execution, and there is no indication yet of a general acceptance of homosexuality in Muslim communities. In fact, the antagonism of traditional Islam to homosexuality has been used politically to attack Islam and contrast it with a more tolerant, secular, or Western world. Whatever one thinks of this strategy, and it is surely based on a dichotomy far too crude to be worth supporting, to argue that Islam should be seen as neutral on sexuality is to play very loosely indeed with the basic texts. The religion however interpreted makes clear its antagonism to sexual acts outside of marriage, which is, of course, entirely a technical problem that could be solved by allowing marriage in Islam between men. However, both the Qur'an and the hadith make it clear that sexual relationships between men and men are thoroughly obnoxious, and if men have feelings that they would like to requite sexually with other men this is something they should initially resist and in time replace with more appropriate attitudes. After all, "And that you should judge between them by what God has revealed, and do not follow their vain desires, and be cautious of them, in case they seduce you from part of what God has revealed to you" (5:49).

What is wrong with progressive Islam?

Islam and its various legal schools have detailed rules on sexuality, since like many religions, it has clear ideas on the roles of the different gender groups and how they should interact. Whatever some may say, it has a highly patriarchal flavor, one that specifies very different roles for men and women across a range of activities and outcomes. In this it is similar to many iterations of the other Abrahamic religions. The early commentators and lawyers in all these religions were men, and still are largely men, so it is hardly surprising that the religions should have taken this tone. There are many references in the Qur'an to differences between men and women, and also many references to where men and women are regarded as equal, in their capacity to believe at least, and that is, of course, a very significant capacity. It is difficult to argue that the Qur'an is bristling with egalitarian ideas, although some have valiantly argued in this way. In particular the progressive Islam lobby are very keen on presenting such an approach (2:34, 17:61). The rest of the tradition and, in particular, the hadith make it clear that complementarity rather than equality is seen as the appropriate way for men and women to relate to each other. However, this goes against much of modern thinking on gender roles and the faith does not seem to accept the same notion of equality as is current. For some people this is an advantage, they want to turn away from modernity and all its horrors. There are a variety of ways of reacting to this potentially disturbing aspect of religion. The individual may reject the religion and adhere to the notion of equality or vice versa. She may think that there might be something defecting about her notion of equality if it does not appear to be validated by God in His Book. The more interesting strategy and the one we shall look at here is to suggest that Islam has all along accepted the modern notion of equality but for one reason or another this has not been sufficiently appreciated until progressive Islam came along. Sometimes this is linked with the idea that the treatment of gender in the Qur'an was progressive for its time and we need to continue with the progressive message in our time by working toward an interpretation that results in the sort of equality that can be recognized now as accurate and acceptable. According to Asma Barlas, "all codes, including the Qur'an, can be read in multiple modes, including egalitarian ones" (2002: 4). This exegetical principle is not restricted to gender but occurs throughout modern approaches to the Book (Duderija 2017). It can be read in a variety of different ways to be in favor of socialism, liberal conceptions of justice, or whatever political aim one sees as valuable. Religions often present their main beliefs in such a general way that they can be made to fit in with a variety of other views, especially religions that have lasted. They have to be fluid enough to compromise with a variety of challenges so that they can survive the buffeting of change. Different people can find a sympathetic response in their doctrines and often these will be entirely different responses.

The question is, though, not whether the Qur'an can be seen in those ways but whether it is plausible to make the effort. This is a question about scriptural hermeneutics in general, about how far we can interpret texts in line with the principles we hold dear and which seem often not to be there explicitly in those texts. When matters are discussed in the Book that seem out of date and old fashioned, they then need to be changed, albeit maintaining the spirit of what God has laid down as the law. Yet, does not the Qur'an warn us about this? For example, there is

> Do you then believe in a part of the Book and disbelieve in the other? What then is the reward of such among you as do this but disgrace in the life of this world, and on the day of resurrection they shall be sent back to the most serious penalty, and God is not unaware of what you do. (2:85)

Even more powerfully we are told: "It is not fitting for a believer, whether man or woman, when a matter has been decided by God and His messenger to have any option about their decision: if any one disobeys God and His messenger, he is indeed on a clearly wrong path" (33:36). The idea of following more egalitarian principles seems to come up against "They have taken as lords besides God their rabbis and their monks and the Messiah son of Maryam, when they were told to worship only one God. There is no God except for Him" (9:31). The rabbis and monks here can be taken to be like the ideas of gender equality that some think need to be followed in their interpretation of religion. They are part of *shirk* since they are principles we often accept yet which do not seem to be part of the Qur'an, quite the contrary. And at 4:48 we are warned that *shirk* can never be forgiven.

The more immediate issue and perhaps rather more manageable is to work out how to link those general moral principles such as justice, equality, fairness, and so on with the specific rules and regulations we find within a religious code, and here within Islam. Advocates for a faith keep on saying that it is based on at least one of these principles, and then produce an argument to show that this is a plausible interpretation of the relevant passages, including those which might seem to be awkward for the main thesis. These general principles are taken to be the *maqasid al-shari'a*, the aims and intentions of the law, and so anything which has become legal and seems to stand in way of those general aims must be wrong. There is probably then a story of how patriarchal society changed the law from the direction it was supposed to go, and made it fit in with its interests but no longer with the aims of the law in general. Clearly, the interpretation and even the identification of law depends heavily on who the lawyers are, and especially the important lawyers.

That is how law works in any system, something is said to be legal, it is appealed and a higher court adjudges on this issue. Often an appeal is made to the general principles that are taken to lie at the basis of the law itself, and specific instances of law need to be in line with those general principles. Progressive Islam bases itself on such an approach, and this is a serious error. But how can we tell if the law is in line with the general principles? It may seem obvious, and sometimes it is. The fact that people of good will and equal intellectual standing may disagree suggests that there is often no easy solution to such an issue. It is certainly the case that the Qur'an makes many references to the attitude of mutual respect that men and women should hold each other, to the importance of justice and fairness, to the disreputable nature of traditional beliefs (which may involve poor behavior and discrimination of men toward women), of the significance of kindness, and yet there are some verses which point in the direction of privileging men over women. They may all be interpreted in such a way that the inequality is only apparent since, as Barlas says quite rightly, there is no limit to how we can take texts. On the other hand, there are limits to plausibility. It is quite possible, as feminists who are also Muslims say, that those verses that could be taken in a patriarchal direction come from the early years of Islam and hence became part of the background to law which in Islam is so crucial. They represent a social system that no longer exists and so are not really relevant to how legislation would be framed for today. The traditions and, of course, the schools of law and commentary constructed around them and the Qur'an were taken in a particular way, and now that forms the concept of the sunna, the appropriate practice of Muslims, but it consists of a considerable variation from the path that Islam could have taken had the local social system been less patriarchal. This is an approach taken in many religions, and it has a lot to be said for it, but in Sunni Islam at least it does call for a very different way of working out the basis for moral behavior. The latter is very much based on the tradition, not just the tradition of the Prophet and what we know of his behavior, but also the tradition of what was done with those reports and how they went on to inform law. The Qur'an criticizes tradition, but only the tradition of those who acted without knowing how they really ought to act. Once we have the Book this tradition can be abandoned and the Qur'an used to re-establish the original monotheism that is really capable of guiding us how to behave. Criticizing *taqlid* or depending on tradition makes sense if we are dubious about the provenance of the tradition or its capacity to continue to energize our religiosity. The first factor at least should not be a concern for Muslims with what they believe about the Qur'an and what goes along with it. There can certainly be debate about the nature of the tradition, and often is. Women do not seem to have had much to do with it, although there are hadith from women closely linked with the Prophet of course, but the relative absence of women has led to a definite flavor of patriarchy in the corpus. Those producing the hadith, those assessing them and commenting on them, are almost entirely men, and like the Church Fathers and the authors of the Talmud, probably did not have a high opinion of the capabilities of women, an attitude, of course, often shared by women themselves at that time. They tended to value hierarchy, and equality does not really fit in with the idea of a ranking of people and their abilities and capacities. They often were not young, and seem to be grumpy, hardly surprising given their age, and their judgments fit in with their background.

Is there any reason not to go back to the Qur'an and put to one side the tradition that has built up around it? We are familiar with this strategy from other religions. They tend to accumulate a lot of additional material of one sort or another as they develop, and a time comes when the religion looks cumbersome and overly complex, and a desire arises to get back to basics. The idea is that over time religions get slanted in particular directions, and not necessarily in the direction that the religion itself sets out to go. One of the stylistic features of Islamic law that is not sufficiently noted is its enthusiasm for codification, for reducing the series of statutes and regulations to a few basic principles and linking the different parts of the legal system to each other in a logical way. The motive here is not so much logical clarity as intellectual bravado. The aim is to show that the law is not an arbitrary sets of commands but a system and it is possible to see how the system is organized if one is clever enough, since the system is perspicuous. Once this is grasped it is much easier to navigate around it, it provides us with a straight path and we can more easily stay on the path because of it. So while law goes into details of particular cases, and explains why it takes a certain position, it also points to the reason for the moves that are made and how they fit in with the system as a whole. This is important since unless one understands why the law is as it is it is difficult to operate with it as we do not really understand its workings. Simplification is a way of making something complex accessible to us, and it is important that users of religion know how to use it, and do not always have to rely on someone else to tell them what to do. This is something the Qur'an stresses a good deal, and rightly so.

The problem with creating a new and more progressive tradition is that what is taken to be the tradition is closer in time and space to the original revelation, and so might be assumed to be better at understanding it. It is not just a matter of understanding the language of the time, although that is a relevant feature, or being close to the main agents of the Qur'an, also far from irrelevant. The hadith are part of the world in which the Qur'an was produced, although of course many of them are taken to be dubious, but even the dubious ones are often in line with the leading teachings of the Qur'an. The hadith tell us how to apply the Qur'an to our practice, and the fact that they often go in a variety of different directions merely means that we have to try to work out which of them gives the most appropriate advice. That does not just mean which hadith are strong as against which hadith are weak, although that is certainly an important consideration. As al-Ghazali argued when his choice of weak hadith in his *Ihya'* was criticized, he could have found stronger ones which made the same point, so it hardly mattered. The important task as always is to strike a degree of balance between the hadith when working out how to proceed and as the Qur'an puts it at 39:18 "find the best meaning." This could mean go for the meaning that fits in with the conception of justice that you have since obviously the Qur'an would want to fit in with that conception. This is how the Mu'tazilites took it, and this is also the approach of progressives. They have a conception of how things ought to be and the Qur'an must have the same view, since how could it be in favor of something that is not just and virtuous? A problem with this view, though, is that it largely separates the Qur'an from ethics, the latter is used as an interpretive tool to investigate the former. Yet for many Muslims the reverse is the case, it is the Qur'an which instructs us on the nature of our duty. This is certainly a claim we find in the Book and we need to take it seriously.

There are a variety of directions one can take here. It can be argued that without the Qur'an or some similar divinely inspired religious work we have no idea how to behave. It could be argued rather less strongly that we can often work out some or much of what we ought to do in another way, and the Qur'an is there to make our moral knowledge much more complete and effective. There is a continuum here of dependence on guidance from a prophet or messenger, sometimes it looks like that is the only sort of moral advice that could operate, and sometimes as though it is helpful but not always essential. What the Qur'an and hadith tend to suggest is that however one sees the relationship between those sources of moral knowledge and our independent ways of working things out, we do need guidance. That is not a controversial point, but the whole point of Islam is to point to a form of guidance and invite people to accept it. They do not have to but it is in their interests to do so, and this is because God really knows the route to salvation and wants to help us get onto it. God knows, we do not know, and if we follow His advice, then we do know what to do. We still may not know why, but it is enough for us that He has told us what to do and then we just know that we should do it. The name of the religion, Islam, is important since it is based on the idea of submission, submission to God not because He is more powerful than us, although He is, but because He knows how we should behave and we need to submit to that information if we are to be rational.

But where do we find the information? Here we have a big problem, since information about ethics is not easy to find. It is not like scientific information, and the Qur'an does seem to advocate that we find out about the world and use that knowledge to improve our lives. The Qur'an and the hadith are full of moral advice but often it goes in a variety of directions and so it is not easy to see it as information. Suggestions, perhaps, is a more accurate description. This is as one expect since moral knowledge is not obviously possible. We can have moral beliefs and yet respect those who have contrary beliefs, and this brings out how difficult it is to call such beliefs knowledge. We find this replicated in religion, different groups in a religion have firm views on what should be done and other groups may have different views. A good example of this is the way that the main legal schools in Sunni Islam respect each other's rulings, although they may not agree with them. Here we really need to pay close attention to the hadith. The argument is that the hadith represent a way of moving the more general ideas in the Qur'an into practice, since the hadith consists of stories and reports that embody religious ideas in practice. They provide accounts of what the Prophet and those close to him did and said on a variety of occasions, and thus offer an example to be followed. But often there are hadith which go in a variety of directions so it is not clear what was done or said in the past, or better, a variety of things were done and said in the past and we need to construct some route for ourselves out of this variety. It is a bit like asking for directions and being given different advice. I remember when I had an allotment and my neighbors gave me advice on how to grow plants the advice was often contrary to each other and I then had to work out how to set about gardening while offending as little as possible anyone around me. It looks as though we are getting back to the idea expressed by many and, here quoted from Barlas, that we can go in whichever direction we wish. That is, we can take the advice as pointing us in any direction we want to go, and if we have progressive views then that is the direction we will choose.

One of the problems with that strategy, though, is that it fails to recognize other voices and opinions. It puts us in charge of interpretation and there is something questionable about that when it is a matter of discussing a religious text. We appear to approach the text with a view already of how it ought to go, since we accept certain principles that we are going to insist on the text following. The principle at stake here is how far we can discern God's intentions when approaching the text. Often religions ask us to do things for reasons we cannot discern, but since we assume that God knows what they are, we can just follow what we are told to do. This happens a lot in the Qur'an, and at length in the confrontation of Musa and Khidr. It is important in religion to accept the idea that God is in charge and can ask us to do things we do not always understand. This gives us a way of dealing with hadith with which we disapprove, we should not necessarily reject them but accept them as important information that we do not really understand. We cannot see how that sort of approach could fit in with how we see Islam, just as Musa could not see why God was allowing all sorts of bad things to happen when he was traveling with Khidr. This represents a difficulty with the progressive view, the difficulty it has with dealing with awkward hadith and passages of the Qur'an. By "awkward" is meant those passages that do not fit into the progressive narrative or versions of the *maqasid al-shari'a*, the latter playing its usual steamrolling part in squashing complexity. In the Qur'an the phenomenon of *naskh* or abrogation of some verses by others can be employed, of course, to discipline the inconvenient verses and in the hadith the mantle of being well-founded can be removed from naughty conversations. This is such a cheap trick though, and we find it played so frequently. It fits in nicely with utilitarianism and the idea that there is some underlying principle that justifies what we do, and religion then serves to illustrate that principle, not as its basis. People often say that given one particular verse a whole load of others cannot be taken at face value, or given a particular hadith then if we accept it we cannot regard as relevant a lot of others. It is like saying of a person whom one likes but who does something wrong that our relationship is now obviously completely at an end. We can say this of course, but we are more likely to try to work out how to preserve the relationship and work out why he did what he did and how we are going to come to terms with it. That does not mean we accept but it does mean that we have to work with him and the obnoxious event and find some way of resolving matters, perhaps temporarily, and think of how we are going to move on, as people say, and learn from what happened.

We seem to have something of a dichotomy here between a policy of strict *taqlid*, just doing what we are told to do by the tradition, imitating those before us, with a naïve approach to knowing how to discern what that tradition actually is, and a policy of anything goes. Surely this is a false choice, these are extremes which are both unattractive. A policy of respecting *wasatiya* or moderation would suggest we find somewhere in the middle which represents a reasonable compromise. We should look to tradition for guidance and at the same time combine it with our experiences and ideas. There are always going to be awkward aspects of both and we have to acknowledge them and find a way to deal with them.

A good example here are the references in the Qur'an to women being a bit lower in status than men, which to be fair has to be seen alongside many far more egalitarian passages about the roles of men and women. There are the laws of inheritance, of course, but also the passage saying that women are a degree below men, and also the passage where corporal punishment for disobedient wives is recommended look impervious to egalitarian interpretation. These are difficult passages for anyone committed to egalitarianism. They seem to imply that women are inferior to men, not just that they are complementary. We could take the attitude that if that is what God says then we just have to act accordingly since He knows and we do not. On the other hand, we could take these passages to illustrate the implications of treating men and women as not being equal. For example, in the passage on the disobedient wife a whole range of reactions is suggested, violence being the last and coming at the end of them all. The idea might be that in a situation of conflict these are the sorts of things that people do. It starts with verbal admonitions and ends with physical violence; the stakes keep on getting higher and in the end we tend to get rough. Should not the Qur'an clearly dismiss the acceptability of such treatment? Perhaps it is just reporting on what people do or say. Similarly, when we hear that men are a degree above women, this could be a reflection on what people say, on familiar social attitudes, and not necessarily advice to be followed. After all, we are also told that Islam is the best religion and pursues the good, rejects evil and adheres to God (3:110); It is not at all clear whether this is taken to be a report on a fact or an aspiration. It surely cannot mean that the community of people who call themselves Muslims is superior to everyone else since that is patently false. It could mean that if there came to be a community who genuinely submitted to God, then that community would be impressive. We cannot always be sure of the voice that remarks in the Qur'an adopt, which makes it look like it can mean anything at all.

The trouble with the *maqasid al-shari'a* approach is that it gets us to stop arguing too early. In 4:34 we have a well-known passage which seems to contemplate with approval a husband striking his wife, if in the end she does not behave properly. This is not the first thing to do, but after trying a range of milder sanctions, this is what he should end up doing, if everything else fails. There are other possible translations, but really no other plausible ones.

On the other hand, some would argue this cannot be the right interpretation since it goes against the aims of Islam. To strike someone in these conditions ignores the fact that God prohibits aggression. To physically beat another person is an act of aggression whatever the circumstances, and yet we are told "do not transgress, God does not like the aggressors" 2:190. Then God commands husbands and wives to treat each other with love and mercy, beating the wife is not a merciful act: "And from His signs is that He created for you mates from yourselves that you may reside with them, and He placed between you affection and mercy. In that are signs for a people who reflect" (30:21). In 4:19 men are told to treat their wives with kindness, which hardly accords with physical or any other kind of violence. Finally, it is worth pointing out that if the heinous sin being dealt with here is adultery, then there is already a punishment established for that (hundred lashes at 24:2) so anything in addition is excessive.

Although these are frequent arguments, they really do not work. Let us look at adultery. Perhaps the husband striking the adulterous wife is an alternative to the hundred lashes, and it certainly seems preferable. Beating someone is aggression but it could be regarded as legitimate aggression, the Qur'an is not a pacifist text. In certain conditions violence is justified, and indeed even requisite. Physically striking someone could be seen as an act of love, in the sense that it is a last attempt at saving the relationship. It might also be seen as merciful, better than the hundred lashes at least or at any of the other consequences of the relationship entirely breaking down. Yet, many today would think that adultery should not be regarded as a crime at all, despite what the Qur'an says; our decisions about how we wish to use our bodies should be left to us. It might not even be the cause of a marital relationship breaking down but could be incorporated in it, as multiple wives and concubines might operate. People do have very complicated lives with marriages, relationships with a variety of people, some sexual, some not but perhaps even closer than those that are, and perhaps people are able to juggle these different people in an appropriate sort of way. The Qur'an only permits marriage to more than one wife if all can be treated fairly, and it may be that an adulterous relationship could be maintained in such a way that all partners felt they were being treated fairly. We could take this principle and use it to replace marriage, itself an institution with something more appropriate to the times we live in and its values.

We are getting a very long way from the Qur'an here, though. We seem to be agreeing with the progressive line that anything goes, that we can interpret a text in any way we wish. A big problem with this is that it collapses the text into a principle, perhaps here an egalitarian principle, and whatever the text says can be ignored or replaced by the principle. Often ethical thinkers do appeal to an absolute idea and everything has to come under if it is to be morally acceptable, and this does not do justice to the variety of situations in which we find ourselves wondering what to do. It would be convenient to have such a general idea, and this is perhaps how the angels in Islam operate. They are always good, they always know what they should do and they always do it. When God tells them to bow down to humanity, in the form of Adam, they wonder at the soundness of the instruction since, as they point out, humanity is a highly imperfect thing. We not only have freedom of choice, which is the conclusion generally drawn from this passage, and this does not just mean we are not constrained in our behavior by force from outside of us. It also means that we can decide how to behave, and an aspect of that is we often do not know how we ought to behave, a reflection of the moral openness of our world. The angels always know and yet God wants them to give priority to those who do not, and this seems to be a celebration of ignorance rather than knowledge, despite His claim that He knows and the angels do not. Perhaps the point is that we are capable of having rich ethical lives since those lives are so complex and ridden with contradictions and contrasting commitments and passions. The angels interpret the text exactly as it ought to be interpreted, they never have to struggle with it or wonder what it means. They are in the position of someone who every time gets the right answer to a mathematical problem, as against someone who knows how to solve the problem but sometimes gets it wrong. Paradoxically, it is the latter who has the better grasp of mathematics since she know how to get the right answer, although she does not always get it. Someone who just gets it automatically is not doing mathematics, she is just always producing the right answer.

This is something that Iblis hints at when he refuses to bow down, pointing out that humans are made of different material from angels and are more imperfect. He is right in the sense that all the angels do what God tells them to do except for Iblis, whereas not many human beings do what God tells them do. Angels are much better submitters than we are, but then that is their nature. God has created the world and Islam to fit our nature but has left us with room to find our own way around both the world and the Qur'an. There are no nice neat solutions to the problematic issues we find in the Book or indeed in the world, and so the progressives are wrong in thinking we can just do what we like with the text.

It is quite common to think that people who are less skilled at an activity are worthy of our contempt, and this is Iblis' point. He is going to dedicate himself to misleading human beings and proving that he is right in his low opinion of us. It is worth noticing that people who are dishonest often enjoy encouraging others to be dishonest and are pleased when they discover that people are dishonest. When somebody does something wrong it is often claimed that everyone is doing it, as though that would make it right or excusable. One of the activities that Iblis is engaged in is leading us away from God, since that serves to show that he was right in thinking that we are not really capable of doing what we are told to do by God. We find it difficult to follow God as a rule and this is not just weakness of will, it is often because we do not know what we should do, how we ought to behave. The Qur'an and the Traditions often leave it open and the task is to work out how to interpret texts to establish a satisfying synthesis blending our experiences, the tradition, and the stories we tell each other. It is worth using this word "task" since the idea of a process is important. So is the product at the end of the process, but as the Prophet is supposed to have said, *al-din nasiha*, religion is advice. In fact, he repeated it three times. Advice is generally quite tentative, rather than a set of precise instructions. He is right, religion is often quite hesitant in what it tells us and encourages us to work out how to behave and what the religion is actually saying. Often we need guidance; indeed, we always need guidance according to the Qur'an, but the problem is knowing where to find it: "O believers, obey God, and obey the Messenger, and those in authority among you" (4:59). The latter phrase *'uli'l-amr'* can be taken to mean "the people of knowledge" or "the people of religion and jurisprudence," or to refer to the imams as in the Shi'i traditions. Those who have knowledge, we are told, "And that those who have been given knowledge may know that it is the truth from your Lord, so that they may believe in it and their hearts may submit humbly to Him. God certainly guides those who believe onto a right path" (22:54). Obviously, we should depend on them. But how do we know who they are?

Perhaps they are the traditional leaders of the community. The Qur'an is rather critical of tradition that after all in its time often represented what the Book saw as regression from pure monotheism. Ibn 'Abd Rabbih refers to a story about al-Ḥajjaj, b. Yusuf al-Thaqafi (d. 95/714), the notoriously harsh governor of Iraq at the time of Caliph 'Abd al-Malik b. Marwan (d. 65–86/685–705). Sulayk b. al-Sulaka complained to Ḥajjāj that he had been punished for an offense committed by someone else from his tribe. Ḥajjāj responds by quoting lines from pre-Islamic poetry that support that sort of punishment, to which Sulayk b. al-Sulaka responds with the story of Joseph and his brothers from 12:78-9. The brothers address Joseph thus when Benjamin is accused of theft: "O gracious prince, he has a father, aged and great with years, so take one of us in his place—we see that you are someone who does good." Joseph replied: "God forbid that we should take any other but him in whose possession we found our property, we would really do the wrong thing." Here, Joseph refuses to punish anyone other than who was at fault. The idea we can take from this is that tradition here is of no guide to how we should act. When Ḥajjaj hears the verses, he relents and agrees that Sulayk b. al-Sulaka should not have been punished. Ibn 'Abd Rabbih uses the Qur'anic quote as an example of the significance of individual autonomy and responsibility, and how only the Qur'an is acceptable as the basis of how to behave. Here we see what is wrong with progressivism and the way it is used. Whatever we think of the progressive principles, they are not to be found in the Qur'an. Perhaps the Qur'an would be better with them, but they are not there. The Qur'an suggests that when it comes to knowing how we should act God knows and we often do not, and we are best off following Him. This is often repeated in the Book and we need to take it seriously.

Bibliography

Abrahamov, Binyamin (1996), *Anthropomorphism and Interpretation of the Qur'an in the Theology of al-Qasim ibn Ibrahim*, Leiden: Brill.

Al-Albani, Muhammad (2002), *Jilbab al-mara'a al-muslimah fi al-kitab wa'l-sunna.* [The Muslim Woman's Covering in the Book and Tradition], Cairo: Dar al-Salam.

Ali, Kecia (2006), *Sexual Ethics and Islam: Feminist Reflections on Qur'an, Hadith, and Jurisprudence*, Oxford: Oneworld.

Alshaar, Nuha (2014a), "An Islamic approach to moral virtue: Fakhr al-Din al-Razi's treatment of Birr (Virtue) in his al-Tafsir al-Kabir," *Mélanges de l'Université Saint-Joseph* 64: 87–100.

Alshaar, Nuha (2014b), *Ethics in Islam: Friendship in the Political Thought of Al-Tawhidi and His Contemporaries*, Abingdon: Routledge.

Amara, Fadela, and Zappi, Sylvia (2003), *Ni putes ni soumises*, Paris: La Découverte.

Antoun, Raymond (1968), "On the modesty of women in Arab Muslim villages: A study in the accommodation of traditions," *American Anthropologist* 70 (1968): 671–97.

Barlas, Asma (2002), *Believing Women in Islam: Unreading Patriarchal Interpretations of the Qur'an*, Austin: University of Texas Press.

Bauer, Karen (2015), *Gender Hierarchy in the Qur'an*, New York: Cambridge University Press.

Boudibha, Abdelwahab (1975), *La sexualité en Islam*, Paris: Presses universitaires de France.

Brown, Jonathan (2017), "A Pre-Modern Defense of the Hadiths on Sodomy," *American Journal of Islamic Social Sciences* 34/3: 1–44.

El Cheikh, Nadia (2010), "Caliphal harems, Household harems: Baghdad in the fourth century of the Islamic era," in *Harem Histories: Envisioning Places and Living Spaces*, Marilyn Booth (ed.), Durham, NC: Duke University Press: 87–103.

Converting to Islam. Available at: http://convertingtoislam.com/circum.html

Delong-Bas, Natana (2004), *Wahhabi Islam: From Revival and Reform to Global Jihad*, New York: Oxford University Press.

Don Alfonso el Sabio (1807), *Las siete partidas del rey*, Madrid: Imprenta Real, vol. 3: 677–78.

Duderija, Adis (2017), *The Imperatives of Progressive Islam*, London: Routledge.

Emon, Anver, Ellis, Mark, and Glahn, Benjamin (eds.) (2012), *Islamic Law and International Human Rights Law: Searching for Common Ground?*, Oxford: Oxford University Press.

El Feki, Shereen (2013), *Sex and the Citadel: Intimate Life in a Changing Arab World*, New York: Vintage.

Göle, Nilüfer (1996), *The Forbidden Modern: Civilization and Veiling*, Ann Arbor: University of Michigan Press.

Göle, Nilüfer (2009), "Turkish Delight in Vienna: Art, Islam and European Public Culture," *Cultural Politics: An International Journal* 5/3: 277–98.

Hamdy, Sherine (2012), *Our Bodies Belong to God: Organ Transplants, Islam, and the Struggle for Human Dignity in Egypt*, Berkeley: University of California Press.

Hart, Kimberley (2013), *And then We Work for God: Rural Sunni Islam in Western Turkey*, Stanford, CA: Stanford University Press.

Hidayatullah, A. (2014), *Feminist Edges of the Qur'an*, New York: Oxford University Press.
Ibn 'Abd Rabbih (2007), *The Unique Necklace: Al-'Iqd al-Farīd*, trans. Issa J. Boullata, Reading: Garnet, vol. 1.
Ibrić, Almir (2010), *Bilder und Tätowierungen in Islam. Eine Einführung in die Ethik und Ästhetik des Polytheismusverbots*, Vienna: LIT Verlag.
Kamali, Mohammed (2002), *The Dignity of Man: An Islamic Perspective*, Cambridge: Islamic Texts Society.
Kane, Cheikh Hamidou (2012), *Ambiguous Adventure*, trans. Katherine Woods, New York: Melville House.
Kassis, Hanna (1990), "Roots of conflict: Aspects of Christian-Muslim confrontation in eleventh century Spain," in *Conversion and Continuity: Indigenous Christian Communities in Islamic Lands, Eighth to Eighteenth Centuries*, Michael Gervers and Ramzi Bikhazi (eds.), Toronto: Pontifical Institute of Medieval Studies: 151–60; 153, 157.
Katz, Marion (2013), *Prayer in Islamic Thought and Practice*, Cambridge: Cambridge University Press.
Kaya, Ali (November 2012), "Euthanasia in Islamic law with respect to the theory of protecting integrity of body and soul," *International Journal of Humanities and Social Science* 2/21: 292–97.
"The Kingdom in the Closet." Available at: https://www.theatlantic.com/magazine/archive/2007/05/the-kingdom-in-the-closet/30577
Kugle, Scott Siraj al-Haqq (2010), *Homosexuality in Islam: Critical Reflections on Gay, Lesbian, and Transgender Muslims*, Oxford: Oneworld.
Larsson, Göran (2011), "Islam and tattooing: An old question, a new research topic." Available at: http://ojs.abo.fi/index.php/scripta/article/view/317
Lazreg, Marnia (2009), *Questioning the Veil: Open Letters to Muslim Women*, Princeton, NJ: Princeton University Press.
Leaman, Oliver (1996), "Secular friendship and religious devotion," in *Friendship East and West: Philosophical Perspectives*, O. Leaman (ed.), Richmond, VA: Curzon: 251–62.
Leaman, Oliver (2013), *Controversies in Contemporary Islam*, London: Routledge: 71–87.
Mahomed, Nadeem, and Esack, Farid (March 2017), "The normal and abnormal: On the politics of being Muslim and relating to same-sex sexuality," *Journal of the American Academy of Religion* 85/1: 224–43.
Mernissi, Fatima (2001), *Scheherezade Goes West: Different Cultures, Different Harems*, New York: Washington Square Press.
Murata, Kazuyo (2017), *Beauty in Sufism: The Teachings of Ruzbihan Baqli*, Albany: State University of New York Press.
Murray, Stephen, Roscoe, Will (1997), *Islamic Homosexualities: Culture, History, and Literature*, New York: New York University Press.
MuslimConverts.Com. Available at: http://www.muslimconverts.com/cosmetics/tattoo.htm
Mussap, Alexander (2009), "Strength of faith and body image in Muslim and non-Muslim women," *Mental Health, Religion & Culture* 12: 121–27.
Mutahhari, Murtada (2010), *Al-Islam wa mutatalibat al-'asr* [Islam and the Demands of the Age], Beirut: Dar al-Amir li'l -Thaqafa wa'l-'Ulum.

Nasr, S. Hossein (2007), *The Garden of Truth: The Vision and Promise of Sufism, Islam's Mystical Tradition*, New York: Harper.
Ni putes ni soumises. Available at: http://www.npns.fr/
Özyürek, Esra (2015), *Becoming Muslim: Race, Religion, and Conversion in the New Europe*, Princeton, NJ: Princeton University Press.
Peumans, Wim (2017), *Queer Muslims in Europe: Sexuality, Religion and Migration in Belgium*, London: I. B. Tauris.
al-Qaradawi, Yusuf Abdallah (2004), *Al-Halal wa'l-haram fi al-Islam* [The Permitted and the Forbidden] (15th ed.), Beirut: al-Maktab al-Islami.
Roderick (1999), *Historia Arabum*, ed. Juan Valverde, Turnhout: Brepols: 87.
El-Rouayheb, Khaled (2005), *Before Homosexuality in the Arab-Islamic World, 1500–1800*, Chicago, IL: University of Chicago Press.
Rowson, Everett (1997), "The effeminates of early Medina," in *Que(e)rying Religion: A Critical Anthology*, Gary David Comstock and Susan E. Henking (eds.), New York: Continuum: 61–88.
Schmidtke, Sabine (1999), "Homoeroticism and homosexuality in Islam: A review article," *Bulletin of the School of Oriental and African Studies* 62/2: 260–66.
Schmitt, Arno (1995), *Bio-bibliography of Male-Male Sexuality and Eroticism in Muslim Societies*, Berlin: Verlag Rosa Winkel.
Schmitt, Arno, and Sofer, Jehoeda (eds.) (1992), *Sexuality and Eroticism among Males in Moslem Societies*, Binghamton, NY: Harrington Park.
Shafi'i (2008), *al-Umm*, ed. R. Fawzi 'Abd al-Muttalib, Mansura: Dar al-Wafa', 6: 373–77.
al-Shahid al-Thani (2016), *Desire of the Aspirant: On the Etiquette of the Teacher and the Student*, trans. A. Khaleeli, London: ICAS Press.
Shaikh, Sa'adiyya (2012), *Sufi Narratives of Intimacy: Ibn 'Arabi, Gender, and Sexuality*, Chapel Hill: University of North Carolina Press.
al-Shatibi, Abu Ishaq (2003), *Al-Muwafaqat fi usul al-shari'a./* [The Reconciliation of the Principles of Islamic Law], Cairo: Al-Maktaba Al-Tawfiqiyya.
Smith, Jane, and Haddad, Yvonne (2003), *The Islamic Understanding of Death and Resurrection*, Oxford: Oxford University Press.
Society for the Protection of the Unborn Child. Available at: http://www.deathrefe rence.com/Ho-Ka/Islam.html#ixzz3X94VXge8https://www.spuc.org.uk/about/ muslim-division/euthanasia
De Sondy, Amanullah (2013), *Crises of Islamic Masculinity*, London: Bloomsbury Academic.
Tarlo, Emma (2010), *Visibly Muslim: Fashion, Politics, Faith*, Oxford: Berg.
Vaid, Mobeen (2007), "Can Islam accommodate homosexual acts? Qur'anic revisionism and the case of Scott Kugle," *American Journal of Islamic Social Sciences* 34/3: 45–97.
William of Auvergne (2009), *De legibus (Opera omnia* 1:18–102), *De virtutibus (opera omnia* 1: 102–91). Translated in *On the Virtues* by Roland Teske, Milwaukee: 113–14.
Wolfson, Harry (1976), *Philosophy of the Kalam*, Cambridge, MA: Harvard University Press.
Woofenden, Heidi (2012), "A call to prayer: A cross-cultural examination of religious faith, modesty, and body image," *Bridgewater State University, Undergraduate Review* 8: 81–87.
Wright, J. W., and Rowson, Everett K. (eds.) (1997), *Homoeroticism in Classical Arabic Literature*, Wright, NY: Columbia University Press.

6

Nature

He only prohibited for you carrion, blood, the flesh of the pig and what was dedicated to other than God, but if one is forced out of necessity rather than desire or greed, then he incurs no sin. God is the forgiver, the merciful. (2:173)

God establishes dietary laws, a bit more restrictive than that applicable to the Christians, and a lot more lenient than the rules for the Jews. The rules for the latter are sometimes described as part of punishment for their poor behavior in the past. If people cannot obey them because they are put in a very difficult position they are allowed to put them aside, and this suggests that there is nothing important in them apart from the fact that God has given us an order. The presence of *darura* or necessity can obviate many rules, but here the possibility of being excused is actually mentioned when the rule is specified. It has to be said that the regulations are actually not that difficult to follow, and like many dietary laws in religion in general, no reason is given for them. There are many references to the natural world in the Qur'an, yet little direct advice or instruction on how to deal with it. This, of course, provides a good deal of rhetorical space for those who have views on these issues to embroider an Islamic line on such issues as how we should treat the environment, what we should eat, and so on. It is a good idea to try to resist this temptation.

The modern halal phenomenon

There is evidence that interest in halal food has increased a great deal in recent years. The size of the industry continues to expand quickly and the certification appears in many shops where previously there would have been nothing. This is often put down to the increasing size of the Muslim community in many countries that in the past had small communities, and, of course, the rapid increase in the Muslim population overall, and no doubt that is a relevant point. The interesting question though is whether the local Muslim population really wants halal food and what it regards as halal. In majority Muslim countries everything is halal and so there is generally no issue about wondering how the animals have been killed or how the food has been prepared. What are the attitudes of Muslims toward halal in the United States and Europe, and what if anything does it have to tell us about the nature of the communities in which they live? This study looks mainly at Muslims in countries where they are not the majority and how significant attitudes to halal might be as part of a general moral position that is taken to be specifically Islamic.

This project involved many interviews with people in various countries where Muslims are minorities and I assured everyone that they would be anonymous, so the detail I give is severely restricted to avoid it being possible to identify anyone. Some people were happy to be identified, but I thought this would be problematic, since it might make what they said be treated differently than others. The people I selected to interview were those involved in halal slaughter, raising animals for such an outcome and those who have various attitudes to halal food and also a variety of ideas of what it means to be halal. I also interviewed some non-Muslims about their opinions of halal. There was no attempt at choosing a representative sample of interviewees and the interviews themselves were loosely structured, so the results suffer from those limitations, but it was never my attempt at carrying out a scientific inquiry. I did manage to talk to people from a wide variety of cultural backgrounds, though, and of course in different countries, so I hope there is some value in the results. Only a very small number of the people I interviewed are mentioned here, and perhaps had I selected other interviewees it would not have been so easy to come out with the conclusions I arrive at here. I should alert readers to this fact and they should, of course, bear it in mind when they assess what they read. It is not customary to include empirical inquiry in work on philosophical ethics, but I think this is a shame. How people from a variety of backgrounds think about what they eat and where it comes from does raise a range of ethical issues and we get some notion of how abstract ideas actually impinge on behavior. There are two instructive aspects to this for philosophers and theologians. Many people have little interest in avoiding contradiction, and the niceties of religious rules are infinitely variable as far as those who identify themselves as members of a religious group are concerned. By contrast, there are plenty of Muslims who only accept a rigid view of their religion and what it demands of them in terms of food. Yet, the rules we see in the Qur'an might not be exhaustive, just minimum guides to what we should and should not consider eating, and perhaps Muslims are supposed to consider also what their wider implications are and act on them.

Is there anything special about Islam?

Many Muslims are eager to practice their faith and part of that practice is to only eat and drink products that are acceptable from an Islamic point of view. There may have been an increase in religiosity in recent years, and this would certainly have gone hand in hand with an increase in enthusiasm for eating and drinking, like everything else, to be in accordance with Islam. It is often said that Islam is unusual as a religion in that it is not just a matter of faith but a whole way of life, and so what Muslims eat and drink is regulated by their faith as are all sorts of other things. This is far from accurate. There are plenty of religions that seek to regulate the whole of the life of their adherents, and even those which do not make some demands on their general activities. In fact, Islam makes fewer demands than many other faiths, and often sees itself as being a moderate religion, occupying a middle position between the materialism of Judaism and the asceticism of Christianity. There are references in the Qur'an to God not wanting religion to be difficult, and the rules of eating and drinking along with many of the other rules of Islam are not extreme. This was a point made in 2015 in parts of Europe where the timing of Ramadan in June and July at the height of summer made the fast very long, since the period of darkness, when eating may take place, is relatively short. Some Muslims, although certainly not most, argued that in situations where this produces hardship people should follow the hours of fasting observed in the Middle East and not in Europe. After all, we are told: "O Believers! Fasting is prescribed for you as it was prescribed for those before you, that you may become conscious of God" (2:183). It has a purpose, and presumably its role in making us think about God can be used to vary how we carry out the ritual. If it becomes very burdensome it can be either postponed or even suspended for those with problems that mean they could not appropriately participate in it. As some defenders of fasting in Islam often say, it could have been more arduous, it could have extended throughout the year, for example. Salat (prayer) is similarly restricted to five a day, it could easily have been more and there are some accounts that suggest that originally it was going to be more.

The increase in interest in non-Muslim majority countries in halal may be a result of the way in which Islam is constantly in the news, largely for negative reasons, and this may have encouraged Muslims to identify more closely with the rules of their religion. That is what some of the respondents of the study I carried out said, that for the first time they felt as Muslims that people were looking at them and if they were going to be singled out as Muslims they might as well be good Muslims. For some it is the fact that they are often regarded as Muslims first and everything else more obliquely that they tried to evade by behaving just like everyone else, and not paying any attention to the halal nature of food and drink. Like most immigrant communities, there is a tremendous push to assimilate into the host community if they are allowed to assimilate. One young Muslim in Chicago said to me that he felt he had to join his colleagues for drinks after work because that was part of the office culture, and it was not acceptable to stick to soft drinks. Some Muslims married to Christians go to church with their wives and eat there also, not caring about what they are eating since it is in that context the normal thing to do. Many young Muslims participate in the ordinary activities of young people in the West and the only thing that differentiates them from everyone else is perhaps their name and ethnicity. It is not difficult in modern Western society for a religious minority to blend in with the majority in this way, and issues of halal fall readily by the wayside as a consequence. No doubt, the different immigrant communities relate to halal in different ways, with some preserving higher levels of observance than others. Income and career levels may be a factor also, and from my interviewees it seems that the higher the level of professional success, the less interest there is in halal, although there still may be an interest. As is often said, we should not speak of the Islamic community, there are many different communities, and within those communities there are significant subgroups where behavior is very much related to the characteristics of the group itself. Here as so often the principles of religion and social inquiry go in different directions. According to many Muslims, there is one Islamic community, and there are rules that that community ought to keep. They are divine rules and so do not change, they represent how God wants us to live. On the other hand, when we observe what actually happens we see that there are many different communities, and a whole variety of ways of interpreting the rules. It is worth highlighting this tension since it arises again and again in this discussion.

Different kinds of Muslims

Although, of course, there are ways of defining who is a Muslim, it is worth noting that many people fall into the category of being what respondents in the United States called being "kinda Muslim." These are often people whose parents are Muslims but who follow no religion themselves; they do not pray or necessarily even adhere to any religious beliefs. Not surprisingly, their commitment to eating halal food is weak, but, on the other hand, some of them told me that eating halal food was the only thing they did that was Muslim. It has to be said also that the very visible nature of Islam in present culture means that even this group felt the need to find out more about the religion that others were constantly associating them with, while all they wanted to do was ignore it. Some responded by saying that if everyone saw them as a Muslim then they ought to be one, at least in behavior. It is worth pointing out, though, that as with many religions in the West the levels of religious commitment vary widely, and this is true, of course, and there is a significant community of "kinda" Muslims who might be better called cultural Muslims rather than anything else. Their relationship to "their" religion is complicated, as is their relationship with halal.

I used this questionnaire to get some idea of commitment to Islam, and it is adapted from an investigation by the Barna organization into degrees of Christian religiosity in the United States. Barna had fifteen factors, I only have ten, but I think it is clear what those classified as post-Muslim or highly post-Muslim do not accept about Islam.

Post-Muslim = meet at least 60 percent of the following 10 factors (6 or more factors)

Highly post-Muslim = meet at least 80 percent of the following 10 factors (8 or more factors)

1   do not believe in God
2   identify as atheist or agnostic
3   disagree that faith is important in their lives
4   have not prayed to God (in the last year)
5   disagree that the Qur'an is accurate
6   have not donated money to an Islamic charity (in the last year)
7   have not attended a mosque (in the last year)
8   agree that the Prophet Muhammad was not perfect
9   do not feel a responsibility to encourage others to embrace Islam
10 have not read the Qur'an (in the last year)

[cities.barna.org/the-most-post-christian-cities-in-america/]

Some highly post-Muslim respondents said that eating halal was important to them, for cultural rather than religious reasons, and it would be interesting to know how large a part of the halal market such people represent. On the other hand, their attitude to halal was often very soft, in the sense that if it was not available they were not that bothered, and they sometimes suggested that they had an interest in trying food that was actually forbidden, such as pork. One of the interesting things that came out was how inconsistent people in the post-Muslim groups were in what they sometimes said about halal. Some people said halal was important to them but admitted to eating anything without worrying about halal. When I asked what they thought halal was they could not really say, although they tended to know it did not include pork products. When asked if they would eat pork many said no, but when asked if they would check that food did not have pork in it, almost no one in this group said yes. So it seems that the preference for halal meant for some that if halal was available they would not avoid it, which is not much of a preference. It has to be said though that views on halal are often confused, in that some respondents would say they had positive views of halal and yet would eat absolutely anything, and often do. We should not be surprised at the fact that people often not only contradict themselves but also seem to have no concerns about doing it.

The halal controversies

One of the factors that make even cultural Muslims identify with halal has been the media controversy over halal slaughter in Europe. There are three aspects to this. One is the major controversy over whether halal slaughter is cruel by comparison with modern industrial practices. The second is whether halal meat is being introduced into general meal preparation without customers knowing about it. Finally, is the ubiquity of halal food an example of the creeping Islamicization of Western society?

How have Muslims responded to the cruelty issue? First of all, they have reiterated the parts of the Qur'an and the hadith of the Prophet which serve to distance Islam from cruelty to animals. There are certainly several such passages. Verses 6:38 and 45:4 say that animals are signs of divine power and design and live in their own communities, and 44:38-39 points out that everything was created not haphazardly but because of justice. The different legal schools tend to take slightly different lines on how animals may be treated, and Sarra Tlili suggests that animals do best under a Shafi'i regime. There are many references in the Qur'an to animals and they are, on the whole, respectful in style, so there are no grounds in the religious literature for many of the ways in which animals are mistreated in any society. The fondness in some communities for hunting for fun is particularly difficult to justify on religious grounds in Islam.

The main issue of potential cruelty in animal slaughter is the use of stunning. In modern slaughterhouses animals are often stunned first, the aim being to make the animal insensible before it is actually killed. This is problematic for both kosher and halal slaughter, which insists that only a living animal can be legally slaughtered and the stunning process leaves the animal in a questionable status. In any case, in both systems of law it is important that as much blood as possible is removed from the dead animal, and it may be that if it is killed without being first stunned then the flow of blood is increased. Both religions insist that their slaughter methods are humane and better than the modern techniques, but this has not prevented some countries such as Denmark from banning both kosher and halal slaughter. Most research suggests that stunning is more humane than any other method of killing, but that, of course, does not establish it is true. On the other hand, it does seem likely to be true, and legislation in Western countries tends to insist on stunning except when there is a religious exception, which, of course, exists in the case of Islam and Judaism.

The issue of cruelty is an interesting one and it is not going to be addressed here as a matter of how to determine what is more or less cruel as far as slaughter is concerned. What is relevant is the use made of the topic by the media and the effect it has had on the Muslim community in Western countries. Many newspapers have highlighted what they say is the cruel nature of halal slaughter, and pictures are shown of animals struggling with blood pouring out of them, the aim being to portray the method as barbaric, with implications for the nature of the community for which the meat is being prepared. Defenders of the traditional practice have often replied in kind, using pictures of slaughterhouses that stun where the process has obviously not worked and the animals look to be in considerable distress. Not surprisingly, some who work in such places may have a casual attitude to animal welfare and this is obvious from their actions when they think they are not being observed and filmed. This is itself a traditional form of response by Muslims to attacks on what they do, it might be called the tu quoque defense. It takes this form: you say that what we do is barbaric, but what you do is just as or even more barbaric. There is usually a rider which goes: in any case, what we do is not barbaric. Such a strategy is often employed nowadays to attacks on Islam because of terrorism or the treatment of women. The response is often that what goes on in the non-Islamic world in this regard is no better or even worse than what Muslims are said to do, and then what Muslims do is not as bad as is commonly thought. Another form of response is to deny that Muslims would ever act in such a way and that the crimes were committed by others to throw a poor light on Islam, or perhaps that Muslims are implicated unfairly due to Islamophobic motives.

Eating animals and Islam

The Qur'an makes clear that eating some animals is permissible (5:1) and adds that forbidding what God has made permissible is wrong (5:87). The hadith speak a lot about how animals are to be treated, and the general approach is that while they may be used, they should not be mistreated or made to suffer unnecessarily. As one might imagine, in the early years of Islam animals played a large part in economic life and issues of how to treat them were important. They are still important, and now in rather different ways, since animals are now used in experiments for medical research and one might wonder how Islam regards such a process. It is perhaps surprising that this is a very little discussed topic, especially as so many Muslims work in the life and medical sciences.

The tu quoque argument is in many ways beside the point since most halal meat comes from animals that are stunned before they are killed. Yet, this is not a universal practice and some are not, often not those animals that are killed by small operations or just by a family member for their personal use. There is certainly scope to challenge the good faith of those criticizing non-stunned slaughter, since slaughterhouses seem to be very unpleasant places however the animals are eventually dispatched, as is even the process of transporting live beasts to such places. On the other hand, for carnivores this might be regarded as unavoidable, whereas not stunning the animal about to be killed is not. From a Muslim point of view, since God prescribed a particular slaughter method, He must know that it is preferable to kill animals in this way and so we can rest assured that this is how they ought to be dispatched. That is not an argument that works for non-Muslims, though, and it does seem reasonable to suggest that it would be less painful to be rendered insensible first and then killed as compared with just being killed, however sharp the knife and skilled the killer. What we can take from the controversy, though, that is important is the fact that many Muslims with whom I spoke felt that the whole issue had been raised in order to attack the community and make it look out of touch with modern Western values. This victimology was common right across the range of Muslims, from those who were very religious to those who were not, although the more observant seemed to embrace the victim status more enthusiastically. Among them the idea that this could be an issue worth discussing tended to be rejected as ridiculous. After all, God has spoken on the issue and they followed a legal school that recommended a particular kind of slaughter, and that is the end of the topic as far as they were concerned. Since obviously there is nothing wrong with halal slaughter, even without stunning, in their view, anyone who thought there was is not only wrong, but must have motives for slandering the community in this way. The idea that there could be a debate on the issue was generally rejected, since Islam had specified a particular course of action and nothing could or should interfere with that.

The greater halal and the lesser halal

Some Muslims, in particular those younger and better educated, were prepared to accept that this is a topic that could be debated. They were less sure of the evil intentions of those criticizing halal, although still predominantly suspicious of those attacks and what lay behind them. A movement has now been created in the Islamic world which is itself critical of many of the things that are done to animals, although it is still a very small movement as of now. One Muslim farmer in Illinois said to me,

> It is like the issue of jihad, where a distinction is made between the lesser and the greater jihad. The lesser is physical struggle while the greater is spiritual improvement. The way I see it there is a lesser and greater halal. The lesser is just following the rules, however they have come down to us. The greater is seeking a closer relationship with our environment and seeking to treat animals well even up to the time we kill them. We then kill them compassionately, in the traditional manner but not in large batches, so they do not see each other being killed, they do not smell the blood of those who preceded them.

Some argue that the greater halal is actually avoiding killing animals at all to eat, although this is a tiny minority among those I interviewed. One of the reasons the halal market is so large is because Muslims, on the whole, are enthusiastic carnivores, if they can afford to be, and vegetarians who travel to Islamic-majority countries are often met with incomprehension. On the other hand, it looks as though there has been a growth in the vegetarian and vegan movements in the West, and it would reasonable to expect that some Muslims would get caught up in those movements. This does seem to have happened, but I met very few people who described themselves as both Muslim and vegetarian, and very few vegans. In the past some Sufi groups have promoted vegetarianism among themselves, but this is not of much relevance since this was probably seen as part of an ascetic lifestyle, and there is no reason to think it should be advocated in general. Yet if it is true that there are health reasons to eat less or no meat, then it would not be difficult to find legal justification for such behavior. For many Muslims the problem in giving up meat is more cultural than religious, but as so often the practice of rejecting meat would be justified in religious rather than in cultural terms. In that way it would acquire a greater gravitas.

One interviewee in Germany of Turkish origin who was vegetarian reported that the imam of his mosque in Bavaria was energetically opposed to his stance when he said that he found difficulties in reconciling the idea of killing innocent animals with worshipping the God who created those animals. This was an interesting case where the halal controversy in Germany alerted people to the ways in which all animals were killed, halal or otherwise. He was appalled by their treatment and decided to avoid meat, and his imam responded that that meant he could not celebrate Bayram or carry out his hajj duties properly. In the end he solved the difficulty by telling the imam that he was a vegetarian for health reasons, an explanation that was immediately accepted since it did not threaten the lifestyle that the community as a whole enjoyed, although the excuse was still treated with suspicion. Until this happened the imam suggested that not eating meat for a Muslim was *bid'a* or innovation, although not *kufr* or disbelief. This point is also made, albeit in a less legalistic manner, by Dien, who points to the centrality of meat in Islamic life. He is right, there are many references to it in the Qur'an and the hadith especially, and the references are uniformly approving of the practice. On the other hand, my interviewee argued quite plausibly that there are also many references to the importance of avoiding cruelty, and often in religion one is confronted with a variety of apparently contrary positions that have to be reconciled in some way. This vegetarian Muslim was however suspicious of the campaign against halal in Germany, yet it was that campaign that got him to change his eating habits. He was also annoyed by the tendency of some local politicians to emphasize the connection between being German and eating pork, a strategy that goes on in other European countries also. As he said, it is never difficult to eat a normal German meal without the pork. Problems of food labeling meant that there have been instances of food containing pork without being so labeled, and he argued that he was able to eat in a more halal way by avoiding halal meat!

Food and fitting in

Food is often used by politicians as a way of appealing to the electorate by showing what regular guys they are and how ordinary their eating habits are. In Europe this works some of the time with the older parts of the electorate who are perplexed at the way in which society is changing and the new people who are around eating and doing different things. Food excludes as well as includes, but modern Europe is now thoroughly "multi-kulti" to use the German expression, it contains large numbers of different communities who are predominantly young and who have, on the whole, integrated very successfully with the host community. Some of them have allegiances elsewhere also, and it usually is also and so not exclusive, and that is common now in Europe, with people travelling from one country to work in another, they may marry someone from a third country and retire to a fourth. Hundreds of thousands of migrants have moved to Europe and the United States and whatever happens there is no doubt but that most of them will stay. Many of them are Muslims, and the towns they eventually live in will no doubt soon produce restaurants and shops selling the food they like to eat, or which their religion says they can eat. The days when the population of European countries were homogenous and more or less ate the same sorts of things are not only in the past but in quite the distant past now, if it was ever true. The debate in Germany and Austria about whether one could be German or Austrian and not eat pork appeals to a certain category of voters but is unlikely to do much to change the general political climate. Modern society contains a diversity of communities and so a diversity of types of food, and refusing to accept this is to look nostalgically toward a past when everything was more simple and straightforward, a past that will never return. Insisting that pork be on the school menu, as has occurred in parts of France ruled by the National Front, for example, is trying to pretend that just one type of food is suitable for everyone, and that was never true, and certainly is not now. Laicism does not mean that everyone has to eat the same food, but that the state should not impose food on anyone for religious reasons, exactly the opposite of what some French educational regions are trying to do. I asked a Muslim girl of sixteen in France if this would be a problem for her and she just shrugged and said that then she would bring in her own food. She interpreted this move as the authorities saying to her that they do not want Muslims in the schools, but she invited me to look around, and there were plenty there already—they are not going anywhere, so the policy is futile. Why not just accept that some people want to eat different things?

Surreptitious halal and Islamicization

The third charge that is made is that the practice of meat being halal without everyone being told about it is a feature of the Islamicization of Western society, often classified as a "creeping" process to bring out its sinister nature. Since many Muslims want to eat halal meat, and since there are many Muslims, meat providers have often just bought halal meat and sold it as meat without telling anyone except those who ask. More problematically perhaps, food providers have sometimes omitted pork products since it is simpler not to have to worry about who might be eating it, keeping it away from allowable kinds of meat. Again, the pig has become a symbol of normality and hostility to it the reverse. An interesting aspect of this is the spoof campaign against Peppa Pig by Muslims, which in turn led to a real campaign to support Peppa Pig from those who are trying apparently, although not in reality, to have it banned. The idea that Muslims would be discouraged from watching Peppa Pig on TV or playing with the toys is not that implausible and there is some evidence that parents do occasionally try to prevent their children from having anything to do with pigs in any form. Those seeking to emphasize the strangeness of Muslims naturally land on facts like this and make something enormous out of them. Pigs are an important part of many cultures, and to have a community living with those cultures and not valuing pigs is shocking to some, in just the same way that many people, although less nowadays, expect families to share certain basic features, or people to wear similar clothes. The critique of multiculturalism is implicit in these complaints, and indeed a theme of this discussion is surely that food is very much an aspect of identity. The idea that halal food may be ubiquitous is profoundly worrying to such critics since it suggests that Islam is becoming part of the mainstream and is not only a fringe minority group. On the other hand, the idea that people should know what they are eating is not unreasonable, except that the difference between halal and other meat cannot be in the taste or the dietary value of the product. It cannot be a matter of whether the meat is stunned or not, since most halal meat is stunned. But not all of it is, so the worry might be that some of the meat comes from animals killed in a different way. This is surely unlikely to be the case, though, since the relatively small number of animals killed without being stunned for Muslims to eat appeals to a limited audience in the Muslim community, or are the products of small farms which sends meat probably to specialist halal butchers, or is consumed at home.

Halal food provided in schools in Michigan have led to a controversy, and I interviewed some of the individuals involved. Parts of Michigan, like Dearborn, now have a large Muslim population, and have had for some time, and the local schools are in some cases providing halal food to cater to this population. Given the radical attempt to separate religion from the state in the United States, this could be regarded as problematic, especially as it is more expensive, although the school authorities in Dearborn are cagey on this issue. Some of the opposition to this accommodation to the religious needs of Muslims comes from people who obviously do not approve of the growing Muslim population of the area. I spoke at length to an older white Catholic woman who clearly objected to this new population "taking over" and expecting special provision to be made for them. But she had a lot of problem with that group in any case, so any provision for them would be objectionable in her eyes, even having them there in the first place. "This was a great neighborhood before they came, and now you can't go to the stores without hearing languages you cannot understand and people dressed in funny clothes," she reported. She objected to halal food not because of slaughter methods but due to its novelty. "I wouldn't want to eat it," she told me firmly. Quite a well-organized campaign against this provision was mounted in Dearborn but has not gained much traction in the neighborhood. It is an important part of the nationwide discussion in the United States, though, and is often seen as another indication of the growing Islamicization of the country. Similar policies to include halal in New York city and state, and San Diego, are being discussed, and it does seem difficult to justify the provision of halal food exclusively; that is, ignoring other religions and their dietary requirements. In many urban centers the meals will be free since a proportion of children attending the school come from low income families, and this places another burden on the finances of the education authority. To some it appears to be an attempt at establishing a religion in the state, in violation of the constitution. To others it is just reflecting the changing demographics of particular neighborhoods and being culturally sensitive to those communities. It has to be said that the financial implications are not that significant. It is easy to accuse people of Islamophobia if they oppose state provision of halal food but in America with its sharp legal divide between the state and religion there are problems in taking account of religion in ordinary schools.

Halal certification and non-Muslims

There has been some research on the effect that halal labeling has on non-Muslim consumers. It is interesting how this diverges from non-Jewish consumers of kosher food. The latter sometimes report that in their view the standards certified by kosher means the food is better than other food, and there is at least in the United States a considerable market for the products from the general community. Kosher food is often more expensive than other food, and this suggests to some that it is then better. This is not the case with halal food, those hostile to Muslims try to avoid it and non-Muslims do not, on the whole, think it is of a higher standard than other food. The price difference is usually minor, or halal food is even cheaper than non-halal products. On the other hand, from my research in London and Berlin where many fast food outlets have halal posters on their premises, few non-Muslim consumers notice them. The words are not usually very large, they are often in Arabic and so largely invisible to many Europeans, and there is often a plethora of notices of one kind or another, and if it has no relevance to a consumer they are unlikely to stop and think about it. In any case in large urban centers consumers are used to multicultural shops and do not notice what is not relevant to them. Some consumers did tell me that they would avoid anywhere that has halal certification since they are not sympathetic to what they take to be the Islamic form of slaughter. Often these were people coming out of halal shops with food in their hands. It is difficult to take seriously the idea that animal welfare is a leading issue here, given the conditions that exist in ordinary slaughterhouses.

Halal certification and the Muslim consumer

Among Muslim consumers the situation is also not entirely clear since the nature of the certification is often relevant. In just the same way that mosques are often differentiated according to the nationality of their clientele, different groups of Muslims are often suspicious of varieties of halal certification unfamiliar to them or that comes from somewhere where they have no connection. There are a variety of authorities and they often have slightly different ways of judging things, and their capacities for inspection also vary widely. In addition, many shops just put up a general halal sign which means little, and if asked what it means they say it means they buy their meat from halal suppliers. Who certifies those supplies is not necessarily known nor is whether everything in the shop comes from those suppliers, since the scope for inspection is weak or nonexistent. One has to rely largely on the conscientiousness of the shopkeeper. Have the halal products been in contact with non-halal meat? What about the shopkeepers? When the meat was delivered what steps were taken to preserve its identity and avoid such contact? Does it matter?

Nowadays these questions have been extended to a degree to include details of how the animals were raised, what they were fed on and how we should regard our relationship with them? Are they there merely to be used or are they partners with us in the created world and creatures for whom we should care even if on occasion we need to make use of them? These wider issues arise increasingly today when considering halal and, to a degree, come under the heading the greater halal, where Muslims do not just stick to the letter of the law but use the law to interrogate their practices and consider refining them in a number of significant ways. One such topic is naturally whether we should really be eating animals at all, given the sorts of things that God says about them in the Qur'an. As a Muslim told me in Montreal, "If we are told that animals live in communities, that they pray each day and are signs of God, I do not see how we can kill and eat them. They seem to be rather like us." He did eat meat but was starting to feel guilty about it, as a result of finding it difficult to reconcile with Islam. His coreligionists were critical of his position, pointing to all those verses in the Qur'an and the hadith that appear to validate meat eating, and his reply was to suggest that these were helpful in telling us what to do if we felt we had to eat meat, a bit like the laws of divorce. Few institutions in Islam are respected more than marriage but the religion accepts that there are circumstances where marriage breaks down and then divorce is necessary, and this is how it should be done. The fact that there are rules for divorce does not establish that divorce is a good thing, on the contrary. By analogy, the fact that there are rules for how to kill animals does not show that killing them is something we ought to do, just that if we have to do it then this is how you should do it. A Muslim from Birmingham told me that the trouble with halal rules is that they persuade some Muslims that once they have ensured that their food is labeled appropriate they have come to the end of the thinking they need to do about what they eat. She suggested that halal is the starting and not the finishing point and, of course, only has meaning if it is part of a lifestyle which itself is halal and not something else. This woman denied she was especially religious and seemed quite hostile to many who are. She was a trade union official and argued that part of halal was how the workforce was treated, what they were paid, and so on. This is part of the trend to compare and contrast the lesser with the greater halal that has arisen several times during the interviews, an approach which has led some Muslims to forego meat entirely or entirely change the way in which they see meat as acceptable. A question that is impossible to resolve here is whether this is a reflection on wider trends in Western society, among which concern over food is now a major issue, or a natural consequence of how the concept of halal would naturally evolve within certain Muslim communities.

The way forward?

It does seem that this wider notion of halal is largely restricted to younger, more upwardly mobile and assimilated Muslims, those who identify themselves firmly as members of the country in which they have grown up and whose language they speak well. The narrower notion is prevalent among first-generation Muslims whose primary identity may still be to their original country and its community. A conversation on this topic within the family of a Turkish origin group in Saarbrücken illustrated this perfectly. The parents who had come from eastern Turkey and were Kurdish were completely amazed at the idea that animals had any rights to anything except to be eaten after having been killed in the right way. Their three children differed on the topic though, one son and one daughter arguing that only organic meat should be consumed and every step taken to prevent suffering in the animals, including not buying meat associated with factory farming. All were in favor of halal, but for the younger family members the idea of not consuming so much meat was acceptable, even not consuming meat at all (the daughter). It is difficult to believe that these ideas came from their meditations on the nature of Islam since in my conversations with them there seemed to be very little meditation, and actually they both told me that they were not that bothered by eating halal at all in any case. It is always difficult to know how to assess what one is told, since during the conversation they both said that halal was very important to them but then they said it was not, and if they were out with their friends it was not something they checked up on specifically. On the other hand, if they were going to eat meat and saw the halal label on the shop, they were pleased.

It would be a mistake to think that, on the whole, older Muslims have different attitudes to halal than younger members of the community. I met many young Muslims who are far more committed to sticking to halal food than their parents, for example, and many parents poked fun at their children's enthusiasm for their religion, including halal. A New York accountant who came originally from Pakistan had children who far outdid him for piety and his comment was that when he came to America no one bothered about halal, by which I assume he meant no one in his group, and of course no one bothered about it in Pakistan since there everything was halal anyway. He was a very secular man and admitted that one of the reasons to come to America was getting away from "all that religious stuff." He disapproved of the ubiquity of the halal label. His children, though, said it was important for them to know that their food was halal, and it was a certification that they actively looked for, although they betrayed a certain naïveté about how reliable it was. We went to a hamburger barrow near the Metropolitan Museum in New York City that announced it was halal, but when I asked the Egyptian purveyor who certified it or where the meat came from he seemed to have no idea. The children said that at least it was better to go to a place that said it was halal than one that did not; you would expect a certain level of honesty from the outlet, and I hope they are right. I asked what they would feel if they found out that some meat that they thought was halal was not, and they were not troubled by this prospect, although, of course they would prefer it to be halal, they said. They did not think it made much legal difference, since so long as they had taken reasonable measures to ensure food is halal, they have done everything that legally can be expected of them. Their motivation was appropriate and if something went wrong then it would not have been their fault. Of course, they would prefer it if nothing went wrong. This preference turned out to be very mild though and it characterizes many Muslim attitudes to halal food.

The more committed to Islam people said they were, the more relevant halal food was to them, which is hardly surprising. On the other hand, a lot of Muslims who are only weakly connected to their religion expressed an interest in it, and it is important to be more sophisticated in measuring levels of commitment than by just relying on behavioral criteria such as those in the adapted series of questions I used here. From the point of view of the *madhhab* (school of law) there are criteria for being a Muslim that many people who regard themselves as Muslims, and perhaps more importantly, who are regarded by others as Muslims, do not in fact accept. From a sociological point of view these people should be treated as Muslims and their views on halal are significant, since it may be that in some countries there are more of them than there are Muslims with the "correct" kinds of beliefs and practices. As suggested earlier, for some of these "kinda, sorta" Muslims halal was important since it was their only contact with the religion. For others it was important since they still wanted to preserve some connection with the ethnic or cultural group from which they had originated. For some, though, the practices of halal slaughter, like all animal slaughter, were regarded as barbaric and indeed a good reason to distance oneself from Islam. Very few people I met thought it was possible to combine being a Muslim with being vegetarian or vegan, although there are Muslim groups in existence defending such ideas. This attitude is itself a good indication of the widely accepted notion that Islam is closely connected with carnivorous behavior. The only vegetarian Muslims I came across were those who followed the Sufi version of Islam, or those who thought it was healthy, and the former used this idea of the greater and lesser halal to defend their position here and its compatibility with Islam. These are people who live in communities that have been constructed round this and associated ideas, they often have their own prayer centers and no longer participate in many of the rituals of their families. They are often highly educated and feel they have the right to put together a form of religion that they find personally satisfying, including their own eating practices. There have always been such groups in the history of Islam, but I get the impression that now they have imbibed the doctrine quite common in wider Western society that what they regard as their religion is something up to them to decide, which is perhaps rather new.

Before we dismiss these unusual approaches as just wrong or deviant we should consider broadening who we count as members of the *umma* (community). To take an example from an entirely different area, gender, there is evidence that millennials often take up diverse approaches to the idea of gender structure (Risman 2017). The idea of gender as binary is rejected by many and yet others insist on an essentialist dichotomy between male and female. Risman calls those who were raised traditionally and continued in thinking in those terms true believers. Their beliefs and practices were highly consistent and they have a firm view on who they are and how they differ in gender terms from others. Then she discusses the innovators, who were critical to a degree of gender roles as traditionally defined, and they are distinguished from the rebels who advocated a society where people do not identify with a particular gender. So far so good, but the really interesting category she identifies is that of those she calls the straddlers, and she uses this label because in some areas of thought they are innovators, in other areas they are true believers, and what they had in common was "inconsistency in their responses" (p. 223). This is so similar to many of my respondents, they were often happy to contradict themselves when describing their religious and other beliefs while, at the same time, claiming to identify with the Muslim community. Those of us who study religion and, in particular, philosophers are very interested in arguments and boundaries in faith and what distinguishes one group from another, and so are many practitioners also, of course. On the other hand, there are also plenty of people in a religion who are not very interested in these issues. The expression just used, "in a religion" is important, it suggests that you are either in or out, and yet it is possible to be half in and half out, or some different proportion may operate here. Using Risman's terminology, there are many straddlers in religion, they accept some basic religious beliefs, or think they do, and yet are very innovative about others, and the mixture that results is more of a variety of ideas than a synthesis. This fact serves to encourage skepticism about the *maqasid al-shari'a* doctrine, the idea that there are other basic principles behind the rules of Islam. A problem with trying to identify such rules is that they are either too narrow and so exclude many Muslims, or that they are too broad and so give us little useful direction. Are there rules that will cover the true believers, the innovators, and the straddlers? That is the challenge for the theory being questioned throughout this book.

Two aspects of halal are likely to feature in the future. It will become much bigger, since the worldwide Muslim population is growing rapidly. Business will cater for this market, and countries will compete with each other to dominate the certification and production business. It is likely that there be no end to the fragmentation of the Islamic world so that it is improbable that any one country will achieve hegemony in this area. Malaysians may be happy with Malaysian certification, but other nations less happy, for example. The idea of a global halal certification is great in theory and yet in reality is unlikely to emerge. The other development is that halal as a concept will become more complex. The bare legal category will be broadened and extended in a variety of directions to take account of more sophisticated views on food and drink. This inquiry has concentrated on food and drink, and of course the halal/haram dichotomy ranges over a vast range of human behavior including clothing, conversation, the media, and so on, and these will also, no doubt, be part of a changing understanding of how to be a Muslim in the future.

Our relationship with nature

There is a line that is often taken on Islam and the natural world and it goes like this. According to the Qur'an, everything in the natural world is a sign (*aya*) of God and is of an orderly and perfect world, inhabited by angels, jinn, human beings, plants, and animals. The world and its organization points to God as its creator (27:88). The Qur'an makes clear that the main purpose of human beings is to serve God, to be grateful to Him, and worship Him alone. Nature exists for us to use but we are not supposed to "corrupt the earth" (*fasad fi'l-ard*), a familiar expression by now. We are told: "We did not create the heavens, the earth, and all between them casually. We created them only for just ends: But most of them do not understand" (44:38-39 and also see 2:1641; 6:97-99; 25:45-46; 88:17-20; 30:22; 3:190-191; 29:20; 24:44; 31:20; 16:12). In an especially elegant phrase we read:

> Behold! In the creation of the heavens and the earth; in the alternation of the night and the day; in the sailing of the ships through the ocean for the profit of mankind; in the rain God sends down from the skies and the life which He gives through it to an earth that is dead; in the beasts of all kinds that He scatters throughout the earth; in the change of the winds and the clouds which they trail like their slaves between the sky and the earth; these are signs for a people that are wise. (2:164)

When God creates anything, He places within it its powers or laws of behavior, called, in the Qur'an, "guidance," "command," or "measure" and this enables it to fit into the rest of the universe: "He gave everything its creation and then guided" (17:44; also see, 57:1; 59:1; 61:1; 24:41). Everything is calculated: "Indeed, We have created everything with a measure" (7:54). The Qur'an speaks frequently of the perfect order in the universe as proof not only of God's existence but also of His unity. According to Iqbal, the Qur'an regards the whole universe as Muslim because everything in it except us has surrendered itself to God's will and so is automatically a Muslim (Iqbal 2013:14). Even the mountains are, like other created things, signs of God's omnipresence, they obey the rules He has set for them (27:88 and 70:9), along with water (21:30) and the sun (69:6). We are called on to reflect that, since everything has been created by design and balance and is interdependent with everything else, we should work out how to interact with the rest of the world. We are not the owners of the world, but entrusted by God with looking after it, and while we can enjoy it and benefit from it, this involves not going to excess and being careful with what we are given. "In fact God will not change the condition of people until they change what is in themselves" (13:12). This is one of the many injunctions in Islam for people to take charge of their affairs in a practical fashion, in so far as we can, and not wait for God to act on our behalf. He has acted on our behalf by presenting us with the world and shaping it in a particular way, the rest is up to us.

What is worth noticing here is that we get no direct advice on how we should actually behave. What is it to avoid corruption on earth and excess? Corruption on earth can be taken to mean many things; that Qur'anic quote was used in Iran as part of a campaign against litter. When we use the resources all around us we change the world, we grow things and take things away and so on, we build and change nature. Presumably, we are allowed to do this, there is no criticism of it in the Qur'an. Some religious thinkers argue that the Qur'an can be taken to argue in favor of a particular attitude to ecological principles. There is no evidence of this. For example, it is sometimes argued that the large amount of cattle and our enthusiasm for eating them and using their bodies for clothing is something we should challenge, since using plants to feed animals is wasteful. We would be better off eating the plants themselves. There is no criticism of cattle and their husbandry in the Qur'an, though, quite the reverse. They are there for our benefit, there is no suggestion that we should not take advantage of them. It might be suggested that at the time cattle were not excessive in numbers and did not produce ecological problems, but that now perhaps they do and need to be restricted in numbers or even not bred at all. Perhaps if the revelation were to be given now the message would include injunctions about following a plant-based diet in order to avoid corruption on the earth.

Our responsibility to look after the world

We are told that the world has a perfect order but does that mean it always has such an order or that it had that order when it was created? It is then perhaps up to us to preserve or maintain it. Presumably, it means the latter since the Qur'an makes it clear that we have choices and if we go awry things will deteriorate around us. God cannot be expected to make everything right again, He only changes things when we ourselves change (13:12). Often religious thinkers use these sorts of statements in their scriptures as indications that we should treat the world carefully and not abuse it, and this seems reasonable. Given the emphasis in Islam on divine forgiveness, we can think of the possibility that after we have treated the world badly and the negative consequences of that are unleashed, that God would forgive us and make everything alright again. That should be accepted as a possibility but hardly as something on which we should rely; for one thing forgiveness often arises after a period of repentance, and it is not clear that enough of us would repent in the face of imminent ecological disaster. The real problem here is not in finding theological grounds for establishing our responsibility for looking after the world, those are readily available in all the major religions. The difficulty is knowing what their practical consequences are. How do we preserve the world? To take an example, we know that species disappear and are under threat. The elephant is a good example, and it might be thought that if we want to preserve the elephant we then do not kill them, we provide them with a habitat in which they can flourish and make illegal the sale of products made from them. Some people argue this is precisely the wrong thing to do, elephants would expand in numbers to such an extent that they would threaten the livelihood and even lives of those living in their vicinity, and such an expansion in their population would harm their welfare. The best thing to do is to encourage the hunting of elephants as an activity that brings in wealthy tourists and so encourages the continued existence and welfare of an elephant population. If elephants were seen as a potential cash crop then their occasional trampling of village produce would not be taken so seriously, and measures by the local population to keep them in existence would be widely encouraged. Now, this is not the place to adjudicate between the different strategies here, but it is the place to point out that it is not obvious what the right strategy is. One should not expect to find it in the Qur'an, but we should expect the Qur'an to help us work out what principles we need to adopt and follow. Yet once we know that we still have to discover the best way of realizing those ends, and this is a matter for debate and experiment, not something whose answer is obvious.

Let us take another example, that of the desirability of the cessation or at least alleviation of poverty. The Qur'an talks about this constantly, as do the other Abrahamic scriptures. One way of helping the poor is by giving them things, and charity is constantly urged on Muslims. But there is no suggestion in any of these religious texts that there is anything wrong with private property, and it is generally accepted that there will be differences between rich and poor. It is wrong to think that an emphasis on charity means that disparities in wealth are wrong. They might be encouraged if it is felt that they lead to the poor being wealthier than they would otherwise be, something that some economists argue is the case. That is, through the free exercise of the market there is a general increase in wealth, on a rising tide all boats rise, and the worst off become much better off than they would be otherwise. Perhaps this theory is wrong, but this is not in itself a religious issue. Perhaps those at the very top of the pyramid will share their wealth with those below them, or perhaps they will not. Perhaps they will make a better job of sharing it than governments would if they take it away through tax or perhaps not. The point here is that it is not obvious from a religious point of view what we should do. It might even be argued that it is better to share a small amount of wealth than to go for larger disparities with the hope that eventually some sharing will take place, even if in the latter case the poorer are better off than in the former.

One way in which religion does help is that it gets us over the objection that we should not care about future generations since their welfare is not part of our welfare. They have no impact on us since right now they do not exist, whereas what we do, of course, has a major impact on them. If climate change is a genuine problem, and a great deal of uncertainty exists around it, then it may not affect us at all, since its effects may be delayed until after we are likely to be gone. Why should we be interested in the welfare of others who do not even exist now, and may never exist? From the point of view of religion, and not only religion, this is a silly question. We live in a world established for the use of human beings and other animals and this is just as much the case for future time as for now. Even without religion we could see this, since so many of our projects are directed to the future, a future in which we will not feature, but whose contemplation is a concern to us now, and so affects our happiness and otherwise. Religion is very good at giving us reasons for thinking time is important, the past and the future and not just our own time. The trouble with utilitarianism, and the legal principle of *maslaha*, is that it gives us a skewed understanding of time and of the narrative unity that we try to make of our lives.

We are told in the Qur'an that we should be grateful to God for what He does for us. After all, His actions are entirely gratuitous, we need Him but He does not need us. He has created us and provided us with an environment within which we can flourish. It is not clear whether we ought to be grateful for just being created, since it is not always the case that people would prefer to be alive than otherwise. It is not obvious what the contrast is anyway as it is difficult to know how to assess the difference between being alive and never having been created in the first place. Some people are terrified at the prospect of oblivion but for others it looks attractive, especially if one has a Buddhist or Vedanta motive for doubting the substantiality of what we experience in the everyday world. Yet here the issue is not whether we ought to be grateful for existing per se, but whether we ought to be grateful for existing in a world in which we can function, and surely there should be no argument about this. If we are going to exist in the first place, then it is worth existing somewhere pleasant. It might follow that we are under an obligation to keep it pleasant, or improve it, or at least not to allow it to deteriorate, but it is difficult to see why. If somebody gives me something then am I obliged to look after it carefully or share it with others? It is a gift, not a loan, after all and surely that means I can do anything I like with it, so long as it does not harm anyone else. The harm to others has nothing to do with the origins of what I have been given, it is true that we should not harm others, on the whole, whatever the origins of the means of harm. When it comes to dealing with the environment it is not obvious what harm is and what risks are acceptable or otherwise. For example, using resources like gas and oil have bad effects on the environment, they deplete natural resources that cannot be renewed, they lead to problems in the atmosphere and accidents on the road, and so on. But they also create great wealth and employment, entire industries and indeed countries depend on them, cities are built and powered, and it may be that in the future we shall discover ways of mitigating environmental damage that is produced. Perhaps God is thinking of the beneficial aspects of exploitation of the environment when He replies to the angels who suggest quite rightly that human beings will be destructive that He knows what they do not. Perhaps it will all have a happy ending.

When we say that we need God but He does not need us, that is literally true, but in a sense does He not need us if He is going to have a relationship with anything a bit similar to how He is? He is said to have friends, and messengers, and there are also, of course, the jinn and angels, but they lack the personality of human beings. We are much more interesting than the angels; they are just good, and while God may be disappointed at some of the things we do, although surely not surprised, it makes for a much more interesting relationship if one side of it at least is capable of behaving in a wide range of different ways. Some of the major characters in the Qur'an are so constantly good that they become rather uninteresting; one does not get the notion that they are really tempted at all in the sense that they might give in to temptation. Musa is a notable exception; he is all over the place when he takes his trip with Khidr, he constantly goes awry and has to be chided on the foolish comments he makes. Many of the other prophets though are outstanding moral exemplars, and one cannot conceive of their doing a wrong thing, even under grave provocation. Yusuf, for example, is totally resolute throughout all his trials and tribulations, and even when women are throwing themselves at him, he is far from being tempted to err. Although Muhammad is only a man, he is sometimes called the perfect man and is taken to encapsulate all the virtues, yet his life is quite difficult. Of humble origin, his message is initially rejected by the Meccans and he has to go into exile, only returning much later to his hometown. The early years of Islam were marked with much success, but also with a good deal of conflict, struggle, and crisis. Muhammad does not have a son who survives to take over, a considerable failure then as often now also. Although as we know Islam grew rapidly, and today is one of the major world religions, perhaps due to be the majority religion in the near future, it very early on splintered into divisions, and remains so today. Muslims sometimes do horrible things, and horrible things are done to them, and a wide variety of different forms of the religion have developed. It could all have been so different if Islam had been launched by angels and they had been put in charge of the world, different but also much less interesting. In so far as God can be said to have a relationship with His creatures, this relationship should be one He accepts is going to be with largely imperfect people.

To give an analogy, a parent may well allow her child to do something silly even though she could easily prevent him from acting in that way. She wants him to find out for himself, to take risks, and assess a variety of experiences. She wants him to have choices, and even if she know how he will eventually decide, as surely God always knows, she thinks it is important for him to work things out for himself and take it from there. We learn a good deal from mistakes, perhaps more than from getting things right, and we also act within a vast realm of uncertainty. We do not know what economic system is going to work out best for most people, we do not know what environmental choices we should make, there is much about the social and natural world that is still a mystery to us. God knows and could just tell us, but perhaps He wants us to work it out for ourselves. The thing is that in a situation where it is difficult to work out which theory is true, we need to consider and assess the alternatives, and although it might be annoying at the time, it is a valuable experience, like getting lost in a maze and trying to find our way out.

The conclusion has to be that the particular strategy we should take to look after the world and the animals in it is far from clear. The Qur'an says it is important to appreciate that nature is created by God and given a shape by him, it has a purpose and plan, yet actually discovering what that is often defeats us. Like enthusiastically selecting a particular diet, we may align ourselves with a certain theory of nature and we should then work with it to look after it better, but there are other diets and theories that might be better, and we may never find out the answer to such issues. A moderate stance here would presumably be to select the approach that seems the best grounded but by no means reject other approaches. This is a very unexciting conclusion, and yet it is hardly a novel one when dealing with moral dilemmas. We may reject what others say we ought to do, and yet can still respect their opinions and the arguments they use to get to them. The one thing we can take from this is that starting a sentence with the expression "As a Muslim . . ." and then presenting some moral account of what we should eat and how we should treat the world is unlikely to be helpful, and the other Abrahamic religions are in exactly the same boat.

Bibliography

Abu-Lughod, L. (1986), *Veiled Sentiments: Honor and Poetry in a Bedouin Society*, Berkeley: University of California Press.

Abu-Lughod, L. (1989), "Zones of theory in the anthropology of the Arab world," *Annual Review of Anthropology* 8: 267–306.

Agrama, Hussein (2012), *Questioning Secularism: Islam, Sovereignty, and the Rule of Law in Modern Egypt*, Chicago, IL: University of Chicago Press.

Armanios, Febe, and Ergene, Bogac (2018), *Halal Food, A History*, New York: Oxford University Press.

Asad, T. (1986), *The Idea of an Anthropology of Islam*, Washington, DC: Centre for Contemporary Arab Studies: 59–88.

Bergeaud-Blackler, Florence, Fischer, Johan, and Lever, John (eds.) (2016), *Halal Matters: Islam, Politics and Markets in Global Perspective*, London: Routledge.

Dien, Mawil Izzi (2000), *The Environmental Dimensions of Islam*, Cambridge: Lutterworth.

Fadil, Nadia, and Fernando, Mayanthi (2015), "Rediscovering the 'everyday' Muslim: Notes on an anthropological divide," *HAU: Journal of Ethnographic Theory* 5/2: 59–88.

Follz, Richard (2001), "Is vegetarianism un-Islamic?," *Studies in Contemporary Islam* 3/1: 39–54.

Hirschkind, Charles (2001), "The ethics of listening: Cassette-Sermon audition in contemporary Egypt," *American Ethnologist* 28/3: 623–49.

Iqbal, Mohammed (2013), *Reconstruction of Religious Thought in Islam*, Stanford, CA: Stanford University Press.

Janmohamed, Shelina (2016), *Generation M: Young Muslims Changing the World*, London: I. B. Tauris.

Kamali, Mohammad (2013), *The Parameters of Halal and Haram in Shariah and the Halal Industry*, Herndon, VA: International Institute of Islamic Thought.

Mahmood, Saba (2003), "Ethical formation and politics of individual autonomy in contemporary Egypt," *Islam: The Public and Private Spheres* 70/3: 837–66.

Mahmood, Saba (2005), *Politics of Piety: The Islamic Revival and the Feminist Subject*, Princeton, NJ: Princeton University Press.
Nasr, Seyyed H. (1996), *Islam and the Role of Nature*, New York: Oxford University Press.
Ramadan, Tariq (2013), "The unethical treatment of animals betrays the spirit of Islam," *ABC Religion and Ethics*, October 15. Available at: http://www.abc.net.au/religion/articles/2013/10/15/3869365.htm
Risman, Barbara (2017), "2016 southern sociological society presidential address: Are millennials cracking the gender structure," *Social Currents* 4/3: 208–27.
Schielke, Samuli (2009), "Being good in Ramadan: Ambivalence, fragmentation, and the moral self in the lives of young Egyptians," *Journal of the Royal Anthropological Institute* 15/1: 524–40.
Tlili, Sarra (2015), "Animals would follow Shafi'ism. Legitimate and illegitimate violence against animals in Islamic medieval texts," in *Violence in Islamic Thought from the Qur'an to the Mongols*, Robert Gleave and Istvan Kristo-Nagy (eds.), Edinburgh: Edinburgh: Edinburgh University Press: 225–44.

7

Choice

It is not appropriate for a believing man or woman to have any choice in a matter, when it has been decided upon by God and His messenger. (3:36)

One of the earliest debates in the *kalam*, Islamic theology, was on the nature of human responsibility. Actually, the debate was about whether any such possibility exists. This is not surprising since the Qur'an itself says on many occasions that we are responsible for what we do and also that we are not, that God is in charge of everything that happens. For example, anyone who has done even a tiny amount of good or bad will be held accountable for it (99:7-8). In fact, before human beings were given the ability to choose how to act this was offered to things like the heavens, the earth, and the mountains but they declined it and only human beings were foolish enough to take it on (33:72). This ability to distinguish between right and wrong, to think about how to act, a faculty which is often taken to define us as human beings, is mentioned in the verse that reads: "It is He who brought you forth from the wombs of your mothers when you knew nothing, and He gave you hearing and sight and intelligence and affections so that you can be grateful" (16:78, see also 23:78, 46:26 and 67:23). We can distinguish between right and wrong (91:7-8). This ability is something we get from our creator, but once we have it does it operate independently of Him or does He continue to influence us through that faculty? Religions often want to do contrasting things, they want to ascribe responsibility to us so that we may be rewarded or punished in response to what we do. After all, religions present us with moral demands and claims and expect us to take up some sort of attitude to them. On the other hand, they often emphasize our lack of power in comparison to the divine, and this might lead us to wonder if we even have the power to make our own moral decisions. If we cannot even be said to throw things, when we appear to have thrown them, because strictly speaking it is God who throws not us, what sense can we make of human independent moral decision?

Jahm ibn Safwan (d. c.745/128) argued that if we think we are free then we are denying the overwhelming power of God to act. He suggests that if we think we can do things ourselves then we think we are like God. This is *shirk*, idolatry, it is to behave like Pharaoh and claim to be gods ourselves (28:38, 79:24). This seems a bit extreme, since to claim we are free to make our own decisions does not mean we are divine, just not coerced by the divine. I may think I was free to type what I have just typed, but I don't usually think of myself as being divine. On the other hand, it is like a servant pretending he or she is of a higher status, and in that sense is clearly to make unjustified claims. It is a familiar phenomenon that patients in psychiatric institutions sometimes identify with and think they are the staff. After all, they understand how to use the language the staff uses and how to behave since they have plenty of experience of observing them. Instead of being dependent on others, they think they are in charge. Rather than being the object of attention, they believe they are organizing their own lives and directing those of others. It is not difficult to move from these examples to suggest that human beings are in a similar position when they think they have autonomy. Jahm goes on to deny the possibility of any understanding of divine properties through our knowledge of our properties, which like our belief in our own power is seen as polytheism, and his theory that God is the creator of everything had the useful political implication for the status quo that we should not get involved in political disputes, since ultimately God was behind everything that happened, including our government. We just have to put up with it since God is behind it. Any other attitude is *shirk*, idolatry.

Is human responsibility an oxymoron?

But if human acts are determined totally by God, then why should He punish us for them on Judgment Day, as we are told many times in the Qur'an that He does? The concept of a Judgment Day implies that we have free will and the ability to take action based on our choices. There is no point in warning us about our behavior if we cannot do anything about it. The Mu'tazilites argued that God gave human beings the ability to do whatever they want, for good or ill. Everything that God does is good while evil comes not from Him but rather from the free choices of creation. This is just. God does not order us to do what we could not do, nor does He want from us what we have no ability to give. God is the creator; if He wished to force people to obey Him and stop them from going against Him, He could do so. Nevertheless, He does not do that because His divine justice allows us to act in the way we want. We can make choices and on the basis of those choices consequences arise. The choices are our own and we have to stand by them.

There are certainly passages which accord with such a view: "Every person is a pledge for what he has earned" (74:38). There is also "Whoever works righteousness benefits his own soul, whoever works evil, it is against his own soul. Your lord is never unjust to his servants" (41:46). This is very much a general theme of the Book, being good is in our own interests, even if we do not realize it. Belief is up to us, as is disbelief, and there are serious consequences to both. "And say: 'The truth is from your Lord.' Then whoever wills, let him believe; and whoever wills, let him disbelieve" (18:29). On the other hand, there are passages suggesting that belief is a matter of what God wants us to do, it is not just up to us. "We showed him the Way: whether he be grateful or ungrateful" (76:3). We are told "No one who is burdened shall bear another's burden. And there is nothing for man except what he strives for" (53:38-39). "We have placed all that is on the earth as an ornament for it so that We may test them on which of them is best in conduct" (18:7; see also 11:7, 67:2), and "Whoever does good it is for his soul, and who does evil it is against it. And your Lord is not unjust to his servants" (41:46). It is up to us how we react to what God does, and there are consequences to making the wrong decision, but we are free to make it and unless we were it would not be just or reasonable to either punish or reward us as a result.

Al-Ghazali was not impressed with this view. Holding an objective standard of justice over God is not appropriate for someone who is far above His creatures. What is just can be discerned from observing what God has done and demanded of us. He created our ability to choose and do things. So our action is both ours and His. Nothing happens except by His ruling; His judgment could not be questioned nor could the fate He set out for us be avoided. The Mu'tazilites argued that God always does what is in people's best interests, He has no choice in the matter. Al-Ghazali countered that God does whatever He wishes to do with His creation, and there is nothing to make him do anything at all or in any way. This is not as different from the Mu'tazilite position as it might seem since he could be arguing that only God knows what is in our interests, and so the fact that He acts in what might appear to be an arbitrary way does not go against our interests in the long run. It is important that we do what God tells us because that is what He tells us, and once we start to wonder why He gives us those orders we risk straying into deciding ourselves which rules to follow and which we can safely put aside, and for al-Ghazali that is a shocking suggestion. On the other hand, he also suggests that there are basic principles of law and these are based on what is in our interests, God does not have to follow such principles, but he does and as a result we have access to how human action is supposed to operate.

There are plenty of passages that fit the view that even belief is really up to God:

> Of them are some who listen to you, but We have placed upon their hearts veils, lest they should understand, and in their ears a deafness.(6:25)

Those who deny our signs are deaf and dumb, in darkness. Who God wills he leads astray, and who he wills he puts on a straight path.(6:39) See also 10:44.

And even if we sent down angels to them, and the dead should speak to them, and we should put everything together before them, they would not believe unless God wished it. (6:111)

Had God willed, they would not have taken up idolatry. (6:107)

And it is God who has created you and what you do. (37:96)

And We decreed in the Book for the children of Israel: You will work corruption in the earth twice, and you will become great tyrants. (17:4)

Indeed, We have made many of the jinn and men for hell. (7:179).

And when we want to destroy a township we command its important inhabitants and they transgress, and ... we annihilate it completely. (17:16) See also 18:28 and 19:83.

This defense of determinism has many echoes in the Qur'an. The idea that all events in the universe including human choices are inevitable because nothing else could have happened implies that human beings have no real freedom of choice. That does not mean they do not have experiences of such freedom, just that it does not accord with any reality. Determinism is often referred to as *jabr* and we get the idea that God obliges things to happen in the way that they do, but there are also often references to human will and motivation, which seems to operate along with divine ordering of the world. One can see why this would be plausible, since if God is omnipotent and omniscient, how could it be that He would not know what decisions we are going to take? He could hardly be surprised at what we do. "This is a warning. Let whoever will take the path to his lord. You will not do it unless God wants it" (76:29-30; see also 7:177-178).

On the other hand, we do have some scope for action: "That is because God never changes the grace he gives anyone until they first change that which is in themselves" (8:53) and also: "But you will not unless God wills it" (76:30) and "And it is God who has created you and what you do" (37:96). Here people ascribe evil events to the Prophet:

Wherever you may be, death will overtake you, even though you were in lofty towers. Yet if good befalls them, they say: This is from God; but if evil befalls them, they say: This is from you. Say: All is from God. What is the matter with these people that they do not understand a single thing? Whatever good befalls you is from God, whatever evil befalls you, it is from your self. We have sent you as a messenger for mankind and God is enough as a witness. (4:78-79; see also 9:50-51)

Determinism and the Qur'an

Here we find two contrasting views: first of all everything comes from God whether good or evil, while in the second verse (79) it is clearly said that the evil comes from us. We are not supposed to see a contradiction here since after all: "Do they not ponder on the Qur'an? If it had been from other than God, they would have found a lot of problems in it (*ikhtilaf*)" (4:82). The idea that everything, whether good or evil, comes from God, runs through much of the Qur'an. Although knowledge of God is natural (7:172-73), we are born in a state of *ghafla* (forgetfulness). We forget our dependence on God and become evil as a result. The personality we have comes from God, like everything else, but we can avoid evil by thinking of God, something He makes possible through His grace: "God does not lead people astray apart from the wrong-doers" (2:26, see also 14:27, 4:55, 9:127, 3:27, 29:69, 6:25, 6:39, and 6:111). The general theme is "You will not will unless God wills" (79:30, see also 6:125). We are told "And as for the boy, his parents were believers and we had knowledge to fear that he would upset them through rebellion and disbelief" (18:80). This refers to the killing of a boy by Khidr on the basis of the knowledge that the boy would grow up to be evil. This is not foreknowledge of what the boy would actually choose freely when he grows up since he never grew up to make that choice. Rather, it refers to the knowledge of something present in the very nature of the boy with which he was born, that is, with which he was created by God and on the basis of which Khidr understood that the boy would choose the wrong path had he lived.

Also relevant is the following verse: "And this was revealed to Noah: None of your people will believe except those who believed already. Do not be distressed because of what they do" (11:36). Once again, this verse is not talking about foreknowledge of the future choice of the disbelievers among his people, but of their inherent inability to choose faith. The revelation to Noah spoke of the nature with which the unbelievers were created and which made it certain that they cannot believe. This is further supported by "And Noah said: 'My Lord! Leave not one of the unbelievers in the land. If You did leave them, they will mislead Your servants and will only breed wicked, ungrateful individuals'" (71:26-27). That the unbelievers will breed none but wicked and ungrateful people implies that the latter would be born with such a character or turned into such characters by parental influence beyond their control and not that wickedness and ingratitude would be their freely chosen way of life. For otherwise the justification given to destroy the parents before they produce children would be difficult to comprehend.

Of course, in the above verses we have only particular cases, but they are enough to establish that in the Qur'anic view working corruption (*fasad*) or disbelief or ingratitude (*kufr*) and rebellion (*tughyan*) can be foreordained by God for a human being. The Qur'an establishes the idea that everything in the future is determined earlier as a general rule at 87:1-3. This verse talks about creation generally. Everything, including humanity is created, is going to follow a certain path in life, which may be good or bad, and is guided toward that destiny. So "no calamity takes place on the earth nor in yourselves but it is in a book before we bring it about" (57:22). The Qur'an does not distinguish between different kinds of evil or good. It uses the same word *sayyi'a* (2:81, 3:120, 30:36, 40:40, and so on) for calamity and "moral" evil, and *hasana* (2:201, 4:40, 78, 13:6, 22, 33:21 etc.) for good fortune and ethical good. Similarly, it uses the same words *sa'id* (11:105, 108) for a fortunate and a morally good person and *shaqiyy* (11:106, 19:32, 19:48, 23:106, 87:11, 91:12, 92:15) for an unfortunate and a morally bad person. Ultimately, fortunate and good are the same, just as the unfortunate and the bad are the same. Here again we see the consequentialist nature of the text and its ethical tenor. Moral good is that which leads to eternal good fortune (paradise) and moral evil is that which leads to eternal ill fortune (hell). There is no independent meaning of good and evil apart from that which leads to human well-being and what leads to his doom. What is at issue here is our responsibility or otherwise for how we end up, and one aspect of this worth emphasizing is that not everything is determined by plain justice. We have to acknowledge the significance of divine grace since God can do anything He likes and often rewards us out of all proportion to anything good we do, and forgives us for unfortunate instances of poor behavior.

In apparent contradiction with the idea of determinism are verses like the following: "And We will certainly put you on trial till We know those of you who strive and are patient and examine your record" (47:31, and 18:7 along with 11:6-7 [discussed later] and 67:2). Verses like this might not be interpreted literally as otherwise they raise the following problem: Since God knows everything, He also knows who will be the best in conduct or who are the ones who will strive or will be patient. So why does God need to try or test people to know what He already knows? This problem arises whenever one knows what the outcome is going to be, even though the agent does not yet know. If I am teaching a child to cycle then I know that for many sessions the only result will be failure, until eventually it clicks and the child takes off under her own power. I know that this stage will come at some stage, God knows precisely when it will happen. God organizes the world in a specific way, and an aspect of this is that He organizes us to do things. When the Qur'an refers to God testing us and setting us tasks to perform and temptations to overcome, He is waiting to see what is going to happen, not how it happens. This interpretation is not only demanded by divine foreknowledge of all events but is also supported by the two verses that precede 47:31 which makes clear that God knows exactly what we are thinking and how we are motivated. God then knows who the hypocrites are, a group who are constantly criticized in the Qur'an.

Verse 47:31 should be understood accordingly. God will put the believers on trial so that those who strive and are patient may be revealed in time, although He already knows who they are. He is hardly going to be surprised by what we do. The case of verses like 18:7 is similar. God will "examine your record" (47:13, see also 10:30 and 3:154). In all these verses we get the idea of God examining and exposing something that is already there and is not necessarily known to the rest of us. Through trials or temptations God brings out those who were foreordained by Him always to be the best and worst in conduct. For us the results are something we have to wait to find out, for Him the knowledge is always there. This interpretation is supported by the fact that the reference to testing us is preceded in 11:7 by a statement that everything is written down in a book (11:6-7), a book that is not being written as events happen but was always there, even before the events happen (57:22). Human beings are included among the living creatures, so that their activities are also in the book and established well in advance of their actually occurring (9:50-51). This reference to *kitab* suggests that the subsequent statement in 11:7 "that He may try you, which of you is best in conduct" should be understood as meaning what is written down in the book.

Does this mean that we are not free to act as we wish? I think right now that I am free to write these words down yet it turns out that for the whole of creation, and indeed perhaps before it, it was determined that I was going to be writing these words in precisely this way, at this time and in this space. On top of that, and perhaps more grimly, you were obliged to read them! What we have to bear in mind here, though, is that just because something is going to happen it does not follow that we have no role to play in bringing it about. When I have breakfast I eat the same things every day when I can and am at home, and anyone could easily predict what I am going to do. It does not follow that I am forced to do it. Similarly with moral behavior, if I am a certain sort of person then I am likely to act in a certain sort of way, and the Qur'an often refers to God making sure that if someone is bad then they carry on being bad so their eventual fate is certain. Does this mean they are not free to repent and become good? They are but not in the sense that they could surprise God. God would already have known that those people would repent, that at some stage they would emerge from the stage of forgetfulness and remember God and turn toward Him. I know that the child will eventually cycle, although she may throw up her arms and say that she will never get it.

Choice and justice

Jahm thought it would not be just for God to create people in this sort of way and then punish them for being bad since it was God himself who made them bad. But that is not quite right. It is God who made them bad, since God is behind everything that happens, He provided them with a personality that developed in a certain way, and as a result of that they behaved accordingly. The thing is that we do not know how we have been made so we have to hope that we are to have the opportunity to thrive and eventually be rewarded as a result of our virtuous behavior, and evil people are a test and a trial for us. Is it fair to blame the evil people for their unpleasant characters since it is God who made them evil, writing it all down in the book and establishing their characters from the beginning? It is useful in general for there to be evil people around, and Satan in particular is given the role of testing us and tempting us, a familiar role for him in religion, of course.

God knows how different people are going to behave, since He knows everything, and He ensures that they behave in accordance with that character. "Then is one who laid the foundation of his building on righteousness from God and His approval better or one who laid the foundation of his building on the edge of a bank about to collapse, so it collapsed with him into the fire of Hell? And God does not guide people who do wrong" (9:109). God knew that those who built the wrong building were going to do so and what the consequences would be. They were always free to change and build in the right sort of way, and if they do so they will be rewarded. But they are not free to surprise God, since He will always know what they are going to do. Does this mean they are not free to take their own decisions? Not really, they are not free to take decisions that are going to surprise God, since nothing surprises Him. To give a different example, any of my neighbors will know that when I appear in the street I will be wearing a hat. This is because I always wear a hat when I go out. That does not mean I am forced to wear a hat and that the idea of not wearing a hat outside leads to sweating palms and heightened blood pressure. It does mean though that as part of my character there is something I tend to do and probably will continue to do unless something else intervenes to make it difficult. This does not mean I am not free not to do it (wearing the hat), it is just that I will probably continue to do it. There is no reason why I should not be punished for it if it became a crime, since I could always set out to try to change my character to avoid doing it.

But does not God influence our thinking? We are told: "O you who believe! Answer God and His messenger when He calls you to that which gives you life; and know that God intervenes between man and his heart, and that to Him you shall be gathered" (8:24). If God controls our thinking and our thinking controls our actions, and on the basis of these we are judged, there seems to be something wrong here. But when we refer to God having an influence on our thinking, surely He is not alone here. We are told that Satan is there to tempt us, other people clearly set out to change our thinking on occasions, and we eventually come to a decision on how to act considering all these different forms of pressure. When we talk of foreign governments meddling in elections, some suggest that the meddling is so powerful that people do not have the power to resist, while others classify this as a form of influence among many others. Some people can resist temptation, others cannot, and when He made us God presumably knows what sorts of people we are going to turn out to be. We do not know, although as we get older we may get to understand more about who we are, and we have to assume (or hope) that there is still scope for us to do well and be good.

Balance and notions of responsibility

In 30:30 we are advised to devote ourselves to God and "follow the nature made by God, the nature with which He created humanity. There is no changing the creation of God. That is the right religion but most people do not understand." Here the idea of creation is linked with our nature, our character, and with this we set out to try to find things out and work out how to behave. This comes out nicely in philosophical stories such as Ibn Tufayl's *Hayy ibn Yaqzan*, where a human child is brought up without any other human beings around and yet still manages to work out the basic truths of religion and morality because of his original character that guides him on how to deal with the variety of experiences he gets as he grows up. That does not mean that everything is plain sailing since, of course, we can follow our character in a variety of ways and we are often impatient (70:19) and forget God (59:19) and do not pray and so on. Fortunately for us God is always ready to forgive us however badly we may turn out, and it might be said that this is only right as He knows right from the start how we are going to behave, since He has created us in a certain way and is aware of how we will respond to temptation.

It is worth reminding ourselves here of the significance of the idea of balance as a leading moral idea in Islam. If we think that everything we do is hopeless since God is behind everything that is over-emphasizing our lack of autonomy. On the other hand, if we think that we are totally in control of our future, that fails to be accurate also. The former position places all power in the hands of God and the latter almost nothing, and we need to find a more middle position here. It is certainly true that according to the Qur'an God is behind everything that happens, but we still have scope to do things. When I teach my child to cycle she will learn how to do it eventually and in a way that I have experienced before with other children, but how she will react to the teaching and how quickly it will be effective is in many ways up to her. The Qur'an gets this balance right nicely by producing a whole variety of ideas on how things come about, both talking about the overwhelming power of God and yet also holding us up as responsible moral beings. Whether this is the correct position is not something to be discussed here, but it is coherent and it is important to understand it, and easy not to.

Who killed Jesus?

In his discussion of the Jews and their attempted murder of Jesus as reported in the Qur'an, Reynolds denies that they killed him. Reynolds assumes that the Jesus of the Injil and the 'Isa of the Qur'an are the same person, and they do share a lot of characteristics. Yet at 4:157 we are told that Jesus was not crucified, although the Jews claimed they did it. A bit of a problem to the

Reynolds thesis is that if Jesus and 'Isa are the same person and his death is a crucial event for Christianity, one wonders how someone could really be the same if they were killed as opposed to, according to many Muslim accounts, being taken up to heaven to await the arrival of the Mahdi. Reynolds gets around this by saying that, in fact, the Qur'an says the Jews were wrong, they did not kill Jesus, God caused him to die and took him up to heaven since God is the person who gives life and death (p. 181). The Jews were guilty of trying to kill him, and their prophets in general, but they were prevented from doing so by God who killed him instead.

This is a strange argument. Of course, God is behind everything that happens and nothing that happens takes place without His knowledge and agreement, so in that sense Reynolds is right. The Qur'an does sometimes push a heavily determinist message in this way (8:17 is a good example of this), but often does not, and the assumption is that the Jews are guilty because they had the choice to try to kill Jesus or not, and they chose to do the wrong thing. Due to mistaken identity they get the wrong man, but their guilty motivation remains. They are often represented in the Qur'an as being mean to the prophets. This view has obviously deep roots in Christianity, and Reynolds details these, but this should not distract us from the issue of whether Jesus and 'Isa are the same people. There seems to be no problem, the Christians have one account of what happened to him at the end of his life, and the Muslims have another, and they are both talking about the same person. Perhaps, but it is worth thinking about the significance of how Jesus died for Christianity. It has an immense significance, and what followed from it, and it might be said that the ubiquity of symbols of Jesus on the cross are highly suggestive of how crucial this event is in Christianity. A Jesus for whom this event did not take place, or take place in that way, might be an entirely different sort of person. That would be awkward for all those commentators on the Qur'an like Reynolds who stress its close connection with the preceding bibles.

What is at issue here though is how far we have room for autonomous behavior. To say that the Jews did not kill Jesus according to the Qur'an because it is really only God who does things is very unbalanced. They killed him and this is something they go in for, since we are told that they have a tendency to be mean to their prophets. It is in their character, just like my putting on a hat when I go out. That does not mean they have to do it, just that they are likely to do it, and God of course knows precisely what they will do long before they even exist. As so often, the Qur'an is far subtler in its treatment of these issues than are its commentators, who fail to grasp the significance of balance as a leading motif in the Book. The point here is not to defend the truth of the Qur'an, just to try to establish what the view is and how it fits in with a reasonable account of how to behave morally.

Bibliography

De Cillis, Maria (2014), *Free Will and Predestination in Islamic Thought: Theoretical Compromises in the Works of Avicenna, al-Ghazali and Ibn 'Arabi*, London: Routledge.
Inati, Shams (2017), *The Problem of Evil: Ibn Sina's Theodicy*, Sheffield: Gorgias.
Reynolds, Gabriel (2018), *The Qur'an and the Bible*, Yale, MI: Yale University Press.
Rosenthal, Franz (1970), *Knowledge Triumphant: The Concept of Knowledge in Medieval Islam*, Leiden: Brill.
Watt, William (1948), *Freewill and Predestination in Early Islam*, London: Luzac.
Wolfson, Harry (1976), *The Philosophy of the Kalam*, Harvard, MA: Harvard University Press.

8

Sufis

Hold fast to the rope of God, and be not divided in groups.
(3:103)

Religions like their followers to do things in groups, on the whole, and Islam is no exception. The social side of religion is always important, and may help keep members in the group and bring others in. Islam suggests on a number of occasions that it is the best religion and also easy to follow, and it includes a variety of social practices which are not difficult to observe. There is, of course, going to the mosque on Fridays, and the name for Friday in Arabic refers to it as the day of gathering together. There are, of course, more strenuous ways of getting together like hajj and *'umra*, the various pilgrimages available and, indeed, incumbent upon Muslims, and these can be unpleasant physically despite the enhanced spirituality that is supposed to accompany those engaged on pilgrimage. In the past the journey itself was often hazardous and full of risk. Even going to the mosque can be unsavory, and the Prophet himself is supposed to have criticized those who eat onions before praying and imposing their heavy odors on others. This suggests that such experiences are not uncommon. The early history of Islam was characterized by splits and controversies, something that persists to this day, and this of course is normal in religion. A variety of ideas about how to interpret the texts occurs and different notions of who has authority, who should lead the community, result as a consequence. For a religion to flourish or at least survive, it needs to attract people to it and continue its beliefs and practices from one generation to another. Hence the significance of doing things with other people; the aim is for people to enjoy those participatory activities and find them a valuable route to their own spiritual growth. These social activities may strengthen faith and commitment to the religion and help weave the religion into many aspects of social and indeed personal life. Many commentators on Islam have pointed to the successful way that Islam does this and see it as one of the excellences of the religion.

A problem with the social side of religion is that people may tend to fall into groups and then set themselves up against each other. Public religion is prone to this. Each group thinks it has access to the truth of how members of the religion should behave and sometimes this leads to groups fighting each other for supremacy. Rope in the *aya* just quoted is interesting material since in the past one strand tends to be woven around another strand, and so on, and a variety of different pieces are bound together and give the object its strength and resilience. There is often no one strand that goes through the whole length of the rope, and no difference between one strand and another. This *aya* could be taken with the verses praising diversity and suggests that God is in favor of a variety of ways of doing things, and interpreting the Qur'an is one of them, although there are plenty of *ayat* which go in other directions also. "Rule is for none but God" (12:40), so ultimately it is not for us to decide how laws should go, it is the divine prerogative to decide on such matters. There is scope for discussion: "And consult with them on the matter. And when you have made a decision place your trust in God, for God certainly loves those who so place their trust" (3:159). But the decisions are taken by God and we need to abide by them. There is no reason though why this means there should not be debate and differences of view as to what the divine decision actually is. On some issues like prayer it is quite clear what it is but on many others, like what is involved in charity, it is not and there exists a variety of views.

On the other hand, this public side of religion is not the only thing it has going for it. There is also the private relationship believers have with God, or which they seek to cultivate. This balancing of public and private duties is not an essentially religious issue, of course. Each individual has both duties to others and duties to himself or herself and we need to find some balance in our lives to deal with both these aspects of our humanity. An entirely secular person has relationships with other people that are, no doubt, important to her but she also needs to think about herself, what she is doing, where she is going, in an entirely personal way, since there is an aspect of all our lives that is private and continues by itself. Should she spend so much time watching TV? Should she go on a gluten-free diet? Should she go for walks in the evening after work? These issues have relevance only to her and need to be reconciled with her social commitments at work or as part of a community of some sort, friends, relatives, acquaintances, and so on. Some people really like to spend time by themselves and will have as little to do with others as possible, whereas for others the reverse is the case. We all need to find some balance that is acceptable to us both psychologically and morally. We might after all want to spend a lot of time by ourselves but feel it is our duty to help others by being with them when they need us and forego what we would otherwise wish to do.

Islam has a variety of customs which bring people together for prayer and celebration of one type or another, and Miskawayh and the *adab* tradition discussed in Chapter 5 points out how the religion builds on what we normally find enjoyable anyway. We are social beings, and we like doing things with other people for at least some of the time, and the religion works with that to devise practices that fit in with our natural inclinations, our *fitra*. Here he is following a persistent claim in Islamic ethics that the religion goes along with how we are and is not devised to make life difficult for us. Why would God, after all, create us in a certain way and then insist that we engage in behavior that goes against how we were created? He could do this, and human beings often do things that are perverse, but it is difficult to see why He would. The customs of Islam are not that onerous as normally interpreted. The dietary restrictions are few and family life including sexual activity within marriage is encouraged. There is the long Ramadan fast, but this is broken by what are often feasts in the evening and at the end there is a big celebration, which is a lot of fun. Even the hardship of the fast as a communal activity has a purpose in deepening solidarity. Five prayers a day are advocated, and the first one is rather early in the morning, but many people enjoy those activities and the prayers are quite short and can be said anywhere. Before prayer there is ablution and this is quite simple, and on Friday the communal prayer may take some time with the sermon and so on, but it is often a pleasant occasion to meet friends and for children to play together and there is often a big meal afterward. Religions need to embody themselves in social life and Islam has had no difficulty doing this. It sees itself as playing a middle role between the materialism of Judaism and the spirituality of Christianity, both of which are seen as excessive, and since it has struck the mean it is naturally well able to reflect how and what we are.

The personal

There is another aspect of religion, though, and that is the personal side. Here one is not so much concerned about the rituals of the religion as about one's private relationship with God. This distinction comes out nicely in the theological controversy that was important in early Islam over what it is to be a believer. Here there are usually three aspects, what you do, what you say, and what you feel in your heart. Some people thought that all one has to do is have the right feelings, action is unimportant, while others stressed action. This is an issue in most religions, one wants to know the link between what we are thinking and what we are doing to count as really being a member of the group. Some people act as though they are members but, in fact, their thoughts are very far from really being in the group, they may just be going through the motions and their beliefs are quite different. By contrast, it is possible to act as though one was not a member but really one is. The consequences are significant, God of course knows the truth, but even for God we might wonder if a grave sinner is able to achieve paradise if he repents in time or whether whatever his beliefs might be his actions condemn him to inevitable punishment in the fire. If action is the criterion then he is in trouble, if thoughts are more important, then, he may still have a chance. Even if his actions are entirely at fault there is always scope for repentance and perhaps forgiveness. Of course, normally everything is synchronized, actions with intentions and words, but when this is not the case difficulties arise for human beings in knowing what is going on. There is no problem for God who can, of course, see into our hearts. One theological school, the Murji'i are supposed to have used this idea to refuse to declare anyone an unbeliever, waiting (*irja*) for God to make the decision.

The private and the institutional

Sufism is very oriented toward this private side to religion. Like all mystics they are interested in achieving a deep personal relationship with God and it may be that on occasion they feel that acting in an ordinary Muslim way would impede their progress. For instance, having to carry out our social functions is distracting and invites us to concentrate on matters of little significance. Long family meals takes up time that could be better spent in contemplation of God. Even going to the mosque may get in the way of doing something much more direct to try to make contact with some level of divinity. Some Sufis valued solitude and isolation, and were reported to have engaged in quite challenging behavior. Perhaps they even abandoned their families, started to eat very limited types of food and gravitated to solitary spaces where they were unlikely to be disturbed. Their hearts were so full of God that they could think of nothing else, and so essentially dropped out of an ordinary Muslim lifestyle. Is it ethical to leave the world of the community? Not perhaps if we have duties to ourselves and this is what the Sufis are intent on developing. In any case, they might well follow a personal ethics which involves paying a good deal of attention to their own behavior and even appearance, but not so much with respect to other people but more with respect to God and to those who are also in the Sufi orbit. The rules for Sufis are often to spend a lot of time on these sorts of issues, as though they could replace their ethical dealings with the external world with an internal ethic. This might seem a bit strange, we know that there can be duties to oneself but all the advice on how we should deal with our own bodies seems to be not very relevant to ethics. On the other hand, we need to take seriously the idea so important to mysticism of the connection between the microcosm with the macrocosm. What happens to the smallest part of the world affects the whole world, and vice versa, so the idea is that by concentrating on cleanliness and directing our minds constantly to God we are a part of the whole world changing in what is seen as a more positive direction.

Advocates of Sufism often deny that it is mystical but claim it is the heart of Islam, making the point that the religion is more than just performance of religious obligations (Leaman 2013: 176–90). Thinking about God is clearly something that religions advocate and no doubt it is true that often we do not do this enough. In many ways religious practices that are apparently designed to help us do this can act in the opposite direction. We can get into a routine and hardly think about what we are doing. The prayers may become so familiar that we no longer consider what the words mean, and our ordinary lives may become so wound up in the religion that we hardly notice what we are doing. Observant people often say that an advantage of being observant is that in many situations they do not have to think what to do since it is obvious given their commitment to the religion. This has the disadvantage though of making more of our daily lives automatic and can lead to less orientation toward God than otherwise. One of the factors that encourage religious people to embrace mysticism is the idea that their religion has become too boring. It is just part of their lifestyle, it has become just something they do and hardly ever think about. The obvious answer then is that this is something they need to start thinking about and the problem is solved. But there is a dynamic in institutions like religion that precisely reflects their status as institutions, their participants become institutionalized and no longer really notice what they are doing. This evidently affects Islam along with other religions, and the evidence is the number of thinkers who have come along to revitalize the faith, the *tajdid* project that has been identified with so many thinkers like al-Ghazali and Said Nursi. The effort is based on a famous hadith where the Prophet says that each century will see someone come and revive Islam, a shrewd comment which could apply to many religions, not only Islam.

We could take another institution, marriage, as a good example here. Marriages also sometimes deteriorate for many people into a set of practices which participants observe but have less and less meaning for them. The passionate love with which it may have started has largely disappeared and something similar needs to be found for the institution to be revived. Indeed, passion may never have really been there in the first place, people may have just drifted into it and various things then happened which resulted in marriage, and after a period, or perhaps quite quickly, the question arises how the participants are going to proceed. They may decide to end their relationship and leave the institution or they may try to revive it in some way, and the aim here will be to do something to energize the participants, give them a motive for being enthusiastic about what they are doing, making them feel personally that they need to take a stand on what the institution means to them. The parallels with mysticism are obvious. As with marriage, those seeking to rekindle enthusiasm about an institution can go in a variety of directions. Groucho Marx is supposed to have said that marriage is a wonderful institution, but who wants to live in an institution? Some people do. One way of coping with the restrictions is to address the problem of a decline in enthusiasm by reapplying oneself to the point of the institution from a personal point of view, but another is to commit oneself more tightly to the rules. We often see this in religion, it is possible to become an enthusiast about a strict and narrow interpretation of the rules after a period of drifting, or have a continuing lax attitude to the rules but concentration on what one takes the point of the institution to be. This could be seen as either a confirmation of the significance of the rules or a retreat from the rules in favor of something more genuine and lasting, what one takes the heart of the matter to be.

That is what the Sufis stress, the orientation of the heart toward God, and that means that we concentrate on God at the expense perhaps of many other things. But is this not to violate the central principle in Islam of balance, *wasatiya*, which we have argued here pervades the Qur'an and other central theological texts? A Sufi might argue that she was more interested in her personal balance, and if by concentrating her thinking on God and perhaps not paying much attention to her links with other people she looks abstracted from the community, then it is preferable for this to be the case than that she follows a version of religion which she finds inauthentic. If she is not happy in her normal role in the community then she is unlikely to experience balance anyway, nor are her relationships with others likely to bring that balance about more generally. Religions tend to favor uniformity but we should take seriously the idea of balance across the whole variety of performers, so that we have some extremes at both ends and many similar levels of behavior in the middle. That would also constitute balance of a kind although not uniformity. If we take those passages in the Qur'an praising diversity seriously, then this is an option we should consider, although it is never clear whether diversity is seen as a good in itself or a state of affairs to be transcended when everyone embraces Islam. This argument extends to more than just attitudes to ordinary religious rituals and could be linked with sexual or gender preferences by different Muslims. Moral rules apply to everyone and yet some people might prefer not to get engaged with the ordinary ethical world, their route to God might be different and so society would be seen as a potential enterprise they could take up but prefer to avoid. There are some people who are very keen to enter the social system and play an active part in it, while others decline to do so, and while each individual life might be unbalanced, overall, there is a balance and this might be the best that we can get in a world where different people want to go in different directions for at least some of the time. It just is the case that some of us prefer to do things with other people, while others like to be by themselves and find a private form of self-expression.

A response might be that the latter group just go wrong. Islam lays out how people are supposed to act; it is worth pointing out also not Muslims alone but everyone, and if they do not, then they are guilty of sin or maybe even *fasad*, corruption, on earth. But we are talking here about people who are involved in social life, and not really those who exclude themselves from it to a large degree. There is a value in some people doing unusual things and seeing what it would be like to live like that, within limits of course. This could be taken to be an Islamic version of what John Stuart Mill calls experiments in living, where diverse lifestyles are tried out to see which work best and which do not. Although many see Islam as a traditional religion supporting what has come to be regarded as the normal heterosexual family, there is no reason to see this conception of what is desirable as a timeless truth. As is familiar to everyone, religions are flexible and can be taken in a variety of ways, and traditional rules can sometimes be seen as rules for a particular time and place and not for everywhere and every time. One needs to present an argument which shows that what might be regarded as basic Islamic principles are violated by a change in rules to do with who can do what with whom, or who is allowed to leave society, to a degree, for a while or perhaps forever in order to pursue their own personal path to God.

Taqwa

Here we seem to be going far beyond what most Sufis regard as their relationship to ordinary views of Islam. Sufis can after all be members of different legal schools, and do not seek to deny or alter any of the principles of Islam. On the other hand, Sufis may be attracted to forms of asceticism and avoid material comfort, emphasizing repentance and humility before God. Transcending the self, cultivating purity of heart, and fighting pride are all aims of Sufism and they share with many forms of Eastern philosophy the attempt at avoiding attachment to the material world. The Prophet himself is supposed to be an example to follow in terms of his enthusiasm for his prayers, his ability to reject material comfort, and his comportment or *adab*, the etiquette with which he controlled his life and his relationships with others. *Taqwa* means piety in the sense of thinking about God and rejecting everyday distractions, and embedding in one's character a moral, along with a physical, cleanliness that brings the individual into a correct physical and spiritual relationship with what is higher than him or her. Sufis often talk about the importance of being guided by someone and of doing what the guide instructs, and of being prepared to engage in spiritual activities that go beyond the common practices of Islam. They follow an esoteric line on the religion, although they accept the main exoteric practices as well, usually, and the particular nature of that line depends upon the school they are in and the guide under whom they have put themselves.

It has already been argued that there are grounds for suggesting that the diversity of approaches in Islam to *taqwa* are not unreasonable in a religion which seeks to establish balance. We can have balance across the community rather than in every lifestyle in the community. In any case, it is not obvious what balance means, so that for one person with particular interests and enthusiasms it can be one thing and for someone else something quite different. On the other hand, there are grounds for thinking that the Sufi approach can be systematically problematic. Emphasizing love sounds very nice, and is no doubt attractive to many, but the process itself of developing in one's attitude to God is a parody of moral development. In the latter, we start off thinking very much in terms of ourselves and then gradually come to take others' interests to heart more and more, we attempt to change our dispositions by engaging in activities which gradually help bring this about. Religions are good at helping us do this, they contain a lot of advice on how to be more charitable, generous, truthful, and so on. There are obviously the general moral principles but built on that we have their application to real life, often via stories and less formal processes. It may even be by what others we know in our community tell us worked for them, we try it out and find it works for us, perhaps with a tweak here and there, and we then pass it on to others, and it helps someone else. Or is ignored and a different way of acting is initiated, which itself may fail or succeed, but is part of a long educational process that any moral actor has to be engaged in. Sufis have something like this, of course, since they may live in a community which talks about how to move from stage to stage of spiritual development, and they should have a guide who is going to counsel them on the way forward. The trouble with the analogy though is that for the Sufi the measure of success is entirely personal. How well is she doing obliterating the self, how well is someone else doing in opening up his heart to God in the widest possible way? There is a science of mysticism in Islam, if that is the appropriate translation of the idea of an *'ilm al-tasawwuf*, and it is right to acknowledge that there is a system here with a hierarchy and a learning process that gets one from one level to another. There is a guide who monitors progress and gives advice, and also others who can make comments. This is not like a moral community though, where our actions and feelings come into contact with other people all the time and can take account of their reaction to what we do and our feelings about it all. A problem with at least this form of mysticism is that like a private language there are no criteria of success (or failure). We need a public arena for this to be possible, and we do not have it in the case of Sufism. This is not to say that there remains anything wrong morally with what Sufis generally do or believe, the claim is that success here is haphazard. It is far from a science or system, despite how it is presented.

Forgetting God

We are told that "in fact, God does not change the condition of a people until they change it themselves" (13:11). This makes it look as though it is very important for us to change what we are thinking and feeling before we can attract the attention of God. One of the things we are not good at doing, according to the Qur'an, is recognizing the role that God plays in our lives. He has gratuitously created us and continues to support and care for us and yet on the whole we do not recognize this or do not recognize it fervently enough. The aim of Sufism is to emphasize the necessity for gratitude and our entire dependence on God. It is true that we do not tend to think who is responsible for how well things go for some of the time, and when they go badly we might suspect that their cause is not someone well intentioned toward us, both attitudes leading to the charge of being ungrateful and actually also to the label of being an unbeliever. Such people go awry, we are told, and fail to acknowledge something which is both true and important to know. Our ordinary lives do not provide evidence of sufficient gratitude, and we tend, in the bustle of the ordinary, to forget what God has done for us or even forget God himself. That does not have to mean that we do not pray but we may not concentrate on the point of the prayer, or where it is supposed to be oriented, and so it becomes just a customary and empty act. How can we remedy the situation? The trouble with the Sufi solution is that it emphasizes the personal at the expense of the communal, and while it might lead to personal growth, it would do little for the participation of the individual as part of a community. It is possible that as the individual progresses from station to station his involvement in society as a whole is enhanced, but it is difficult to see why this would be the case since his attention is directed elsewhere. That is what makes the mystical path a mystical path, it is a path to individual enlightenment, and there does not exist with the Sufi tradition the sort of Mahayana principle in Buddhism where the person becoming enlightened stops at the last moment because he does not want to be enlightened unless everyone can be enlightened. This is a consequence of the compassion which lies at the heart of Buddhism and brings the individual back to the community he has spiritually outstripped. It seems a rather cruel thing to say since surely the Sufi seeks to embody all the virtues as perfectly as he can. On the other hand, Rumi in the *Mathnawi* produces the idea of a candle becoming entirely flame and so being annihilated. He goes on to describe that state as of someone being completely safe and beyond good and evil. Clearly *fana'* or annihilation, the summit of mystical achievement, is amoral, whereas in most varieties of Islam where we should be trying to get to is very different. We leave behind morality at the summit of our experience because it is so personal and individual, we are not then concerned with our relationships with others and so on, the common stuff of morality. We transcend such concerns.

This may show that the aim of Sufism is to leave morality behind but does not establish that en route it will be left behind. After all, if I try to increase my gratitude for divine blessings, might I not think that one of these blessings is my links with other people and that should cause me to think carefully about my relationships with them. If as a sign of my gratitude I try to help other people since I think that is what God would like me to do, would this not serve to make me a better person in my community? It might but it is worth looking at the literature on spiritual growth here and it does seem very self-focused. For example, in the *Ihya'* al-Ghazali stresses the value of visiting people less fortunate than ourselves, people who are sick, in prison, or have some problem in their lives in order to become more aware of how good things generally are for us. It is a Sufi theme that we are stimulated to be grateful by special favor but in the main we just accept the normal run of things going well and do not think of the creator sufficiently. Said Nursi does the same thing, he spends a lot of time talking about the importance of understanding the world around us and where everything good originates, and one way of appreciating this is to contemplate how things are when they are not going well, so that we better appreciate He who acts to help us, in general. Nursi is not officially a Sufi but it has often been argued that there is not much difference between his general strategy and Sufism. His work lacks the systematic nature of the Sufi methodology but works to a very similar conclusion, the need to move from a public religion to a private realm of feeling, and then use that as a way of reinvigorating the public religion (Leaman 1999). It is worth noting in these examples from the *Ihya'* by al-Ghazali that when we observe people who are in difficulties he does not suggest that we help them or take any practical steps to alleviate their problems, we use what we can observe to help ourselves to acquire a better attitude to God. The focus is on God and in the response to death with "My Lord, allow me to return, so that I might do good" (23:99-100), is the good mentioned here a matter of addressing myself in a better way to God, or helping other people? Or of course both? It could be both but does not have to be. We are told in the hadith, "He who knows himself knows his Lord." It looks as though we have ourselves and then an attitude to God and that might exclude ethical life. But what about the doctrine of *wahdat al-wujud* (unity of existence)? This famous slogan, often attributed to Ibn al-'Arabi but in fact never directly used by him, introduces a complication in the notion of ethical life, that is, the necessity of balancing our moral and other demands. After all, for Ibn al-'Arabi *tawhid* (oneness) is equivalent to "Wherever you turn, there is the face of God" (2:115).

For Ibn al-'Arabi, concentrating on God is part of developing our awareness of the meaning of the world. God is not above us somewhere, but here in the world, albeit hidden. The more we understand the world, the more its secrets become unveiled, and the more this happens the closer we come to God. We need to approach the texts appropriately, seeking within them the secret meanings that are missed by a literal interpretation and yet which bring us closer to how things really are, how both the world and God really are. God reveals himself through the world, but for Ibn al-'Arabi never finally, as it is an infinite task to grasp him, hardly surprising since He is Himself infinite. There are different levels of human understanding here, and in line with much of the Qur'an the implication is that it is God who positions different people at different levels of understanding.

We are told that "God has given some of you more than others" (16:71) and "We raise in degrees whoever we will, and above each one who possesses knowledge is someone who knows more" (12:76), and the Qur'an asks, "Are they equal, those who know and those who do not know?" (39:9). This is a rhetorical question, it is supposed to be answered negatively. As is the normal state of affairs in mysticism, human beings are a microcosm reflecting the macrocosm of God. Some are closer to God's perfection than others. God is available to those prepared to undertake the arduous journey to find Him. A hadith popular with the Sufis is: "I was a hidden treasure and I loved to be known so I created the world that I might be known." Everything in the world is a reflection of God, including the negative or evil aspects of life. They are there to contrast with the positive and bring out their nature, and so there are two kinds of names of God, the pleasant ones and the more severe ones, and the contrast is important here epistemologically. Everything in creation needs something opposite to it to bring out its features, like the contrast between the low earth and the high sky. It would be impossible to understand either unless it was related to what is opposite it.

Evil and Iblis

In the *Mathnawi*, Rumi compares the world of good and evil to anger and mercy being linked with each other. The opposite of good is evil. So the existence of evil should not be regarded as a problem, rather, it is linked with the existence of good. God himself is neither good nor evil, he unlike everything else in existence, lacks contrast and differentiation, although when we think of Him we naturally take account of His attributes of beauty (*jamal*) and majesty (*jalal*). To be a witness of divine unity we really have to stop thinking in our ordinary ways, since the idea of something existing which is not in any way complex and differentiated and goes against the character of our language. Not only is this a difficult way for us to think, it is particularly difficult given our nature. We are a mixture of the angel and animal, the intellect (*'aql*) and sensuality (*nafs*), spirit (*ruh*) and matter (*jism*) (Rumi 1961: 89–90). God uniquely is not a mixture at all, and that is why He is so difficult to contemplate.

The human being is the microcosm, the mirror in which all the divine names and properties are reflected, and perfectly in the perfected man (*al-insan al-kamil*), the central theophany (*tajalli*) of the divine names and attributes. When Adam, the first man and prophet was created, God commanded the angels to bow down before him, proclaiming the unique station of humanity in God's creation. All the angels prostrated before Adam except Iblis. Iblis disobeyed God because he believed Adam to be inferior since Adam was created from clay and he from fire (7:11-12). Rumi's view is that Iblis' disobedience stems essentially from spiritual blindness, that is, the inability to distinguish essence (*ma'na*) from form (*surat*). Iblis was right in thinking that we are only created from clay but not right in thinking that our form as rooted in matter entirely determined by what we are capable of becoming. This is a point God makes to the angels as a whole and most of them accept this and do what they are told. Iblis stands out by not going along with what God tells him to do, and it is often thought that this primary disobedience is based on this refusal. On Rumi's approach though it is more that Iblis has such a strong sense of his own self that he is unwilling to allow his own opinion to be suborned by anyone else's, even by God. He is going to stick with what he thinks is right come what may, and in being given the role of deceiving us perhaps his technique is not to get us to believe things which are damaging to us and false but encouraging us to think we can work things out for ourselves. That belief is based on a strong sense of the *nafs*, the self, precisely what we need to relinquish if we are to acquire proximity to God and a greater understanding of our role in the universe. Iblis was full of this when he rejected the divine command to bow down to Adam, something made of clay and despite what God said having no more significance in his eyes than just being some kind of stuff. The Qur'an often contrasts our partial view with the complete view available to God. The use of language to describe us as servants or slaves appears to be servile, and yet it is designed perhaps to encourage us to weaken our sense of our own *nafs*, such a significant source of evil.

When Iblis was expelled from Heaven by God, he was not in any way sorry about his act of disobedience. Instead, he challenged God that he was going to lead as many of Adam's descendants away from an orientation toward God (7:13-16). Iblis becomes the symbol of the qualities of arrogance, pride, envy, anger, disobedience, and spiritual blindness which are the source of evil. Hence, he is in an excellent position to tempt us and lead us astray, he represents what happens when someone is completely concentrated on his notion of his own self-importance. His main ally is our self (*nafs*), it is when we give a lot of importance to our senses and what they can bring to us that we become very much at the mercy of temptation. We should not emphasize the senses entirely here, even if someone is fairly abstracted from his physical side and has a sense of satisfaction in having accomplished this, they are still candidates for Iblis since they have created a strong sense of their own individuality and autonomy. They have set themselves up against God as not dependent on him, Rumi would suggest, and this is classic temptation territory. If we see ourselves as servants or slaves, our dependency is acknowledged.

Escaping from the self

Given his theory that every created thing has an opposite or a contrast that brings out its nature, the self (*nafs*) has a contrast in the intellect (*'aql*). The intellect is the angelic part of man and it is identified with light (*nur*) and what is above us and is very much concerned with acting well. Perhaps it is the link between fire and light that makes Iblis regard it as superior to clay. In Rumi's view, it is only by means of the eye (*'ayn*) of the intellect awakened through spiritual purification and growth that someone becomes enlightened and is able to participate in the divine vision of creation. This eye of the intellect can appreciate the divine unity concealed behind the constant interplay between mercy and anger, beauty and majesty. The ability to see balance is important here, it is very easy to see things from just one point of view, like Iblis. It is not at all clear how much of this seeing involves doing things, how far we need to embed ourselves in the world of action and morality. Before we can be a witness (*shahid*) to this unity we have to first free ourselves intellectually from the domination of our bodies which are very much seen as the enemy from within. This might suggest abstracting ourselves from our social life. In many ways those physical and social feelings are the toughest enemies to beat since they are so difficult for us to identify and confront. Al-Ghazali makes a similar point, our world of matter is related to the hidden and real world in the same way as sleeping is linked with waking. There is nothing particularly wrong with this world, but if we take it to be real and the source of our important distinctions, we are going to be confused by it. This world is a test for us and if we want to pass the test, we need to renounce things in this world if they stand in the way of our spiritual growth. We represent a combination of intellect and appetite, and we need to use our intelligence to control our desires and regulate them in a way that is going to help us on the route to salvation.

For many people as time proceeds their appetites grow and rule their lives, and this is very unhelpful since it directs our attention toward our immediate interests and embeds us in a material notion of the afterlife. There is nothing wrong with the latter, it is there in the Qur'an after all, but really we should see the afterlife as an aspect of our relationship with God in this life. The literal understanding is a bit limiting since it suggests that our physicality is what we should largely be concerned with, whereas of course the opposite is the case. Our spiritual growth starts with the fear that most people feel at the prospect of an afterlife of pain and punishment and then develops into love for God and a gradual winding down of our sense of ourselves as persons and absorption into the idea of the unity of everything and its identity with God. For many, though, this development does not really take place and they are left at the level of fear. A problem of balance again, this is more balanced than thinking that the only thing that is important is this world (*dunya*), but not as balanced as linking the next world with God as a reflection of His love as well as divine retribution. In the same way that we can think of spiritual growth as a process and a development, so we should think about balance. It is not just something we can achieve and then we have it, like a bag of sweets. It is a state we try to achieve and sometimes we are more successful than at other times, and sometimes we get to the right sort of place only to lose it shortly afterward.

This balance can only come about through a process. Human perfection can only be attained after long periods of time when the soul patiently undergoes a painful process of radical transformation. Only a self completely purged of vices and base qualities arising from the dominance of the *nafs* and adorned itself instead with virtues and attributes of God is perfect, and consequently, attains the utmost limits of the innate potential of the human state. Thus, to be a witness to the divine unity, *tawhid*, is in the evocative language of Rumi, to burn one's self before the one (Rumi 1982, I 3008). No self then remains, only God, the ultimate balance.

God and evil

Although God wills both good and evil, it should be noted that He only approves of the good. The divine command to man to do good and the divine prohibition against doing evil are only appropriate or meaningful if there is an ego or aspect of man which desires evil. In the *Fihi mafihi* (What it is), Rumi likens God to the teacher who, on the one hand, requires the ignorance of the student in order that he may teach him, but does not approve of the student's ignorance, on the other. For if he did, then he would not painstakingly teach him:

> God ... wills both good and evil, but only approves the good. ... For commandment to do good and prohibition against evil rightly to apply, one cannot dispense with a soul desiring evil. To will the existence of such a soul is to will evil. But God does not approve of evil, otherwise He would not have commanded the good. ... Hence it is realized that God wills evil in one way and does not will it another way. (Rumi 1961: 187)

In conclusion, it can be stated that for Rumi, there is no evil in God. However, evil exists in the created order. Creation or manifestation which involves separation from God is based on the fundamental principle of contrast and opposition. Evil is a result of separation from God. If God is symbolized by light, then evil can be symbolized by darkness. Darkness is not a reality as is, rather it arises as a result of the lack or absence of light. The presence of darkness is relative to the existence of light. Unlike light, darkness does not possess an independent reality. Thus, evil exists only relatively, not as something that always has to exist. After all, evil is limited and relative in nature, God is absolute and infinite. On the other hand, it could be argued that given the material nature of the world, evil is just as eternal as the world is. Normally, it would not be regarded as eternal but created in time by God and one day it will be brought to an end by him, but the issue is whether the contrast between good and evil is temporary or permanent. If we follow Rumi's argument it is as permanent as the existence of the world, at least in pre-Mahdi times, and even after that time it is difficult to see how people would be able to act well unless they understand the link between virtue and vice. Vice would have to exist at least as an option, although perhaps not as one that anyone would actually initiate. The idea of light only existing if darkness also exists as at least an idea is relevant here. We should not think of light as being real and darkness as only the absence of light. Darkness has its own reality and we often enjoy being in the dark, and not only as a contrast with light. In the language of the Qur'an light is often used as a symbol of knowledge, and darkness as the reverse, and yet we should not be too impressed by this symbolic dichotomy, there are things we can know and experience in darkness that are not available to us in the light, as Nina Edwards has shown recently (Edwards 2018). One of the positive features of contemporary culture is that we often start to query the easy dichotomies that seem to characterize reality, man and woman, light and dark, good and evil being good examples. Of course, some people go further and include God and humanity here. With its emphasis on the significance of being moderate and balanced Islam might be seen as arguing in the same way. We should not emphasize the differences between things but often what they have in common with each other, what we can learn from them. For some sympathetic to Sufism this is true of the relationship between God and His creation also, a view with which Ibn al-'Arabi is sometimes criticized (Campanini 2018). Blind people often complain that religion does not have good things to say about darkness and knowledge should not be identified with light and sight as though it were obvious. Rumi asserts that in creation evil functions as the contrasting manifestation of good. Without evil, good will not be distinct. All the pain and suffering we experience as a result of evil are only preparation for the eventual experience of good. Evil is not created or valued for its own sake, its role is to help us finally be good. So evil, in itself limited and relative in nature, is a necessary stop on the route to the good. This is the account we are given, but then we have the problem of understanding how we can continue to be good when evil disappears. Hence, the idea that is certainly there in Rumi that when we achieve eventual enlightenment good and evil disappear would make more sense, if evil goes then so does good. If we are like angels then moral choice is taken from us, or we transcend it, and so morality is left behind.

The persistence of evil

The idea that evil remains when we come close to God, or when the world is redeemed by the Mahdi, is probably designed to sound different from pre-Islamic religious ideas such as Manicheanism where good and evil are eternal forces battling each other for all time. This seems to challenge the power of God to defeat evil. On the other hand, if action is to continue it is difficult to see how moral choice would come to an end. The idea of identifying with God and thereby avoiding the good/evil dichotomy surely means an end to normal human activity. A relevant observation here is that it looks like a revival of the Aristotelian idea that morality is a secondary virtue, it is a stage in our lives and is important to get us to the ultimate stage but has no ultimate importance of its own. It is not difficult to see why Sufis are sometimes regarded as antinomian since the persistence of morality and law seems to be limited in scope. Some Sufis might wonder whether they need to continue to obey the rules for social life if they could come close to God without them. Of course, the literature insists that they should continue to use them yet it is by no means obvious why. To use a Buddhist example identifying language with the spiritual path, if you get across a river in a boat, once you get to where you are going you do not drag the boat around with you afterward. You do not need morality once you come close to God since action in its normal sense disappears. Only God and divine unity becomes of concern to us, and everything else drops out.

Evil arises from the *nafs* or self. The process of spiritual growth involves the transformation of the *nafs* through developing stages of closeness to God, beginning from its most base state which is that of the *al-nafs al-ammara* or "the soul which incites to evil" (Leaman 2016: 49, 84) to the highest which is its total extinction in God (*fana' fi Allah*). When the self or *nafs* is extinguished in God, we are no longer separated from Him, although what that means is difficult to say. At the level of *fana'* or extinction of the self in God, we do not think of ourselves at all, but only the *shahada*: *La ilaha ill al-Allah* or "there is no god but God" remains. The concept of other gods in *shirk* or idolatry include the *nafs*, our sense of our sense-importance and individuality, our preconceived ideas and enthusiasms, and once that is dissipated, the gap between us and God also disappears. There is a familiar problem here that it is difficult to know what this would be like since so much of our language is based precisely on that gap, on our ability to use our sense of who we are to make sense of the world and what is other than us. Although evil is part and parcel of the ordinary world and enables us to understand what is good, we can set out to remove evil from ourselves, and the notion of repentance is based on the idea of doing this and hence reducing our distance from God.

Balance and mysticism

Although the language of mysticism often seems extreme, it is worth reminding ourselves here of the role of moderation. We are creatures in the middle, in between angels and animals, and although the Sufi path sounds very difficult and extreme, it is actually supposed to be a gradual process where the seeker after truth moves step-by-step over time in the right direction. It is a moderate path, one where he continues to act in his normal role in the world and carry out his ethical duties in the usual sort of way, at least for most of the time. It is Iblis who goes to extremes, when he looks at Adam all he can see is what he is made from, clay, yet he is more than that. Being moderate involves examining things carefully and being aware of their complexity. We are aware of the world as a place of good and evil, we seek to encourage the former and distance ourselves from the latter, yet we have to acknowledge the existence of both. Iblis cannot do this, he sees us as just material and so irredeemable. We have to try to balance these factors in human life so that we are neither overcome by the darkness of our characters nor blinded by their light when they appear to be very positive and aligned with the divine attributes.

There is nothing in Sufism that resembles the moral discussion in Buddhism between the Mahayana and Hinayana or Theravada schools. According to the Mahayana or Greater Vehicle school, a Buddhist should not be enlightened unless everyone is enlightened, so she would hold off from taking that last step. She would instead dedicate her life to helping others get to the stage she almost attained, and presumably then she would suggest they wait before they become enlightened to help others emulate them, and so on. Eventually everyone is ready for the last step and they can all jump in together, as it were. The Hinayana, the lesser vehicle, a diminutive expression, have a smaller notion of enlightenment as personal and more limited. It should be accomplished one person at one time even if no one else is joining him on this occasion. On the whole, the descriptions of the process of getting close to being enlightened and actually achieving it are amoral, since the person undergoing the experience is orienting herself away from everyone and everything else toward something they take to be much more important. Meditation is often solitary and inward looking, the very reverse of ethical life. The more we get away from other people, both in our thoughts and in space, the less need we have of wondering how we should deal with them and balance our various commitments and obligations. It might be argued that this is a rather immoderate form of enterprise, one where we do not seek to balance concerns for ourselves (our *nafs*) and others, but where we try to do without the self at all. Of course, if the self is seen as the source of all evil, as it is with Rumi and many Sufis, then the more we can get demote the better it is. Notice here how far we are getting from the idea of moderation and balance, and perhaps more significantly from moral agency.

The end of morality?

This is in no way an attack on Sufism or mysticism, only of the idea that as we advance through the spiritual trajectory morality is important. We are told it is, but there is no good argument for such a conclusion. Commentators on Islamic philosophy often say with some justification that there is little discussion of moral philosophy within the canon. This is hardly surprising though since many Islamic philosophers were committed to one form of mysticism or another, and so our interaction with other people is not their primary focus. Those thinkers who were more aligned with Aristotle and the idea of morality as among the secondary virtues were hardly likely to spend much time discussing them since they are secondary. They are important in the sense of helping us get to where we want to go, but in the sense that they smooth the path, not in the sense that they move us along it. An appropriate attitude to moral behavior means that one will not be bothered and so can get on with coming closer to what one takes to be one's ultimate aim, an intellectual grasp of reality, perhaps, and the ultimate happiness that success in this enterprise brings with it. The trouble with morality is that like human life it often does not provide us with clear answers or easy solutions. In one set of circumstances an action may seem right, yet in another not, and it is not obvious what accounts for this. This is not the language that philosophers and mystics like to use, they like certainty and clarity, and so it is not difficult to see the relative lack of interest in discussing ethics.

This might appear to be misleading since surely the highest level that people can reach is that of the "complete or perfect human being" (*insan kamil*). This is someone who integrates the divine attributes to constitute a perfect balance. We are representatives of God and it is our responsibility to represent as many of his qualities as we can. The perfect person is distinct morally from most people since, unlike them, he has discovered all of the divine attributes and integrated them within himself and his actions. In our experience of the moral world there are a variety of degrees of these attributes and sometimes they are balanced within the individual and sometimes they are not. Sometimes perhaps as we have seen they are balanced across a range of individuals. This world is the developing manifestation of God through these attributes as we seek to imitate Him, and we may achieve different types of balance at some points, and at others we are less successful in this direction.

The role of morality in spirituality

An important implication of this approach is that we cannot become virtuous through just trying to be good or helping people. Ethics has to be based on both our ability to act and also our knowledge of how to behave if it is to serve as part of a balanced lifestyle. The point is that all negative behavior, or all that is interpreted as evil (or sin) is merely imbalance, negative character traits characterizing a person. Spiritual and moral growth are then seen to advance hand in hand, as it were, and not in opposition to each other. The concepts or states (*ahwal*) such as *tawba* (repentance), *muhasaba* (self-discipline), and *sidq* (correctness) structure the major techniques through which Sufi notions of morality are grounded as embodied practical, emotional, and conceptual dispositions. These states are not expressed in completely personal terms, they need to be expressed in deeds and actions (*'amal*) in order to be recognized as legitimate grounds for Sufi identity. The necessity of establishing the reality of mystical states through deeds ranging from the performance of miracles to the practical enactment of *adab*, the cultural rules about how we should live, as some kind of moral performance is a recurrent theme in the Sufi tradition. Ibn al-'Arabi and al-Ghazali spend a lot of time talking about the importance of the ritual prayers in Islam and their deeper meaning, and it is clear that even if we grasp that deeper meaning we are not exempt from performing them along with everyone else. Adam was taught all the names and given a rank over the angels. This was not because we are better than them but because we are created in the divine form. Angels do not have any choice, they are always good and could not be anything else, but we can improve morally and come closer to God and vice versa.

The Prophet is said to possess an excellent character (68:4) and was sent as a mercy to all the world (21:107) because he incorporates the character traits of God, in so far as a human being can. As a result we are supposed to emulate him. In particular, he represents the mercy and love with which God approaches His creation and also the *tawhid* of everything in the universe, since these attitudes are linked with factors that balance them and make them perfect. So we seem to have a perfectly good working model of Sufi ethics. Morality is to be derived from ontology, the nature of being, which is, of course, something that cannot really be separated from God. We have to try to behave as well as we can to imitate the attributes of God, which means that in our moral thinking we are not only oriented toward each other but also to God. After all, it is from our attempts at getting some grasp of God that we can get some awareness of His attributes. One important way of doing this in Islam is, of course, to use the Qur'an and hadith as a source of information, and also to think about exemplars like the Prophet Muhammad and, for some Muslims, 'Ali and the imams who are regarded as *ma'sum* or infallible. We need guidance, as the Qur'an often tells us, and we may be guided both by it and by remarkable individuals like the prophets and the messengers and others. This is not a principle exclusive to Islam, many religions have the concept of a particularly gifted or noble individual to whom we should look for advice on how to live and think. The traditions in Islam, the hadith literature, are basically premised on the idea that the sayings and practices of some people are worth emulating and that is very much the theme of Sufism also. The Sufi has a guide and the guide is the person to be followed and copied, without his assistance there is no prospect of spiritual growth. It is worth emphasizing again the significance of balance here, since the idea of following a guide and an exemplar is very much part and parcel of doing things like thinking about how far our behavior fits the model we are following, how sure we are that we are not going too far or not going far enough to get it right.

The role of the exemplar

However divine the law may be, it has to be used and interpreted in everyday life, and the concept of moderation is useful in explaining how this is to be done. Moderation can be linked with the idea of considering the consequences of what might happen if a particular decision is taken since it involves considering a wide range of examples that might be relevant in deciding what to do in such a case. It is opposed to the idea of just sticking to a formula and following it. Here we again find the idea that Qur'anic ethics is predominantly utilitarian, it is the consequences that are important and might be used to moderate the application of the moral rule. We do this all the time, someone is on their way to fulfill an obligation and something happens so they cannot do it, perhaps help is required for a person who suddenly falls sick in the street. The idea that because one had promised to meet a friend for a cup of coffee then nothing else could intervene is ridiculous. Promises are important but we need to balance the different commitments we have in life, and in this case the promise would turn out to be thoroughly breakable.

There are a variety ways of decision-making in ethics, one that relies on absolute principles and one dependent on the consequences of action. Another relies on the virtues and how they are to be adapted to action, and the effects that action has on them. The argument in this book is that all are involved and that Islam suggests this by its emphasis on moderation and through the whole hermeneutic process of considering a wide range of sources of authority. Nowhere is this more important than in issues to do with conflict since here the passions of the participants are often raised to such a level that their capacity for calmly and properly assessing the situation before them is diminished. Is the idea of an exemplar just such a simple formula that we should try to avoid? It certainly is true that people often put their trust in unsatisfactory people and as a consequence are misled or exploited. It is also true that there are aspects of even the best people that might not be suitable for us to copy. We are all fallible human beings and likely to go awry. It is not like following someone who has a specialized skill when we need to know how to act. There are no moral experts. The problem with the idea that ontology leads to morality is that the idea of moral experts seems plausible, since these are the people who are the best guides to incorporating the divine qualities in the right sort of way. Then there is only one way of getting it right, and that seems to make sense also, presumably the way that God knows is the right way is just the right way to behave. This is what it takes Musa a long time to understand in his journey with Khidr as described in the Qur'an.

The right way incorporates both the positive moral traits and also the rather darker ones such as *al-darr*, the distressor, as we are told: "If God touches you with adversity, only He can remove it" (6:17). Most of the divine names are positive but some are not and refer to divine power and to the use of that power to establish justice, which is itself, of course, one of God's names. This accounts for the fact that thinkers like al-Ghazali who are seeking to strengthen their ability to feel gratitude toward God sometimes concentrate on the negative aspects of life, with the view to reflecting on the fact that those things are not happening to them, at that moment at least, and this is something for which we should feel gratitude. It might be said that it is a shame that there are people in prison or poor or unfortunate in some way for this sort of reflection to work, given that God might have sought to relieve their problems. We have to believe that God knows and we do not know why these things are happening. But here we have a problem, like that represented by the panhandler approaching us on the street. Does he deserve our charity? Are his problems his own fault, and so God allows them to continue? Or are they undeserved and so his sufferings are a test, for him and/or for us, or for some other reason. We just don't know and we might think that in that case we need to help him, just in case he deserves that help. Were we to think that because things are going badly for him God is not helping him and it is his fault that he is in that position we miss the opportunity to exercise charity, a key demand of the Qur'an. In any case, how could we know? Musa did not know in his journey with Khidr, and if he did not know, what chance have we to find out, at least in this life?

The important thing is to get away from the idea that the moral point of view we should adopt follows from ontology, from the nature of things, despite what Ibn al-'Arabi suggests. It is obviously false since we can understand the situation where two conscientious agents, nonetheless, disagree on the course of action they should follow in a particular situation. We have emphasized this point when we considered, and rejected, the idea of an Islamic bioethics, or an Islamic business ethics, or any other sort of religious ethical system. The idea of a guide is not the idea of someone pointing us in the right direction, but rather someone pointing us in the right direction to think about where the right direction might be situated. This offends against the idea of religion as a simple code to explain how to live and think and we need only follow it to achieve a reasonable chance of salvation. It is that for many religious believers, those whom al-Ghazali describes as concentrating on the fear of God and its consequences. For those who are more motivated by the love of God, and who have a more sophisticated idea of how to relate to Him, the code is more complex. We do know how we are supposed to act in many cases, but in some we need to work this out ourselves, not without assistance, of course, in the sacred literature and from those who interpret it, yet how we approach it will still need to come from us. It is more than solving an intellectual problem, the solution will have to feel right and not just be something formal and automatic. This is important since it represents a stage on the path of spiritual development and so we need to use it to help us get somewhere else.

This brings us back to the role of the exemplar as someone who shows us how to be good. As so often, balance is important here in showing us how to move from principles to practice, and balance is constantly emphasized in the Qur'an. There is a tendency to think of exemplars as people like saints but there is room for heroes also, people who just seem to be nice and ordinary. People critical of Islam often criticize the Prophet Muhammad for having so many wives and being a fighter, but those defending him would highlight his ability to live a full and virtuous life despite his commitments to a wider cause. The fact that Muslims try to emulate him brings out something important in religious life, not that we need to be slavish followers of great leaders, but that in order to be virtuous we often have to try to follow others. As has often been noted, charisma is important in religion, and a great leader or exemplar can attract people to him in ways that are difficult to explain. The soccer player Mo Salah who plays for Liverpool has had such an effect in Liverpool, in a city with a small but growing Muslim presence, that he has managed to transform a largely negative image of Islam. He seems to be a nice guy, he finances various charitable enterprises in his native Egypt and he is an efficient goal scorer, but he is by no means the only Muslim player for his team, or for English teams as a whole. There are many Muslim players in the Premier League in England, coming from all over the world, and many of them might be as or even more devout and charitable than Salah, but for some reason he has struck a nerve. One reason might be that he seems to be very modest about his achievements and restrained in his attitude to others, emphasizing not his abilities but how he plays as part of a team and enjoys success only because others assist and cooperate with him. As an exemplar he is making very useful points here about morality, of course; it is a largely social activity and requires us to think constantly about our relationships with others. It is not just the application of general principles to our lives.

One of the useful achievements of Sufism to the understanding of morality is its emphasis on the role of the guide or exemplar. As with our relationship to God, this can be seen as objectionable and as something that makes us like slaves or servants. If the way we follow someone is uncritical, then it might look as though we are behaving in a servile manner. It does not have to be like that though since it can be seen as working out ways of embodying principles in practice, in similar ways to that of the exemplar. A problem with abstract principles is knowing how to apply them to the world of human behavior, and the exemplar suggests a way. The exemplar can be another human being, or even God, and religions like Islam are useful in helping us work out how to balance our practical lives with the moral principles we try to follow.

Bibliography

Campanini, Massimo (2018), *Al-Ghazali and the Divine*, London: Routledge.
Chittick, W. (1983), *The Sufi Path of Love: The Spiritual Teachings of Rumi*, Albany: State University of New York Press.
Edwards, Nina (2018), *Darkness: A Cultural History*, London: Reaktion Books.
Al-Ghazali (1957), *Ihya' 'ulum al-din* [Revival of the Religious Sciences], Cairo: Dar Ihya' al-kutub al-'arabiya.
Leaman, Oliver (1999), "Nursi's place in the Ihya' tradition," *Muslim World* 89/3–4: 314–24.

Leaman, Oliver (2013), *Controversies in Contemporary Islam*, London: Routledge.
Leaman, Oliver (2016), *The Qur'an: A Philosophical Guide*, London: Bloomsbury.
Rumi (1961), *The Discourses of Rumi*, trans. A. J. Arberry, London: John Murray.
Rumi (1982), *The Mathnawi of Jalaluddin Rumi*, trans. R. A. Nicholson, London: Luzac.

9

Principles

Being faithful to God, turning away from everything that is false, if anyone assigns partners to God is like someone who is hurtling down from the sky and has been snatched up by birds, or the wind blows him away into a distant place. (22:31)

It has been argued throughout this discussion that there is a persistent difficulty in Islamic ethics in reconciling *maslaha* or welfare and the *maqasid al-shariʿa*, the aims of the law. This is surprising since one of the reasons for the law is supposed to be its contribution to our welfare. It is a familiar process in Islamic law to not only look at the detail of the law but also the principles which the law is trying to establish, since that provides the court and others with guidelines as to how far they should go in their application of the letter of the law. After all, the law is there for a purpose and once we understand the purpose we know how to apply it in difficult cases, or even how to change it to make it adapt to new conditions. In many ways the purpose of something is what it means, and if the law is there to do something, and it is not, or if it could be done in some other way, this gives scope to us to change things around. For example, Islam prioritizes human life and is not keen on the idea of people killing either themselves or others. Such life and death decisions should be left to God. On the other hand, there are conditions of conflict or illness where it looks like human life could be expended, and here we need to look at what the point of the principle in question is. There is no blanket ban on taking life in Islam; there are conditions in which it is acceptable, and so we need to think about what principles are at stake here. Many religious thinkers are profoundly dishonest in their presentation of their faith on such issues. They quote a passage or two from their sacred books to show how nice their religion is and ignore all the other passages that take an entirely different and perhaps much harsher line. Even the "nice" quotations do very little to show how we ought to behave. They are very general expressions of opinion on something, so general that they seem to describe nothing useful at all, despite their author being God.

It seems unhelpful to talk about the sanctity of human life when someone is dying and in considerable pain and discomfort from which there is no tolerable respite, although we often do. For such people there is nothing in their future except more unpleasant events, and clearly they are getting nothing out of being alive except suffering and perhaps also a profound embarrassment that others are viewing them in this condition and need to attend to them. Some secular legislatures have concluded that in such a situation people are entitled to end their lives earlier than would otherwise be the case, with appropriate safeguards, of course, to ensure this was really their decision, and a reasonable decision. This is problematic for some religions, including Islam, for whom the time of death should be left to God and His decision not preempted. What are the *maqasid al-shari'a* here? Sanctity of life is one obviously, but suppose this clashes with other desirable aims such as human dignity, individual autonomy, and so on? It might be that the overriding aim of the law here is really balance, achieving an acceptable balance between all these conflicting norms, and this quite accurately represents the thinking of most people who are in this sort of difficult situation, either personally or where someone close to them is suffering. Even if we agree on one aim of the law, there are others often going in different directions.

The role of the principles of law

In such a thought process how far are the aims of the law helpful? This might seem a ridiculous question since they might seem to serve rather like the axioms of our legal and moral system. These are the principles, we often say, of our religion, and everything else stems from them. In cases of doubt we can refer back to the principles and be guided appropriately. We can, of course, identify pillars of Islam and the very general ideas that occur throughout the Qur'an, but it is difficult to argue that these lead to firm principles of conduct. To take an example, there are practices which many Muslim legal authorities do not favor, such as mixed dancing, tattoos, some kinds of pictorial art, music, and so on, but which are not clearly condemned in the main sources of law. These might be regarded as encouraging *shirk*, idolatry, in one form or another, or they could be associated with secularity and regarded as the thin end of the wedge in establishing what is appropriate behavior for Muslims. Modesty is a desirable aim, we are told, and any activity that threatens it is questionable. What are the *maslaha* implications of modesty, however, and how does it lead to welfare? We might say it helps with preserving dignity, for example, but in many circumstances this seems implausible. For example, it does not seem to be directed at welfare when people, mainly women, in very hot weather are obliged to wear a lot of clothes. Many people enjoy sunning themselves, if they can, and we are told that it is good for us to do so, in moderation. On the other hand, if the aims of the law are doing what God wants, and we assume that as the Qur'an tells us, He knows and we do not, then preserving modesty is in our interests, but we do not have to understand why. It is enough that God tells us to act in a particular way. Even if the purpose is not obvious in this world, or realized in this world, it will have a result in the next world, and in fact the difficulties in preserving modesty in this world only adds to the merit of acting in accordance with the law. For such behavior our reward is eventually available in the next world. Or so we should hope since, of course, we do not know how we will end up, the final decision is up to God. There are instances when modesty as traditionally interpreted may stand in the way of something else important, a particularly virtuous political or military end, for instance, and in such circumstances both the *maqasid* and *maslaha* seem to suggest we should suspend the rule and seek to attain the desirable end. When normal conditions resume we can go back to the rule.

This is how the argument has gone to permit certain sorts of behavior which would in themselves be immodest, but given the political purpose they are done for, they become acceptable. As we saw in the discussion of conflict, there is a well-known conversation in a prison in the Islamic Republic of Iran when a prisoner questioned the acceptability of the torture and other horrible methods of dealing with opposition, real or imaginary. Torture and killing were common occurrences in Iran both before and after the Islamic revolution, and as is the case with many revolutions, their supporters end up being persecuted and are shocked at what is happening. Is Islam in favor of torture? Of course not, but the answer was that in a *fatwa* Ayatollah Khomayni, the founder of the Islamic revolution, had said that the most important thing was the preservation of the Islamic Republic (Iran Human Rights, Momeni). The implication is that any measures at all serving this end are acceptable. They are what God would want his representatives on earth to do. This is a very good example of the *maqasid* doctrine. The specific nature of the actions themselves drop out and the only really relevant moral factors here are the ends of the action. One might think that moral agents would immediately reject torture because they would think it is wrong whatever advantages might accrue from it. To take another example, modesty is important but when it interferes with the aims of the *umma* (community), it becomes secondary and variable since other things are more important. If I agree to meet someone for tea at a certain time and place and am prevented from doing so because someone else suddenly required my assistance, no reasonable person would reject that as an excuse. The stronger obligation came into play at the expense of the weaker. I should still feel guilty at missing my appointment, though, as that obligation does not disappear. It is wrong to agree to do something and then not do it. In the case of torture, it is possible that the torturer feels genuine remorse at what he has to do to preserve the state, but from what we hear of such cases this is unlikely. They seem to set about their grisly work with enthusiasm and skill, and are rewarded accordingly, and any regret they may feel at what they do is well hidden. We are often encouraged to display flexibility in morality and yet is everything up for change in the appropriate circumstances? If it is we may have to accept the concept of the virtuous torturer and we might want to suggest that whatever the consequences, torture cannot be acceptable morally. This might seem an extreme example, and of course it is, but there are many rules and regulations of religion that could be suspended in favor of some broader purpose, perhaps most of them on occasion, and the scope for self-deception here is, of course, considerable. I would like to obey the law, one says, but on this particular occasion, as I "reluctantly" uncork another bottle of wine, to do so would be to go against the principles of the law, so I will have to desist.

Another problem with using *maslaha* and *maqasid* as major ethical principles is the logical issue of their status. Are they themselves ethical principles or rather, like balance, second-order principles designed to help organize rules in ethics? The duty to be modest is an ethical principle, well-articulated in the Qur'an and the hadith, and its rationale is grounded, no doubt, in both the *maslaha* and the *maqasid*. There are extreme cases where these second-order principles will justify a radical variation in the rules of modesty, perhaps where life itself is at risk. But for the general round of questions to do with the ethical application of the rules of modesty such dramatic examples are irrelevant. The tradition itself, including the particular legal school of which one is a member, responds to those sorts of questions. Treating *maslaha* and *maqasid* as just ethical principles along with others is to convert all Islamic ethical reasoning into a form of consequentialism. It is quite clear from the Qur'an, though, that many ethical principles are taken to be absolute and not to be abandoned when they become inconvenient. Second-order principles show us in general how the ethical rules themselves are supposed to operate, and do not enter directly into the moral calculus. Once they do they damage the integrity of the Islamic moral system since everything then becomes instrumental and relative to the general rules themselves. That is how we end up with torture chambers in what calls itself an Islamic state.

Legal terms tend to be used in relation to the particular *madhhab*, school of law, that an individual or group adhere to, and within Sunni Islam the competing *madhahib* (schools of law) are treated with respect, and their potential rulings discussed also. The meaning of those terms is derived from that context, and not from the *maqasid*. For example, some Muslim legal thinkers disapprove of music, while others accept some music but not other types, and the grounds for this are not difficult to discover. Music influences the emotions and can turn people away from appropriate religious attitudes, and the occasions in which music is played may encourage loose behavior and dress and, on the whole, orient participants away from *taqwa* or piety.

Yet the Prophet himself is said to have supported the idea of certain kinds of celebration and perhaps music was part of them, and if he approved of the music of his time, perhaps he would approve of music in general, provided it was being used to encourage people to behave well (Leaman 2013: 195–98). This does not mean that music must have such a direct purpose, it could also be an aspect of our lives where we relax and think about a whole variety of things and experience emotions and this in itself is a useful function like eating and sleeping and he expects us to do this sort of thing as part of a balanced life style. It could also be that music has an important political role to play in bringing like-minded people together and inspiring them to do things that are, on the whole, valuable, so there is obviously a continuum of views here in the legal tradition. On the other hand, similar things could be said about pubs and pop concerts. The question is how they relate to the principles of the law. What anchors judgments on this topic are the particular ways of working of the individual schools of law, not the general principles, which are surely shared by all the schools and Shi'a law also.

The attraction of general principles

The temptation in using *maqasid* is that it puts the (generally male) legal thinker in much more control of his material. The traditional view within a particular school may take one form but all one needs to do to transform the judgment is apply to the *maqasid* and one is liberated from those constraints. This is very helpful when political considerations mean that a certain judgment is required, perhaps at odds with a previous ruling. The principles of the law can suddenly be found to validate a different approach and the appropriate ruling is made. This has the advantage of allowing law to change to take account of other changes, and that is obviously a good thing. On the other hand, the principles of Islam do not change, so the only way to use them to countenance other changes is to reinterpret them. There is nothing wrong with that, but to argue that the *maqasid* are the ultimate rationale for such change is problematic. They are so broad that almost anything can be described as fitting in with them, like *maslaha*. Does music contribute to our welfare? Many would say it does but others would disagree and yet would allow it if it was used for a purpose that eventually is likely to improve welfare. Here we would need to ask is this the welfare of everyone, the welfare of those who deserve an increase in it, the welfare of the *umma* as a whole or what. These are familiar issues in moral philosophy and they suggest that using some principle like welfare to justify legal decisions is not as simple as it might seem. On the contrary, there is the danger that it might look as though all one has to do when wanting to legitimize something is appeal to the *maqasid* and suddenly all is well. It used to be cynically remarked in Egypt that the Grand Mufti of al-Azhar always produced *fatawa* (legal judgments) in accordance with the views of the current government. Often these refer to *maqasid*. It is not an indication of rigor in any system of law or anything else if legal argument can suddenly be derailed in this manner. Characterizing an Islamic legal path through using notions like *maslaha* and *darura* is to put the carriage before the horse and is unlikely to be helpful.

Some legal thinkers stress the significance of *ijtihad* or independent legal judgment, especially those within the Shi'a tradition. It is the role of the legal authority to use independent judgment, based obviously on appropriate texts, to examine an issue and think about how to resolve it. Change is often necessary since the material world changes and we need to work out how to adapt divine law to those changes. The assumption is, of course, that such law remains valid for all time, and yet we have to work out precisely what implications it has for practice in new situations. To take an example, most understandings of Islam and the Qur'an regard interest as forbidden, and yet even Islamic banks operate in a financial world in which there are institutions that provide interest on deposits. When the funds of Islamic banks are moved out of the Islamic sector they could be placed in accounts that bear no interest, and one might think that would be the obvious move to make to ensure the Islamic nature of the banking operation. On the other hand, that would mean that the funds of those using the sector would grow at a slower rate than those funds that are in other sectors, and disadvantage Islamic bank users. It has sometimes been argued that provided the interest is not actually levied by the Islamic bank itself, it is acceptable. It is not like the case where the bank offers profit-sharing in place of interest and the profit-sharing rate is less than the interest would be, which is sometimes called the "piety premium" that is paid to keep investments in line with Islam. Here the difference between the two rates can go in either direction, of course. Also, we often have the choice between doing the right thing and the reverse, and the latter might be in our interests, but we can persevere and do the right thing regardless, since that is where we believe our duty takes us. If the Islamic bank participates in the world financial system, as it must in order to offer its clients a comprehensive service, then it needs to act as any other bank would, since presumably if it did not it would come under regulatory investigation. It is a bit like a cab driver who picks up any fare, sometimes they might be carrying alcohol, or they might be wearing clothes which the driver disapproves on religious grounds, but he or she is just providing a service and has to take anyone who wishes to ride in the cab. In some countries the cab rank principle is cited when a lawyer takes on the next client to require representation, it does not mean that the lawyer agrees with the client or thinks the client is innocent or even pleasant, a job is being done and everyone deserves assistance if one is in the business of providing it.

This might seem to be disingenuous. If there are religious objections in Islam to interest, should Muslims participate in an economy based on interest? After all, society has all sorts of features with which religious people disagree and they manage, on the whole, to separate themselves from those if they can. It is possible not to have a television, for example, even though television is ubiquitous in modern Western societies. It is possible not to explore the raunchier reaches of the internet, or even to listen to music. If one is walking down the road and hears music blaring from the radio of a passing car, that is probably acceptable, but if you go somewhere because you hope to hear such forbidden music, and yet think it is immoral, that is problematic. Is the Islamic bank using interest more of the former or the latter? Do they have the status of someone doing something forbidden because it is part of something else they are doing that is acceptable? Or are they doing something forbidden because they really want to do it, but are too ashamed to admit it? The use of interest is not casual or accidental, so it is not like the former case. The deposits do not wander around and end up haphazardly in interest-bearing vehicles. The bank chooses to place the money there. On the other hand, the bank would prefer not to have to do this, and they do not do it because they enjoy it, as in the latter example. The bank thinks it has to do this in order to stay in business, it has to offer a full service in a world where most banking is not Islamic, although its own products are certified halal by religious authorities and so in a sense escape the contagion of interest. Even if all the banks in a country are Islamic and there are no alternatives, the fact that those institutions play a role in a world of non-Islamic finance as well, since money moves around the world, leads to contamination issues. Despite the financial instruments called Islamic being structured in a distinct way, it is uncanny how close the rate of return is on such products with the general interest rates that prevail at the same time. It looks very much as though there is a fairly universal rate of return on money at a particular time and place and however the product is structured, it is going to be the leading indicator of what the *rentier* community receives.

This might seem to be an issue limited to finance, and finance is, of course, famously global. We are told quite rightly how large the Islamic financial sector is becoming, and yet we are not told how well integrated it is in the ordinary way of banking, with the inevitable problems this causes for its purity as a sector obeying what God is taken to have demanded of us. It is worth restating again that the Qur'an is not a guide for Muslims alone but for everyone, and if people use interest in their affairs they go awry, in the words of the Book, all people, not just a specific group. Although we are told that God created us in different ways and we live in different communities, it is not obvious that this is a state of affairs expected to persist, or just the starting position from which we should move to more doctrinal unity and agreement. We are also told that God chose Islam as the best religion (5:3) and so why would He want people to go through their lives with an inferior religion? Although we are often told that one of the *maqasid* is this commitment to diversity, this seems improbable. Interest is fine for some people, that would suggest, and not for others, so do whatever you feel like, is not a principle of Islamic law. Does that mean that people should be forced to behave in a certain way and forbidden from doing things that go against (what is taken to be) Islam? Should this apply to all people or just to Muslims, or to no one at all? After all, we are told that there is no compulsion in religion (2:256), and that makes it look like everyone should just do what they think is right according to their religious principles. Even in secular societies we do not operate like that, though, we do not allow behavior we regard as immoral just because a religion approves of it. On the contrary, particular practices sanctioned by religion are made illegal in many cases, even though no doubt they have sincere supporters from within some faith group. Of course, perhaps Islam is more liberal than that and would allow anyone to do anything that some religious group advocated, but it seems unlikely this is what the Qur'an is suggesting. Progressives often quote those passages that appear to celebrate diversity as among the *maqasid* which should be used as the basis of a more liberal interpretation of legal rules, but this really does not make any sense at all. It is this picking and choosing passages and prioritizing some and downplaying others that gives religion such a bad name intellectually.

Islamic principles and Islamic society

It is often said that the apparent harshness of the *hudud* punishments in Islamic law is mitigated by the fact that they are really only to be implemented in an Islamic society, and we are far from such an environment so far anywhere in the world. If there was a society which operated on the principles of Islam, so there was a genuine commitment to sharing wealth, to respecting each other and preserving modesty, where people on the whole behaved in accordance with piety and generosity, then those who had other ideas and did not wish to participate in the general harmony of society should be treated roughly. They should be tried carefully through the legal process, of course, but if found guilty, the punishments can be quite extreme. Given the general utilitarian flavor of Islamic ethics, one can see why, since such treatment of a few malefactors may lead to much greater welfare in general. As we know from the countries that call themselves Islamic today this state of affairs does not in any way exist. Corruption and inequality are rife, and social harmony, where it exists at all, rests on the power of the state to impose its authority on a cowed citizenry.

One of the few advantages of the *maqasid* language, though, is to help us think about the general principles that an Islamic community should be based upon that would allow us to call it an Islamic community. Here there would be frequent differences of opinion, yet on some criteria the situation is quite clear, and one of them is morality. Are people good? Not everyone of course, but are most people virtuous in their behavior? Do they tell the truth, are they charitable, do they respect others? One of the points of law is to encourage such behavior, using both sanctions and rewards, but essentially by trying to enshrine values in our culture. If we behave well we will all benefit, we are told, both in this world and the next, while the reverse is true of poor behavior. One good way of checking on how Islamic a society is involves looking at its moral practices, not its rules about bank interest or personal appearance. On these criteria it is clear that no states are Islamic, but some societies probably are. These smaller groups of people encourage each other to behave well and, on the whole, succeed, and within that context are very successful in bringing up children and supporting families. Some of these groups are Muslim but some are not, and it is not clear how religion contributes, if at all, to the maintenance of such a state of affairs. The Qur'an hints at this when it suggests that different communities compete with each other in good works, it is almost as though it were agreeing with John Stuart Mill that we need varying experiments in living to discover the very best way. This is obviously not the case, the Qur'an has no doubt that its way is the best, yet, it is modest enough to challenge others to see if Islamic standards of morality can be shown to be inferior to others. It is a bit like someone who is the fastest runner challenging others to beat him, he knows he is going to win but is prepared to see if he is right. Better, he is ready to show others that he is right and has no objection to their competing and losing. Then if they are rational they will acknowledge him as superior, and if we are rational and find that our attempts at being good are less effective or productive than the Islamic system, we should acknowledge Islam as representing the better approach to being good.

How the Qur'an talks about ethics

The Qur'an often expresses itself in this sort of way, it does not insist on our accepting what it says but calls for calm and rational consideration of its main points, a weighing of the evidence and a conclusion which agrees with its claims. This is a bold strategy and is not clear how it would work for morality. The evidence right now is that Muslims do not lead better lives than those of other religious communities or those without any religious affiliation. This is where, of course, we do not include the ritual duties incumbent on Muslims, where obviously they are well in advance of others. The *maqasid al-shari'a* approach is particularly unhelpful here. Islamic finance is supposed to be based on the aim of improving society and doing good, yet how does the careful management of the funds of the very rich do this? It might in that if some people have a lot of money then, they can be charitable with it, and the more money they retain, the more charitable they can be, but that is not much of an argument unless it can be shown that Muslims are more charitable than others, and moreover they are more charitable because they are Muslims. No doubt many Muslims are charitable, it is after all a pillar or one of the principles of Islam, yet so are many other people, Muslim or otherwise. Do Muslims lie less than other people, or steal or cheat less? That does not seem to be the case.

These comments are not criticisms of the passage in the Qur'an calling for competition (5:48), it is a criticism of the idea that the competition has been settled. Perhaps we should apply the same argument to the challenge to create a book like the Qur'an. This is supposed to be another test of the veracity and value of the Book, it could only have been produced by a divine author if no human being could produce anything like it. A lot of energy and ink has been spent on proving the miraculous nature of the Book and since miracles require a deity, its supernatural origins. The Qur'an sets us the challenge of showing that it could have been produced in any other way, in just the way that it sets the challenge of seeing if another community could be as good as the Islamic community. This is a challenge which points to the future and to the desirability of establishing a community that could live up to the challenge, and perhaps the same could be said of the *i'jaz al-Qur'an* doctrine. It is not so much as showing that now we have evidence that it is miraculous, it is more that we are going to use it in such a way that its miraculous nature will emerge. This is not just a matter of its style but also of how we use that style and context to make our lives better, more authentic, and generally benevolent. That could be the *tahaddi* or challenge. It does not only look back to how the Qur'an was created but also forward, to how it is implemented. If a society were to emerge in which morality thrived and piety overcame the desire for personal advantage, then we might have evidence of the divine nature of the message on which that society was based. The challenge to Muslims is to produce such a society. Right now there is no evidence that it has been done or even approached.

Is there any evidence that Qur'anic verses point to the future in this sort of way? For example, we are told that "God has promised to those of you who believe and do good that He will certainly make them rulers in the earth as He made rulers those before them, and He will certainly establish for them their religion which He chose for them, and He will certainly replace their fear with security" (24:55). Yet this is obviously not true for many occasions, where the status of Islam is far from established and believers are justified in feeling nervous about their personal safety. They will, of course, be confident that what is happening is something that God is controlling so that it has a purpose and that nothing happens without His willing it (9:51). In the end everything will end up in the right way. We are told at 5:66. "And if only they had acted according to the Torah, the Injil, and what was sent down to them from their Lord, they would surely have attained happiness from every side." If things are not working out well, then we only have ourselves to blame, although we might wonder what role God plays in directing us to obedience or otherwise. The Qur'an mentions the promise that God has multiplied His people throughout the earth and will eventually gather them together and wonders when this will happen (67:24-25), and the answer is "'Say', as to the knowledge of the time, it is with God alone"

(67:26). The whole concept of judgment and the next world refers to the future and so much of the Qur'an is concerned with those ideas. We have the opportunity to change throughout our lives and we can repent the bad decisions we may have made. When our behavior is assessed at the end of our lives we get the notion of a time span and taking the future seriously. The concept of character is in itself time-based, since it is something that changes and develops over time. Religions are rather good at pointing out the ways that we can gradually change to make ourselves better people, and often rituals are designed to make this easier or even possible in the first place. Rituals can be boring and repetitive, and this instils patience in us, and they can bring us together with other people, useful for humility, and they can regulate our material lives, which helps us think of higher things. We often think of someone adopting a religion at a certain stage, such as when they convert, for example, yet we should perhaps think of it more like passing a driving test. Passing the test means someone is now a person able to drive legally but does not mean that they are good drivers, for that they need practice and experience. It is just the start of their lives as drivers. Similarly, being in a religion is not a one-off event for most of us, it is a stage along which we need to pass to other stages. Religions do not then just talk of the past and present but also of the future, and many of the *ayat* in the Qur'an can be read from such a perspective.

Al-Shatibi suggests: "The rules of the shari'a have been designed to produce goods *(masalih)* and remove evil *(mafasid)* and these are certainly their ends and objects. And the *masalih* are those which promote the preservation and fulfillment of human life, and the realization of all that the human nature, animal and rational demands, till one is happy in every aspect" (al-Shatibi 2005: 195). It is worth pointing out that it is not only broad moral principles that can try to be the basis of explaining why we do things. Custom (*'urf*) can be seen not just as what people do but also as the collective wisdom of a community. A lot of what became Islamic law started off as Arab custom, some of which was certainly condemned and replaced, but much of which survived and came to be endorsed by Islam. This leads to thinkers like Liyakat claiming that "using concepts like *'urf* and *sirah 'uqala'iyyah* (what rationally minded people deem to be proper) will also lead to newer considerations ... such revisions should not be seen as repugnant or violating rational and moral norms as conceived by reasonable people" (2018: 168). The idea is that reasonable people will agree on what we ought to do when a range of hard cases arise and we then just change what we take to be how we should behave despite the existing law. There is a feeling here that what we often regard as acceptable from a religious point of view is based on custom and not on law, and different situations call for different customs. This attitude runs through the *maqasid* literature, everything changes and the rules we have may no longer be relevant, and so they need to change. The trouble is that this makes it look as though anything goes. We escape this by using the idea of *maqasid* to control the scope of acceptable change, provided the new *'urf* fits in with the general principles that underlie Islam. A problem with this view is that it seems to assume that everything in religion is assessable in terms of welfare.

We need to think about the significance of balance again. Ethics involves balance between the use of principles and experience. On one side we have abstract ideas and general, concepts, while on the other hand we have facts, and this is the case for all religions. They have a sacred book, often, with a range of general ideas and instructions, along with some historical information. Then they also use more facts, in Islam taken from the hadith, from the *sira* of the Prophet, and so on. Judgment involves balancing the general ideas with the facts. The *maqasid* idea is that the basic rules of morality do not change but the facts might, not the religious reports from the past, of course, but modern scientific developments often mean that we consider changing what we allow and disallow. For example, it is often thought that a fetus is provided with its soul at a stage of its development in the body of its mother, and that before then abortion is not so much of a problem, since the fetus has not become a person before that stage. It might be that we shall decide that the physical constituents that make a fetus unique occur much earlier, or later, and this could change how we see abortion and when it can take place, if at all. The general principles on the importance of life would not have changed, but when we apply them would. A problem with this suggestion though is that the principle is so general it really fails to get a grip on the data it is supposed to be describing. To say that life is valuable is really to say very little about what we should actually do. Even those religions that proscribe killing under any circumstances, like Jainism and some varieties of Buddhism and Hinduism, allow for cases where innocent people are in danger, or cases of need. Gandhi gave the example of a tiger breaking into the cowshed in a village, or a rabid dog approaching children. In such cases is it right to do nothing? How to work out an answer is to think about linking the general principle with the facts of the case and finding a solution that seems to work with both. That makes it sound like a very rough and ready process, but it does have the merit of actually representing accurately how we do things, and perhaps how we should do them. Both the facts and the principles are important and we have to consider them together. This sometimes makes for difficult decisions, but then so do most things in life, and going for a mechanical solution in every case does not look tempting.

One of the themes of the Qur'an and other similar religious texts is that we do not know and God does, on many occasions. That means that we should not always expect to understand exactly what the situation requires, but should look to guidance and then follow it, wherever it leads. This sounds like conservative advice, we should then just follow the general principles and the traditional ways of understanding them, even if in a particular case we are unhappy with the consequences. That is not necessarily the case, though, on the contrary, it might be that we are tempted to continue to follow tradition and yet are led by new facts to do something different, albeit reluctantly. To take an example, a fund which purports to be Islamic would try to avoid a variety of problematic areas, like alcohol, for example, and would also not be involved in interest. Yet, some of the products it invests in might be heavily invested in those areas. Many stores sell alcohol and companies in general are involved in financing with interest-bearing bonds. A strict refusal to engage with such enterprises might preserve religious purity but would at the same time cut off the investor from leading businesses in the general economy. Many grocery stores sell alcohol, service stations and distribution companies are all involved with it, while hotels and restaurants generally supply it. To avoid all such enterprises would hugely restrict the scope of the investor, and it might be thought appropriate to put her funds in those sectors of the economy, while of course regretting the fact that so many people are apparently not obeying the divine injunction against alcohol consumption. Is this tacit acceptance of alcohol? Not really, it is open acceptance of a fact of life that for most people alcohol is part of their lives, and we should take that into account when we work out where to apply our funds. The principle of avoiding alcohol might be thought to lead to an avoidance of anything to do with it, were we to be guided just by the principle. Yet our experience of the world brings out the ubiquity of alcohol, the fact that its consumption is often without obvious negative effects on both those who drink and those who do not, and the need for us to invest wisely in areas of growth and profitability. That is not to say there is nothing wrong with it, just that we should avoid it but perhaps not all manifestations of it. Ideally, we could do the latter but in an interconnected world in which many people live with different ideas of how they should behave, we need to cope with this diversity, perhaps basing ourselves on the *aya* that is often quoted by those advocating pluralism, where God has made of us many communities and wants us to learn from each other.

The *maqasid* are designed to establish the limits of such learning. They express the basic values that cannot change but within that framework all kinds of change are possible. That at least is the theory and it has been challenged here. The framework turns out to be far too general and vague to do the work it is designed to accomplish. If we agree that the *maqasid* are there for our welfare, and that alcohol is contrary to our welfare, as God tells us in the Qur'an, this still does not tell us how far we can do business with people who use alcohol. Can we transport them in our cars? The various schools of Islamic law answer these questions for us, or rather for those adhering to the various different schools, but they do not pretend to extend to all Muslims, although all Muslims are supposed to respect their findings. The Qur'an suggests that the truth will out and the false will retreat: "Nay, We hurl truth against falsehood, and it knocks out its brain, and behold, falsehood doth perish! Ah! woe be to you for the things you ascribe" (21:18). There is also: "And say: 'Truth has arrived, and falsehood has perished: for falsehood is bound to perish'" (17:81). This optimism about truth and its role in our thinking is worth noting, and the Qur'an does seem to think that people can tell it is true just by reading or hearing it, and that they can continue to use it to make sense of their duties and ultimately, of course, their lives. There is nothing here about the principles behind it all, we are supposed to accept the details of the law as we have them and act on them. Often we just cannot tell what the ultimate reasons for them are, it is after all divine legislation, and we do our best to work out how to behave within the terms of the law and how we understand it. To give a secular example, when I do my taxes in the United States I give the information I have to the preparer and he or she uses their knowledge (and generally a computer) to work out my liabilities or otherwise at the end of each tax year. In the end I sign a document and if anything is wrong I know I am responsible, although I have no idea what is going on in the tax system, a fiendishly complicated system of rules. I suppose I could understand it if I was to spend a lot of time thinking about it, but I prefer not to do this, I leave it for someone to guide me. That is what religion does, it guides us and we often do not really understand why we are told to do what we do, but we do it. We believe the Book is true in the same way that we believe many other things are true, without knowing how they are true.

Believers sometimes say that the good thing about being religious is that we always know what we are supposed to be doing, since our religion tells us. This is far from the truth as we have seen throughout this book. Revealed books do give us lots of rules to follow but they leave a great deal open, and we have to use what we find in them and from other sources to work out how to behave. It has been argued that not only do we often not know what to do but we also do not know what the principles behind religious law are. Although this seems implausible, it accords well with the whole tenor at least of the Qur'an, where we are constantly being told that we do not know and God does. Given the nature of the difference between his creatures and the creator, this is hardly surprising. Any attempt at dealing with the concept of ethics in Islam should take this idea seriously, and few of them do. This book is modest proposal for returning to the Qur'an in trying to understand the nature of how we should think about morality and Islam. The idea that there could be such an area of expertise as "Islamic ethics" really offends the notions of humility and piety, it has been argued throughout, and we need to start again if we are to discuss the role of ethics in Islam. This is not a very satisfying conclusion, since it is always agreeable to derive a clear solution to a problem set by a text, but it is a conclusion that the tenor of the Qur'an suggests. In the end the issue is about how far we expect sacred books to provide us with answers to moral issues as opposed to how far they help us pose questions and supply us with ideas to help deal with those questions. It is this more hesitant approach to religious ethics that has been advocated here and often also in the Qur'an.

Bibliography

Auda, Jasser (2008), *Maqasid al-shari'a as Philosophy of Islamic Law: A Systems Approach*, Herndon, VA: IIIT.

Bälz, Kilian (2008), *Shari'a Risk? How Islamic Finance Has Transformed Islamic Contract Law*, Cambridge, MA: Harvard Law School Islamic Legal Studies Program.

Al-Buti, Ramadan M. Sa'id (2001), *Dawabit al-maslahah* [The Rules of Welfare], Damascus: Waqf al-Risala.

Campanini, Massimo (2016), *Philosophical Perspectives on Modern Qur'anic Exegesis: Key Paradigms and Concepts*, Sheffield: Equinox.

Esposito, John, and Delong-Bas, Natana (2018), *Shariah: What Everyone Needs to Know*, New York: Oxford University Press.

Fadel, Mohammed (2008), "The true, the good and the reasonable: The theological and ethical roots of public reason in Islamic law," *Canadian Journal of Law and Jurisprudence* 21/1: 5–69.

Gleave, Robin (2013), *Islam and Literalism: Literal Meaning and Interpretation in Islamic Legal Theory*, Edinburgh: Edinburgh University Press.

Iran Human Rights. Available at: http://www.iranhrdc.org/english/publications/reports/3158-deadly-fatwa-iran-s-1988-prison-massacre.html

Khan, L. Ali, and Ramadan, Hisham (2011), *Contemporary Ijtihad: Limits and Controversy*, Edinburgh: Edinburgh University Press.

Leaman, Oliver (2013), *Controversies in Contemporary Islam*, London: Routledge.

Momeni Momeni. Available at: http://www.iranhumanrights.org/2010/09/letter-momeni-khamanei

al-Qahtani, M. bin 'Ali (2015), *Understanding maqasid al-shari'a*, Herndon, VA: International Institute of Islamic Theory.

Shabana, Ayman (2010), *Custom in Islamic Law and Legal Theory: The Development of the Concepts of 'Urf and 'Adah in the Islamic Legal Tradition*, New York: Palgrave.

al-Shatibi, A. S. Abu Ishaq (2005), *al-Muwafaqat fi usul al-shari'a* [The Reconciliation of the Principles of Islamic Law], ed. 'Abdullah al-Darraz, Cairo: Dar al Kutub al 'Ilmiyya, vol. 1: 195.

Takim, Liyakat (2018), "The role of custom in shaping Islamic law," in 168 *Proceedings of the Second Annual International Conference on Shi'i Studies*, 2016. London: ICAS Press: 157–69.

INDEX

'abd 9
abortion 75, 78–9, 81, 196
Abraham 111
Abrahamic 8, 43, 98, 106, 111, 144, 147
abrogation 31, 99, 117
adab 95, 100, 108, 162, 167, 178
Adam 49, 102, 120, 171–2, 176, 179
adoption 76
afterlife 17, 27, 85–6, 173
akhlaq 1, 95–6
AKP 93
Alagha, J. 30–1
al-Albani 93
alcohol 31, 47–8, 51–2, 57–8, 62, 190, 197
'alim 33
Allam 28–9
'Amr b. Hisham 35
angel 6, 39, 74, 75, 77, 78, 102, 119–20, 141, 145, 146, 152, 171, 172, 175, 176, 179
apostasy 44, 106
'aqida 33, 73
'aql 73, 171, 172
Aristotle 69, 75, 95, 96, 177
asbab al-nuzul 32
Ash'ari 83
Ash'arites 9–12, 17, 20, 21, 67–8, 70, 82, 85
authoritarian 34
'awra 90–2
'ayn 172

balance 21, 38–9, 50, 56, 62, 63, 71, 72, 73, 86, 93, 95–9, 109, 115, 142, 157–8, 162, 166–7, 173–4, 175, 176–82, 186, 188–9, 196, *see also* body
and mysticism 176–7

Barlas, A. 93, 112–13, 117
barzakh 83
batin 73
belief in God 1, 46, 55, 104, 140, 157, 163, *see also* apostasy; *kufr*
Bhagavad Gita 98
Bible 7, 16, 30, 101, 158
bid'a 71, 133
body, *see* modesty
Buddhism 169, 177

childlessness 7, 83–4
choice 155–6
Christianity, Christians viii, 7, 11, 28–9, 38, 55, 71, 89, 90, 109, 111, 125, 127, 128, 129, 158, 163
circumcision 45, 103
cloning 78, 80–1
clothes 46, 47, 72, 91, 94–5, 135–6, 187, 190, *see also* modesty
compensation 15, 17, 21, 59, 70, 78
competition in ethics 194
consequentialism 24, 25, 27, 28, 35, 48, 52, 62, 154, 188
cruelty 16, 130, 133, 169
customs 3, 46, 92, 94, 103, 162, 163, 195

Dajjal 39
dancing 31, 105, 186
darr 180
darura 20, 28, 30, 79, 94, 98, 125, 190
daruriyyat 52
death viii, 12, 17, 23, 24, 35, 52, 66, 83, 85–6, 89–90, 106, 152, 158, 170, 185–6

determinism 152–5, 158
dietary laws, *see* halal
disability 74–6
DNA 80
dunya 173

El Bernoussi, Z. 76
El Cheikh, N. 100
El-Rouayheb, K. 108–9
embryo 78–83, 85
enlightenment 86, 169, 175, 177
equality 44, 55, 103–4, 112–14
eudaemonia 69
euthanasia 66, 77
evil 1, 5, 6, 13, 15, 16–17, 20, 39–40, 44, 50, 53, 96, 101–2, 118, 132, 150, 151, 152, 153, 154, 156, 169, 171–2, 174–5, 175–8, 195

fadl 5
fairness 50–1, 55, 113
fana' 97, 169, 176
fasad 29, 61, 141, 153, 166
fasting 12–13, 127, 163
fatalism 62
fatiha 13
fatwa 187
fetus 66, 67, 74–9, 82, 84, 196
fitna 34
fitra 29, 163
food, *see* halal
fostering 76–7

gambling 47–9, 51–9, 61–2
gazing 108, 110
genes 67, 70, 74–85
genomics 68, 70, 84–5
ghafla 153
gharar 53–5
al-Ghazali 11, 14, 17, 53, 63, 77–8, 115, 151, 165, 169, 170, 173, 178, 180
Göle, Nilüfer 93
grace 4–5, 9, 18, 101–2, 152–4
gratitude 13, 60, 62, 168–9, 180–1
Greek philosophy 69
guidance 4, 9, 28, 55, 60, 73, 116, 118, 121, 142, 179, 196

hadith vii, ix, x, 2, 13, 20, 30, 32, 33, 34, 36, 37, 39, 41, 44, 49, 54, 66, 69, 71, 75, 77, 78, 81, 83, 84, 92, 95, 101, 105, 106, 107, 111, 112, 114, 115, 116, 117, 130, 131, 133, 137, 165, 170, 171, 179, 196
hajiyyat 52
halal vi, 58, 125–8, 129, 130–41
Hanafi 91–2, 106
Hanbali 91–2, 106
hasan 154
Hazara 109
Hinduism 98–9, 196
homosexuality 105, 106–11
hudud 192
human freedom 12, 19, 26, 44, 61, 120, 152

Ibadi 2
Iblis 39–40, 49, 73, 120, 171–3, 176
Ibn al-'Arabi 170, 175, 178, 181
Ibn Qayyim al-Jawziyya 110
Ibn Safwan, Jahm 150, 155
Ibn Taymiya 110
Ibn Tufayl 68, 157
i'jaz al-qur'an 194
ijtihad 190
imagination 37–8, 101
imam (Shi'ite) x, 2, 18, 20, 30, 33, 36, 41, 71, 121, 179
imams vii, 72, 133
inheritance 38, 78, 118
insan al-kamil 171, 178
insurance 59, 61, 70
interest 50–4, 56–61, 62, 190–1, 193, 197
in vitro fertilization (IVF) 6, 76, 78–9, 81
'Isa, *see* Jesus
Islamic banking 191, *see also* speculation; *sukuk*
Islamicization 130, 134–6
istihsan 81

al-Jabbar, 'Abd 82–1
al-Jabri 33
Jacob 101
jalal 171
jamal 171

INDEX

Jesus ix, 7, 39, 157–8
Jews 7, 11, 28–9, 38, 125, 157–8
jihad 25–5, 32–4, 49, 132
jinn 39, 74, 141, 145, 152
jism 171
Joseph 3, 121, 146
al-Jubba'i 82–3
Judgment Day 18, 55, 112, 150
justice 1, 3, 5, 11, 12, 15, 17, 19, 20, 21, 33, 38, 50, 71, 83, 97, 102, 112, 113, 115, 130, 150–1, 154, 155–6, 180

kalam 67, 73, 149
Kant, Immanuel 36–7, 52
Karbala 35
karma 98
khaliq 1
Khamenei, A. 38
Khidr 3, 39–40, 73, 82, 83, 117, 146, 153, 180–1
Khomayni, A. 187
kill/killing 19, 24, 25, 27–30, 34, 40, 75, 76, 79, 81, 82, 85, 98, 126, 130–3, 135, 137, 138, 143, 153, 157–8, 185, 187, 196
kitab 155
kosher 130, 136
kufr 71, 133, 153

language vii, x, 2, 10–12, 14, 18, 21, 34, 35, 62, 63, 70, 75, 86, 90, 93, 95, 96, 99, 103, 115, 136, 138, 150, 168, 171, 172, 174, 175, 176, 178, 192
law vii, viii, x, 1–9, 15–16, 18, 21, 32, 36, 37, 38, 39, 40–1, 43–4, 47, 48, 49, 52, 53, 57, 63, 68, 69, 70, 71, 72, 73, 74, 76, 77, 80, 84, 89, 91, 93, 97, 101, 104, 105, 112, 113, 114, 115, 118, 125, 130, 137, 138, 139, 142, 151, 162, 176, 179, 185, 186, 187, 188, 189, 190–2, 195, 197, 198
life, value of viii, 6, 7, 9, 12, 13, 15, 16, 17, 20, 23, 24, 26, 28, 29, 30, 31, 37, 40, 41, 45, 46, 52, 53, 55, 59, 61, 63, 65, 66–8, 69, 70, 71, 74, 75, 76, 77–8, 79, 80, 82, 83, 84–5, 86, 89, 90, 94, 95, 96, 100, 102, 104, 112, 127, 133, 138, 142, 146, 153, 154, 156, 158, 161, 163, 164, 165, 166, 167, 168, 170, 171, 173, 176, 177, 178, 179, 180, 181, 182, 185, 186, 188, 189, 195, 196, 197, *see also* afterlife; *maqasid al-shari'a*
lineage 7, 47, 77, 80
liwat 106–7
love 18, 40, 101, 102, 103, 108, 109, 110, 119, 162, 167, 171, 173, 179, 181
lutf 70

makhluq 1
maharim 91–2
Mahdi 24, 39, 158, 174–5
Maliki 91–2, 106
ma'na 171
Manicheanism 175
maqasid al-shari'a 44, 46, 47, 48–53, 59, 77, 104–5, 113, 117–18, 141, 185–7, 193
mashsha'i 6, 68
maslaha 28, 52–3, 54, 81, 82, 84, 104–5, 145, 185–90
ma'sum 179
maysir 53
medical treatment 66, 69
Medina 33, 101
mercy 3, 18, 58, 105, 119, 171, 172
Mernissi, F. 93
middle 38–9
Mill, J.S. 166
Miskawayh 96–7, 162–3
moderation 179–80
modesty 90–4, 105, 186
motives 99–102
Mu'awiyya 33
Muhammad, Prophet ix, 11, 26, 29, 31, 33, 35, 90, 94, 129, 146, 179, 181
muhasaba 178
mulk 33
Murji'i 164
Musa 3, 39–40, 73, 82, 83, 117, 146, 180–1

music 40, 105, 186, 188–9, 191
Mu'tazilah, Mu'tazilites 5, 8, 9,
    14–15, 17, 19, 20, 21, 68, 70, 76,
    82, 83, 85, 101–2, 115, 150–1

al-Nabulusi 110
nafs 34, 171–3, 176–7
naql 73
nasiha 121
naskh, see abrogation
nature 9, 13, 49, 68, 70, 75, 86,
    100–4, 111, 120, 125–7, 141–7,
    153, 157, 171, 179, 181, 195,
    198
Neoplatonism 96, 97
Noah 153
nur 172
Nursi, S. 69, 165, 170
Nusseibeh, S. 14
nutfa 77, 79

orientalism 94

paradise 83, 89, 154, 163
Pashtun 109
paternalism 45, 63
patience 28, 39, 65, 66, 73, 82,
    102, 195
patriarchy 34, 114
peace 18, 23, 32, 33, 35, 36
Pharaoh 3, 86, 150
Plato 19, 95, 96
prayer 4, 6, 13, 40, 66, 92, 127, 140,
    162, 163, 165, 167, 169, 179
principles 68, 72, 74, 77, 81, 82–5,
    95, 98, 105, 108, 112, 113, 114,
    117, 121, 128, 141, 142, 144,
    151, 167, 168, 180, 181, 182,
    185–98
private ownership 57
progressive Islam 93, 111–20, 192
Prophets 3, 5, 18, 32, 41, 97, 116,
    146, 158, 171, 179, *see also*
    Muhammad
punishment 5, 8, 16, 20, 23–4, 25,
    30, 44, 57, 73, 83, 85, 92, 99,
    105, 106–7, 118, 119, 121, 125,
    149, 150, 151, 155, 156, 163,
    173, 192

qabila 33
qamar 53
al-Qaradawi 15, 91
qital 32, *see also* kill

Rahman, F. 61
rationality viii, 9, 12, 14–17, 96
religiosity 114, 127, 129
revelation x, 3, 4, 9, 11–13, 14, 32,
    115, 143, 153
Reynolds, G. 157–8
riba, see interest
rights 26, 43, 45, 46, 76, 78, 89,
    138, 140
risk 9, 16, 45, 46, 48–51, 54, 56,
    58–9, 60, 61, 70, 97, 145–6, 151,
    161
Risman, B. 140
rituals 46–8, 92, 140, 163, 166, 195
Rowson, E. 107–8
Rumi 169, 171–5, 177
Ruzbihan Baqli 108

sabr 82
sa'id 154
Salafi 93, 109
sayyi'a 154
schematism 37
sex 30, 52, 89, 90, 91, 100–1,
    103–5, 106–11, 119, 163,
    166
Shafi'i 91–2, 103, 106, 130
shahada/shahid 173, 176
Al-Shahid al-Thani 96
shaqiyy 154
shari'a 7, 8, 13, 36, 41, 97, 195,
    see also maqasid al-shari'a, law
Shatibi 52, 92, 195
Shaybani 15
Shi'a x, 2, 18, 30, 31, 33, 34, 36, 71,
    189, 190
shirk 29, 105, 113, 150, 176, 186
Shuayb 50
sidq 178
sins ix, 1, 43–62, 106
sira ix, 25, 30, 34, 36, 83, 196
slavery 6, 10, 43
sodomy, *see liwat*
soldier 25, 28, 40

INDEX

soul 34, 69, 75, 77–80, 84, 90, 93, 96, 97, 98, 151, 173, 174, 176, 196
speculation 53, 58–9
stunning 130–2
Sufi 34, 90, 97, 100, 103, 108, 109, 137, 140, 161–82
sukuk 53–5
sunna ix, 20, 41, 71, 114
Sunni 2, 26, 31, 34, 91, 109, 114, 116, 188
surat 171

tahsiniyyat 52
tajalli 171
tajdid 165
takaful 59
tanzih 73, 90
taqiya 31
taqlid 63, 114, 118
taqwa 11, 60, 82, 167–8
tasawwuf 73, 168
tashbih 73, 90
tawba 178
tawhid 170, 174, 179
ta'wil 2
Tlili, S. 130

torture 187–8
tradition, traditional vii, viii, 2, 3, 11, 12, 14, 16, 34, 39, 46, 58, 69, 73, 77, 78, 80, 86, 93, 94, 95, 105, 106, 107, 108, 109, 110, 111, 112, 113, 114, 115, 118, 120, 121, 131, 140, 162, 167, 169, 178, 179, 187, 188, 189, 190, 196, 197, *see also* hadith
tribalism 33–4
tughyan 153

umma 11, 36, 140, 187, 189
'urf 47, 72, 77, 195–6
utilitarianism 10, 21, 25, 52, 53, 56–61, 79, 117, 144, 180, 192

Wahhabi 89
war 15, 24, 25–41, 72, 101
wasat, wasatiya 27, 38, 71, 118, 166
welfare, *see maslaha*

Yusuf, *see* Joseph

zahir 73
zikr 97